THE WILD GULF ALMANAC

**EDUCATIONAL
RESOURCES
ABOUT HABITATS
AND ECOSYSTEMS
IN THE GULF
OF MAINE
WATERSHED**

PRODUCED BY

 The Chewonki Foundation

 The U.S. Fish and Wildlife Service Gulf of Maine Project

 The Wells National Estuarine Research Reserve

WITH SUPPORT FROM
the National Fish and Wildlife Foundation,
Gulf of Maine Council on the Marine Environment,
and other matching grant contributors

WRITTEN AND EDITED BY
Sarah S. Bright
Wiscasset, Maine
1995

#34532590

Funding for the *Wild Gulf Almanac* was provided by a grant from the National Fish and Wildlife Foundation, with additional support from the Gulf of Maine Council on the Marine Environment, the Collaboration of Community Foundations for the Gulf of Maine Environment, BankAmerica Foundation, Bass Pro Shops, Maine Yankee, the Henry B. Plant Memorial Fund, the Libra Foundation, Poland Spring Water Company, and private contributions.

WILD GULF ALMANAC EDITORIAL BOARD

Lois Winter, U.S. Fish and Wildlife Service, Gulf of Maine Project
Henrietta List, Wells National Estuarine Research Reserve
Tom Howick, University of Southern Maine
Alan Lishness, Gulf of Maine Aquarium

THE WILD GULF PROJECT DIRECTORS

W. Donald Hudson, Jr., The Chewonki Foundation
Stewart I. Fefer, U.S. Fish and Wildlife Service, Gulf of Maine Project

EDITOR

Sarah S. Bright

CONTRIBUTING EDITORS

Lois Winter
Marina Schauffler
Tatiana Brailovskaya

DESIGN

Mahan Graphics
Bath, Maine

Printed by J.S. McCarthy, Augusta, Maine, on recycled paper.

Published by the Osprey Press of the Chewonki Foundation.

For additional copies or more information about *The Wild Gulf Almanac*, contact The Chewonki Foundation, RR2 Box 1200, Wiscasset, Maine 04578, tel. (207) 882–7323 or the U.S. Fish and Wildlife Service Gulf of Maine Project, 4R Fundy Road, Falmouth, Maine 04105, tel. (207) 781–8364.

Contents

HOW TO USE THIS ALMANAC

More than one hundred organizations and agencies in the Gulf of Maine watershed submitted materials for the *Wild Gulf Almanac*. In order to make these resources easy to find, we've organized the *Almanac* by major ecological systems, rather than by individual organizations or their geographic location within the watershed.

The first chapter discusses materials that help to introduce the watershed concept and environmental education in general. Following chapters focus primarily on terrestrial, freshwater, estuarine, and coastal and marine systems. The last chapter describes several resources, activities, and materials dealing within the effects of human actions on natural systems in the watershed. As is the case with natural systems themselves, the materials discussed in the *Almanac* inevitably overlap—freshwater systems are, of course, part of terrestrial systems; estuaries combine freshwater and marine systems, human actions affect all systems, and so on.

Each entry begins with the same basic information about the category of material (poster, book, video, etc.), intended audience (K-6, teachers, general public, high school grades, etc.), how to order it or where to get information, and cost. A brief comment follows, intended to give you a quick idea of the format, content, and applicability of the material, along with some subjective perspectives about what we found particularly useful, or even fun.

For the most part, however, we want the material to speak for itself, so each entry includes excerpts from the original text. Many of these excerpts are accompanied by illustrations, tables, lists, and charts to give you a "hands-on" sense of the material and, we hope, some interesting and usable information.

Finally, the directory of resources at the end of the *Almanac* can help you find new contacts, additional resources and more materials. Listings are arranged by category or type of resource and then grouped by state or province.

Whether you browse through the *Almanac* as you would a catalog (or a bookstore), or turn to it for a specific need (where to find information about harbor seals, for example), we hope you enjoy using it as much as we have enjoyed putting it together. Send us your comments, and let us know what you think.

THE WILD GULF ALAMANAC

By reading and using the resources in this book, you are becoming part of a growing network of people who are combining skills, sharing information, and joining forces to learn about and protect the Gulf of Maine environment and all of its living resources. We welcome you to this network and to the *Wild Gulf Almanac*. Its subtitle—*Educational Resources About the Gulf of Maine Watershed*—tells you something about its purpose, but it's important to let you know how and why the *Almanac* came into being, and how you as a reader—and as a participant in all that this book offers—are a key facet of the Wild Gulf Project.

The *Wild Gulf Almanac* is the centerpiece of an environmental education partnership between the Chewonki Foundation and the U.S. Fish and Wildlife Service Gulf of Maine Project—different Maine-based organizations sharing a commitment to understanding and protecting the natural systems that surround and sustain our lives. That partnership is the Wild Gulf Project: An Educational Initiative for the Gulf of Maine.

The Chewonki Foundation and the U.S. Fish and Wildlife Service view education as a critical factor in responsible human interaction with the natural world and its living resources. The Chewonki Foundation is dedicated to helping people grow individually and in community with others by providing educational experiences that foster an understanding and appreciation of the natural world and that emphasize the power of focused, collective effort. Over 2,500 elementary and secondary school students come to Chewonki every year for environmental education programs. Another 25,000 students participate in a Chewonki Outreach Program brought to schools throughout the State of Maine. The Maine Coast Semester for eleventh graders brings students from the United States and Canada each fall and spring to study the natural history of the coast, along with environmental issues and ethics. Faculty at Chewonki teach group problem-solving, integrated and interdisciplinary studies, and "hands-on" learning in the field as well as in the classroom. In all of its programs, Chewonki is committed to creating a sense of community through responsibility and participation in caring for the environment.

The U.S. Fish and Wildlife Service Gulf of Maine Project is part of the Service's Coastal Ecosystems Program, established to identify ecologically important coastal resources in the Gulf of Maine watershed; provide a bridge between a variety of Service programs to protect coastal and estuarine habitats; translate existing scientific information into action plans for conservation and management of public resources; and work with federal, state, local, and nongovernmental partners to implement plans to minimize or eliminate threats facing fish and wildlife resources in coastal areas. The Gulf of Maine Project supports the Gulf of Maine Council on the Marine Environment and the Environmental Protection Agency's National Estuary Programs in Massachusetts Bay, Casco Bay, Maine, and Great Bay, New Hampshire, with biological information and technical expertise on fish and wildlife habitat needs. The Project is also coordinating an effort to identify and analyze regionally significant habitats, organizing multi-partner undertakings to protect wildlife habitat on Maine islands and coastal areas. Another major initiative involves recommending protection strategies for Atlantic salmon along Maine rivers. The Gulf of Maine Project has conducted wetland trends analyses in the watershed to target specific areas for local protection, has developed a Geographic Information System that shares data with state and provincial fish and wildlife agencies, and has produced various education and outreach materials about living resources.

INTRODUCTION

The Wild Gulf initiative began with a grant from the National Fish and Wildlife Foundation in Washington, D.C., an organization created by the United States Congress to support public and private partnerships for conservation of fish, wildlife, and plant resources throughout the world. The Foundation's significant body of work and valuable contributions to conservation is manifest in their generous awards, which provide challenge grants using federal funds to match private funding. In 1993, the Foundation began a far-reaching program for conservation education in order to support projects that inform people about the need to conserve and protect natural habitats and ecosystems, and "to give them the knowledge to become responsible land stewards, because the fate of our natural resources—and ultimately that of our own species—depends on an educated citizenry."

The focus of this effort is to improve teachers' access to quality conservation curricula and outdoor education programs; prepare teachers to become knowledgeable, effective environmental educators; integrate conservation education into current school curricula; increase the use of existing education resources, such as wildlife refuges, parks, forests, aquariums, and zoos; and promote careers in conservation, fish and wildlife management, and environmental research and education. In keeping with these goals, the *Wild Gulf Almanac* is designed to give teachers, students, and the public access to the wealth of information and educational tools currently available about the vast biological region defined by the Gulf of Maine and the 69,000 square miles of land in its watershed. Together, land and sea constitute a beautiful and complex ecosystem of global importance. However, the Gulf of Maine and its watershed are in jeopardy as a result of the cumulative impacts of human population growth and development.

The purpose of the *Wild Gulf Almanac* is to give the Gulf of Maine region the visibility it merits as an extraordinary global ecosystem, to put information about the Gulf in the hands of educators, and to put people who live and work on its shores in touch with one another to help protect and restore its natural abundance. This first issue of the *Wild Gulf Almanac* only begins the process; it is the first volume of what we hope will become an accessible, up-to-date guide for people who want to learn more about the Gulf of Maine and how they can affect its future.

The *Almanac* is the product of an unprecedented collaboration among nearly one hundred environmental and education organizations and agencies that responded to our request for materials. We received books, notebooks, pamphlets, posters, videos, maps, software, and data from every corner of the Gulf of Maine watershed.

At the beginning of this effort, the Chewonki Foundation and the U.S. Fish and Wildlife Service were joined by Wells National Estuarine Research Reserve, which had developed *DEPTHS: Discovering Ecology, Pathway to Science*, a comprehensive curriculum in estuarine ecology for early elementary school students. As part of the Wild Gulf initiative, the Wells Reserve expanded that curriculum through the eighth grade, providing a much-needed bridge for education in ecology through the middle school years. This expanded curriculum became the first major contribution to the *Almanac* (it is described in the chapter on estuarine systems), and we wish to specifically acknowledge the Reserve for its help in the initial, formative months of the *Almanac* and for its ongoing editorial and conceptual involvement.

Other major collaborators in the early stages of the *Almanac's* design were the Gulf of Maine Aquarium (who offered to include the *Almanac* among the resources on its Internet server, provided by a generous grant from NASA), the Manomet Observatory, the New England Aquarium, and the Quebec-Labrador Foundation's Atlantic Center for the Environment. Their support and creativity were instrumental in shaping the idea of the *Almanac* and giving it substance and direction.

We know that materials and catalogs can quickly become outdated. As new materials are developed and our network of communication grows, there will always be a need for another, better, updated issue of the *Almanac*. Your interest and help in reviewing and using the first *Wild Gulf Almanac* will be essential in making subsequent issues more accurate and more comprehensive than the first. We hope you will join the list of contributors in the future, or encourage someone else to do so. It is our intention to keep the *Almanac* growing, so each volume will build upon and complement previous ones, bringing you access to new materials, new issues, and new perspectives on the Gulf of Maine watershed.

Let us know how the *Wild Gulf Almanac* is working for you; perhaps something on these pages will bring you in touch with colleagues you didn't know you had; or you may find activities and materials that suddenly bring an issue to life in your classroom. Let us know if your students and friends are prompted to ask new questions and to explore new answers, or if they become intrigued with an extraordinary fact somewhere in these pages. Please tell us, by all means, if they arrive at new and inspired places in their appreciation and commitment to resource protection. We are all residents of this watershed; we can help each other learn about it. And together we can protect it.

The initial grant for the Wild Gulf initiative from the National Fish and Wildlife Foundation was matched with support from the Gulf of Maine Council on the Marine Environment, the Collaboration of Community Foundations for the Gulf of Maine Environment, BankAmerica Foundation, Poland Spring Water Company, Bass Pro Shops, Maine Yankee, the Henry B. Plant Memorial Fund, the Libra Foundation, and private contributions. We are grateful for their commitment to and support of this effort. For their insight, patience, and inspiration in helping us to imagine the *Almanac* in the first place and then bring it into being, we also want to thank the members of our Editorial Board—Stewart Fefer, Tom Howick, Alan Lishness, and especially Lois Winter, Henrietta List, and Marina Schauffler who gave their time and energy to reviewing the *Almanac* at various stages. Their editorial comments and suggestions have proved invaluable. To Project Directors Don Hudson and Stew Fefer go a thousand thanks for their extraordinary patience and support, and for the vision of what this work could be. And finally, we thank every one of our contributors for their enthusiasm, their generosity, and their understanding of the need to create an "educational watershed" of resources that we can all share. This is their *Almanac*, and yours.

—The Editors

WATERSHED-WIDE INFORMATION

For over five million of us—in Maine, Massachusetts, New Brunswick, New Hampshire, and Nova Scotia—who live on the 69,115 square miles of land that constitutes the Gulf of Maine watershed, environmental education can begin right here. We live within a complex and beautiful network of interconnected systems and habitats that are a vital part of the Gulf: what we do in this watershed has a direct impact on the vast marine system touching our shores.

"There's no place like home."
—Frank Baum,
The Wizard of Oz

The Gulf of Maine watershed comprises an extensive network of rivers, forests, fields, lakes, wetlands, and estuaries which collect all the freshwater that flows into the Gulf from major rivers (including the Merrimack, Kennebec, Androscoggin, Penobscot, and St. John). Hundreds of miles from the coast, every rivulet, creek, stream, and river within this huge basin forms part of a local watershed that fits like a puzzle piece into the whole. Fish, birds, and mammals inhabiting all parts of this region share a diversity of habitats. Some of the planet's most biologically productive areas are created by the Gulf's unique marine habitats which have historically sustained major fishing, tourist, and recreation industries. The health of these marine systems depends not only on how we treat the Gulf directly, but also on our actions on land which ultimately filter toward the sea.

Perhaps the time will come when the old Iroquois vision of the eagle is finally installed in our statute books and when the eagle bird is flourishing—not just de-listed as an endangered species, but flourishing—throughout all of its habitat. Perhaps then I and the others can all return to Bear Valley, at a time when our eagle girls and boys may have eagle daughters and sons of their own. And we can stand there together in the beginnings of dawn, three generations of us or more, and see and feel the glides and swoops and the long lazy curves and the majesty and dignity of these beings that, inexplicably, embody both mortality and eternity. And when that early morning comes, and when the eagle bird begins to pull the blanket off from the eastern sky, we will have no doubt in our souls that we were right to take on this long and sacred task.

—Charles F. Wilkinson, Eagle Bird, *New York: Vintage Press, 1993, p. 20*

Unfortunately, the ecological integrity of the watershed and the Gulf has been seriously compromised by escalating human population growth, demands for resources, and the accompanying pollution, wetland loss, and habitat fragmentation resulting from cumulative effects of development. Human activities have led to serious declines in species abundance. One tragic example is the virtual "commercial extinction" of traditionally plentiful groundfish in the Gulf of Maine. Such declines in fish and wildlife resources have reached proportions that threaten both the ecological and economic health of the watershed and all its residents.

Environmental education organizations, government agencies, and private conservation groups are working to develop a watershed-wide approach to understanding and managing species, habitats, and ecosystems in the Gulf of Maine watershed. If we can comprehend the watershed as a whole, we can work together to protect and restore its parts. Materials described in this chapter provide information about the watershed and offer basic references and resources about environmental topics and issues. Here—and now—is a good place to begin your own environmental exploration of this extraordinary and intricate global resource.

13

The Gulf of Maine Watershed
A Beautiful Place to Start Your Environmental Education

Endangered and Threatened Species in the Gulf of Maine Watershed (1994)
(U.S. Fish and Wildlife Service, Maine Department of Inland Fisheries and Wildlife, and Maine Audubon Society.)

Threatened Species (Species that will become endangered if current populations experience further decline)

Bald eagle
Seabeach amaranth
Small whorled pogonia
Eastern prairie fringed orchid
Puritan title beetle
Northeastern beach tiger beetle
Green turtle
Loggerhead turtle

Endangered (Species in immediate danger of extinction)

Blue whale
Finback whale
Humpback whale
Right whale
Sei whale
Sperm whale
Peregrine falcon
Piping plover
Roseate tern
Least tern
Shortnose sturgeon
American burying beetle
Karner blue butterfly
Jesup's milk-vetch
Furbish lousewort
Sandplain gerardia
Robbinson's cinquefoil
American chaffseed
Northeastern bulrush
Atlantic Ridley turtle
Leatherback turtle
Hawksbill turtle
Plymouth red-bellied turtle

Extirpated in Maine (Species of wildlife that were once indigenous to Maine but have not been found in the state for the past fifty years)

Woodland caribou
Sea mink
Eastern cougar
Grey wolf
Labrador duck
Eastern Anatum Peregrine falcon
Eskimo curlew
Great auk
Passenger pigeon
Loggerhead shrike
Timber rattlesnake

"Environmental education is distinct from previous educational strategies. It stresses the combination of values exploration, knowledge and skill development, and a commitment to action. By including both the natural and human-built environment, and by encouraging people to develop both a sense of wonder and a sense of responsibility for their environment, environmental education addresses the heart of environmental problems and solutions—that is, human behavior."
—*National Consortium for Environmental Education and Training* Getting Started, A Guide to Bringing Environmental Education Into Your Classroom

14

Title: EE Toolbox Catalog—A Comprehensive Set of Tools for Environmental Education In-service Providers and Educators

Target Group: Educators K-12, teacher trainers

Available from: The National Consortium for Environmental Education and Training (NCEET), School of Natural Resources & Environment, University of Michigan, Dana Building 430 E. University, Ann Arbor, MI 48109-1115; telephone (313) 998-6726; fax (313) 936-2195

Cost: Free

COMMENT

NCEET's EE Toolbox is "an organized collection of publications for educators who conduct environmental education (EE) teacher in-service training programs. The EE Toolbox is intended to advance EE in-service programs towards the goal of empowering teachers to help students carefully consider the environment and develop the skills that will enable them to take responsible actions." The *EE Toolbox Catalog* explains each component of the Toolbox and provides an order form and details about getting your hands on the materials. The components of the Toolbox, designed to be integrated into any subject or topic, are: the *Workshop Resource Manual* in which there are nine individual units; *Getting Started: A Guide to Bringing Environmental Education Into Your Classroom*; the *EE Reference Collection*, a series of articles by EE leaders to complement the *Manual*; a *National Survey of EE Teacher Inservice Education*; and a *Slide Resource Kit*. NCEET was initially funded by the U.S. Environmental Protection Agency and now has a wide base of support through a variety of partnerships including Apple Computer, General Motors, the Amway Corporation, U.S. Fish and Wildlife Service, and several other state universities and nonprofit environmental organizations. Entries on following pages describe more from NCEET's EE Toolbox.

> "NCEET's goal is to encourage individuals to incorporate environmental strategies into their lives, while working to develop citizenry that appreciates and respects the total environment."

EXCERPTS

"When it comes to the environment, kids want to know. They want to know how to clean up their neighborhoods and what they can do to save energy. They want to know how global environmental issues might affect their futures.

In 1992, the U.S. Environmental Protection Agency provided funding for the National Consortium for Environmental Education and Training. The Consortium, led by the University of Michigan, is now coordinating a national effort to improve the efficiency and effectiveness of environmental education.

NCEET works to support, enhance, and extend effective environmental education in grades K-12. To achieve this on a national level, NCEET has created a core set of initiatives that provide a diverse framework for enhancing environmental education."
—NCEET

Title: Katahdin to the Sea: Aquatic Environments in Maine Poster

Target Group: General audience

Available from: The Wild Gulf Poster Series, The Chewonki Foundation, Wiscasset, ME 04578; telephone (207) 882–7323; fax (207) 882-4074

Cost: Free to teachers as part of the Wild Gulf Poster Series while supplies last; $30 plus shipping for the general public to purchase set of four posters

COMMENT

Copies of this multicolored poster are hanging in hallways and offices from state and federal agencies to environmental organizations, and now—as part of the Wild Gulf Poster Series—in classrooms throughout the Gulf of Maine watershed. A joint project of the Gulf of Maine Aquarium and the Poland Spring Company, this is one of the most attractive and popular posters about the Gulf of Maine currently in print. It's fun to look at and fun to read, with beautiful color illustrations and photos. In creating a "cross section" of the Gulf of Maine watershed, the poster focuses on the essential role that water plays in the environment—from uplands to estuaries, shore, and sea, describing the major habitats and plant and animal communities found along the way. And if this weren't already enough for one poster, there are also classroom activities suggested for each habitat study area. This is a poster you'll probably want to frame.

EXCERPTS

"To tap the groundwater in an aquifer, wells are dug until they reach the top layer of the aquifer, the water table. The water table is not flat as its name suggests. It has peaks and valleys that repeat the shape of the land above it. When a lot of water is pumped from an aquifer, or when there is a dry spell, the water table sinks lower..."—*Gulf of Maine Aquarium*

"...Spongy sphagnum moss soaks up warmth, oxygen, and rainwater and keeps them from reaching the bog below. Sphagnum is so absorbent it was used for diapers by the Indians and for bandages in battlefield hospitals in World War I. When sphagnum moss dies and decays, it makes the water in the bog as acid as orange juice."—*Gulf of Maine Aquarium*

Title: On Water, On Wings, In the Woods: A Guide for Maine Wildlife Watchers

Target Group: General audience

Available from: Maine Department of Inland Fisheries and Wildlife, State House Station 41, Augusta, ME 04333-0041; telephone (207) 287-3371; fax (207) 287-6395

Cost: $4.95, plus $1 for shipping and handling

COMMENT

This 64-page basic guide book to wildlife watching in Maine provides a list of reference books; a short section on creating wildlife habitat on your own property; a list of state headquarters, offices, and fish hatcheries; and a list of wildlife management areas. Interpretive signs and regional maps are explained in the front of the book.

EXCERPTS

"The softcover book, which is the result of a year-long effort by staff of *Maine Fish and Wildlife Magazine*, contains more than two dozen full-color wildlife photographs and describes 62 places in Maine to view wildlife in its natural setting. Most sites listed are on publicly owned land and all are open for careful public use and enjoyment. The book is organized by geographic regions and describes each site in detail—how to get there, the wildlife species you might expect to see, details on the availability of restrooms, parking, and other facilities, and much more, including information on access for persons with disabilities."—*Maine Department of Inland Fisheries and Wildlife*

"Signs of wildlife are all around. Tracks in mud, snow, or sand are easy to spot. Nibbled branches, cracked acorns or beechnuts, rubs and scratches on tree trunks, holes pecked in trees, chewed and stripped bark, broken vegetation along a well-used path, and partially eaten fruit under a wild apple tree are all signs that wildlife is around. Recognize these signs, and you will find a variety of wildlife are in the area!

Cynthia Curtis

Do a little homework about the species you really want to see. Read up on its natural history and habits. Learn in what habitats the critter is most likely to be found. For example in Maine, you generally won't find an eider duck on an inland lake, or a loon with young off the coast. Learn what it likes to eat and where it prefers to rest, hide, and socialize." —*Maine Department of Inland Fisheries and Wildlife*

How Close is Too Close?

• Watching songbirds at nest sites, especially when adults are incubating eggs or feeding young, keeps parents away from nests for long periods and causes chilling of eggs or nestlings, or nest abandonment by the adults.

• Human intrusions near colonies of great blue herons and other birds that congregate in large numbers can be harmful to entire local populations.

• The pursuit of family flocks of waterfowl or loons, in boats, canoes or kayaks, 'just to get a little closer,' may lead to repeated distress calls, diving and eventually, exhausted young birds or chicks separated from adults.

• Cow moose and their calves are sometimes pursued by one group of people after another during the course of a day, all trying for a good look or 'that perfect photograph.' This can lead to exhaustion in young animals and possible separation of mother and young.

Dr. Jim Parker

REMEMBER, your encounter alone may not be a disturbance to wildlife, but several such encounters over a period of time can cause cumulative effects. If you care about wildlife, observe, enjoy, but don't encroach.—*Maine Department of Inland Fisheries and Wildlife*

What Are the Odds of Seeing Them?

Finding wildlife, and having them stay put long enough to watch or photograph, is not always easy. The species mentioned under the site descriptions in this book can all be seen, but there are no guarantees. They are after all, free-roaming animals. Most are elusive and avoid contact with humans....

Successful wildlife viewing requires knowledge of the animals' habits and habitats, and knowing when to look for them. A good deal of patience often helps, too!
—*Maine Department of Inland Fisheries and Wildlife*

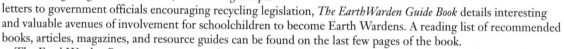

The Earth

The Earth is coloured
blue and green
So we must help keep
it clean.
Canadian, American,
Japanese,
And other people just
like these.
Our earth is dying as we
know,
So clean it up and make
it glow.

—*Rebecca Crossman, age 11*
Grade4/5M
Arnold H. McLeod Elementary
Moncton, New Brunswick; excerpted
from the EarthWarden Guide Book.

Title: EarthWarden Guide Book, Living Lightly on Planet Earth

Target Group: Grades K-8

Available from: EarthWardens Office, 327
Chartersville Road Dieppe, NB, E1A 1K5 Canada;
telephone (506) 852–4483

Cost: $10

COMMENT

The *EarthWarden Guide Book* contains seven chapters of
teaching suggestions and environmental education
activities for creating environmental education programs. Its pages are laced with original drawings and
writings from schoolchildren who have participated in
the program. From creating a scavenger hunt as an
introduction to nature, to developing a "Trash Attack
Team" for fighting waste reduction, to outlining sample
letters to government officials encouraging recycling legislation, *The EarthWarden Guide Book* details interesting
and valuable avenues of involvement for schoolchildren to become Earth Wardens. A reading list of recommended
books, articles, magazines, and resource guides can be found on the last few pages of the book.

The EarthWarden Program operates on the premise that "Every little bit helps. Everyone working together can
make a difference in improving our environment." Not bad food for thought. Browse through the book, and consider the student work highlighted in the margins of the pages—this tenet is taken to heart. Another nice thing
about the *EarthWarden Guide Book:* it heartily encourages parent participation.

The *EarthWardenGuide Book* is the result of a collaborative and innovative partnership between parents and
teachers in the Moncton, New Brunswick, area to promote environmental awareness and stewardship. In one year,
the partnership grew from a single-school pilot project geared for 650 students to one that served several schools
and over 3,000 students. A French version of the guide, funded by the provincial Environmental Trust Fund is
available. For more information on programs and projects from New Brunswick Environment, see page 104.

EXCERPT

"The EarthWarden Program is
more than just getting outdoors
into nature or learning about recycling. It reveals to children that
the Earth is a living thing, as we
are, and needs love and care to
grow strong and healthy. The
Earth is not to be used, but cared
for, like a friend. The
EarthWarden program provides
opportunities for children to form
a friendship with the Earth as
unique as they are themselves.

This program carries my hope, a
hope that all children will be
touched by the wonders of our
environment. Every child should
have the opportunity to experience
the simple joys of hearing waves
wash up on a shore, feel and smell
the scent of freshly turned earth, to
see the natural world around
them."—*Shirley St. Pierre,*
EarthWarden Program

Amazing Facts

- *From the* EarthWarden Guide
Book, *the EarthWarden Program.*

Car pollution does not necessarily
stop when a car is junked and
hauled to a dump or junkyard.
Rusting car bodies clutter the landscape and piles of used tires can
turn into an environmental disas-
ter. Some examples:
- Hagersville, Ontario, February
12, 1990. Over 13 million tires
caught fire at a tire depot near
this town and burned out of control for over 17 days! Oil and
dangerous compounds melted
from the tires and seeped into
the land and groundwater below,
causing serious contamination.
- A tire plant in Ohio dumped
so much hazardous waste
into the Cuyahoga River
that the water caught
fire! Happily, 20 years
after that fire, the river
is recovering and
being restored to its
original beauty.

Amazing Facts

Among the worst of the toxins that
travel in our air is a chemical called
sulphur dioxide. It is one of the
leading causes of acid rain and also
helps create smog—a nasty mixture
of smoke and fog that sometimes
settles over cities. Here are some
of the worst cases of smog ever
recorded:
- Donoara, Pennsylvania, 1948.
Smog there was so bad that the
people of the town could not
even see as far away as their
hands!
- London, England, 1952. A dead-
ly smog in that city killed 4,000
people!
- Mexico City. The air over this
city is sometimes so filthy that
birds flying through it sometimes drop out of the sky
dead!

Kendra Attis

Title: AWARE (Annapolis Watershed Aquatic Resource Enquirer) Software Program

Target Group: General audience/community groups, leaders, businesses

Available from: Clean Annapolis River Project (CARP), PO Box 395, Annapolis Royal, NS BOS 1AO Canada; telephone (902) 532-7533; fax (902) 678-1253; e-mail shawbold@fox.nstn.ca

Cost: Contact for additional information

COMMENT

AWARE is the latest product developed by CARP's Annapolis Basin Coastal Zone Project. The Coastal Zone Project was designated in 1993 to develop a computerized information system linking economic and environmental interests. As "a non-governmental community-based organization devoted to promoting the conservation and wise use of the natural resources of the Annapolis River watershed," CARP is committed to empowering communities to promote and care for natural resources and local economies in mutually beneficial ways. CARP has subsequently developed many educational materials, systems, and articles to demonstrate "how the combined efforts of local residents, businesses, governments, industries, and scientists can be effective in charting a course for the future management of the river and its watershed."

CARP's specific objectives are "to assist in the rehabilitation and protection of the Annapolis River watershed by encouraging cooperation between public, private, and government organizations; to promote the concept of multiple use of estuarine resources; and to foster the involvement of local residents in the process of decision-making with regard to the future of the Annapolis River and Estuary." CARP has been involved in several facets of conservation in Nova Scotia: water and energy conservation, restoration of fish habitat, river water-quality monitoring, and the dissemination of information about the Annapolis River. AWARE is the organization's latest brainchild.

A description of the functions of AWARE follows, but it should be noted that the software is still in its developmental stage. It is an exciting prototype for computer buffs, nonetheless. For more on the Clean Annapolis River Project and its series of "River Issues" articles see page 22.

EXCERPTS

"This is an integrated information management system that comprises a variety of program application modules linked together in a coherent manner that can access, display, and manipulate a wide range of GIS (Geographic Information System) coverages and other environmental information pertaining to the study area.

The AWARE prototype, although far from complete, clearly demonstrates the general architecture, flexible functionality and ease of use of such an integrated software package that can meet the information management and ecological modeling needs of community-based groups and local decision-makers concerned with sustainable economic development and environmental conservation. It is designed to permit rapid access to regional environmental and other relevant information, facilitate simple manipulation of selected geographically referenced databases, allow modeling of selected ecological processes, and expedite the generation of maps and other graphics that are suitable for public presentations...

The prototype AWARE program is PC-based, modular, runs under MS-Windows and is extremely user-friendly... Community based environmental management is a rapidly emerging trend at the provincial, national and international level. The AWARE software developed as part of this project is positioned to capitalize on that trend as it provides community groups with the computer-based tools to enhance local decisionmaking. As a result, it is envisaged that this software will be of interest to many emerging community groups."—*Clean Annapolis River Project*

Title: Video Programs

Target Group: General audience

Available from: Maine State Library Educational Video Services at Station 64, LMA Building, Augusta, ME 04333-0064; telephone (207) 287-5620; fax (207) 287-5624

Cost: Free, if a blank tape is provided; $5 without the tape

COMMENT

All of the Maine Department of Inland Fisheries and Wildlife video programs are available free to teachers (in Maine only) through the Maine State Library's Educational Video Services. All a teacher needs to do is send a brand-new, blank video tape to the library with a request for whatever specific program he/she would like to have taped. Catalogs of available programs through this service are mailed to all school libraries throughout the state; teachers should check with their school librarians for this catalog.

A Sample of Available Titles from the Maine State Library:

- Maine Department of Inland Fisheries and Wildlife: Preserving, Protecting, and Managing our Wildlife Resource

- Catch and Release Fishing in Maine

- Bald Eagle—Rebirth in Maine

- Cobscook—Of Boiling Waters

- Maine's Fish and Wildlife—What Are They Worth?

- Maine Birds— Managing for Their Future

- Maine's Wildlife Management Areas

- Protecting Maine's Endangered Species

- Warden Search and Rescue

18

Mark Marcuson

Title: EE Toolbox—Workshop Resource Manual

Target Group: Educators K-12, teacher trainers

Available from: The National Consortium for Environmental Education and Training (NCEET), School of Natural Resources & Environment, University of Michigan, Dana Building 430 E. University, Ann Arbor, MI 48109-1115; telephone (313) 998-6726; fax (313) 936-2195

Cost: $35 each; for orders of twenty or more, bulk rates available

COMMENT

The *Workshop Resource Manual*, providing background information, workshop activities, master copies for handouts and overheads, and checklists for workshop facilitators, is one of the centerpieces of the EE Toolbox. Nine individual units make up the manual, including topics such as "Designing Effective Workshops and Defining EE," "Multicultural and Urban EE," "Integrating EE," and "Computer-Aided EE." All units are germane to the host of different issues that arise when bringing environmental education into classrooms in a variety of circumstances. Though intended to be used together, these units can also be used separately. Each unit alone is substantial enough to create a complete workshop, particularly one with specific needs. The *Workshop Resource Manual* can be purchased either as individual units or in its nine-unit entirety.

Endangered Species:
What you can do to help

• Find out which species in your area are endangered or threatened by writing your state wildlife or conservation department. Be informed about other wildlife issues in your area and tell others about what you have learned.

• Visit one of the more than 500 National Wildlife Refuges. Become a volunteer at a refuge.

• Join a conservation group; many have local chapters.

• Check the law before buying wildlife products. Before traveling overseas, write the U.S. Fish and Wildlife Service, Publications, 130 Arlington Square, Washington, D.C. 20240, for a copy of *Buyer Beware* and *Facts About Federal Wildlife Laws.*

• Report violations of wildlife laws to your local game warden. Many states have a special "hotline" number for this.

• Set an example by recycling and being careful not to litter. Some kinds of litter such as balloons, discarded fishing line, and plastic six-pack rings can suffocate, entrap, or strangle wildlife.

• Avoid using unnecessary lawn and garden chemicals, improperly disposing of household chemicals, and causing water pollution or erosion.

• Buy a Federal Duck Stamp at your local post office. By law, money from Duck Stamp sales goes directly into a special fund used only to buy prime wetland habitat. A great variety of wildlife, including many endangered species, depends on wetlands.

• Plan a vacation around observing wildlife in its natural habitat, such as a marsh or forest. Look for state, federal, or private wildlife conservation areas near your destination.

—Prepared by U.S. Fish and Wildlife Service

EXCERPTS

"This unit ['Approaching Environmental Education in the Classroom'] is for any workshop facilitator who wants to help teachers address environmental issues in their classrooms. This unit covers the benefits to students and teachers and describes how to get around common barriers. It gives you a framework for understanding the problem-solving process and explains three ways to help students become skilled in it. The 'Activities' section suggests ideas for your workshops, whether you focus on a specific environmental problem or on the process of approaching environmental issues in general. Throughout the unit are guidelines, examples, and sample discussion questions for your workshops."—*NCEET,* The Workshop Resource Manual: Approaching Environmental Education in the Classroom, *Margaret T. Pennock, Lisa V. Bardwell.*

"A key point is that advocacy is not the same as education. A teacher may do both, but they have different purposes. To advocate for a solution or behavior change is akin to telling people what to do, rather than educating them (with information and skills) to make their own choices. Teachers may advocate certain behaviors ('Don't hit kids on the playground' and 'Wash your hands before lunch') to promote social norms or protect students' well-being. Regarding controversial issues, however, an approach that 'educates' is often the best route.

This line gets very fuzzy, however, when younger students want to do something about the environment and tend to see the world in terms of 'good guys and bad guys.' It is important to help students understand the complexity of most environmental issues: Americans want things like cars, TVs, and convenience; that desire creates problems like habitat destruction and pollution. Helping students develop the skills and commitment to balance both needs—for a comfortable life and for environmental protection—is the essence of environmental education."—*NCEET, "EE Toolbox—Workshop Resource Manual"*

One Fish, Two Fish...?

During one investigation project, students in a humanities class were studying the heritage of fishing on the New England coast. Interviews with local fishers uncovered a complex problem related to their way of life, livelihoods, and resource management: overfishing. The class focused on understanding all aspects of this problem by gathering information from local newspapers and both environmental and fishing groups, visiting fish markets, and interviewing many people on all sides of the issue.—*NCEET, "The Workshop Resource Manual, Approaching Environmental Issues in the Classroom."*

"It has been estimated that there are almost 80,000 species of edible plants, of which fewer than 20 produce 90 percent of the world's food. If under-utilized species are conserved, they could help to feed growing populations."—*U.S. Fish and Wildlife Service*

Endangered means there is still time, but *extinction* means forever.
—*U.S. Fish and Wildlife Service*

Title: Rare and Endangered Species Fact Sheets

Target: General public

Available from: U.S. Fish and Wildlife Service, New England Field Offices, 22 Bridge Street, Room 400, Concord, NH 03301; telephone (603) 225-1411; fax (603) 225-1467

Cost: Free

COMMENT

Succinct and to-the-point, these fact sheets from the New England Field Office of the U.S. Fish and Wildlife Service provide valuable information on the habitats and life histories of the American Burying Beetle, the Karner Blue Butterfly, and the Roseate Tern. They convey basic facts relating to each species, and they do it well. They are interesting—albeit disturbing—reports on the status of species at risk, reminding us that we are losing species at an unprecedented rate. These fact sheets are good teaching and research tools for projects or simply for general interest.

EXCERPTS

"Since the landing of the Pilgrims in 1620, more than 500 species, subspecies, and varieties of our Nation's plants and animals are known to have become extinct. In contrast, during the Pleistocene Ice Age, all of North America lost only about three species every 100 years."—*U.S. Fish and Wildlife Service, "The Karner Blue Butterfly Rare Species Fact Sheet"*

"The tern species and most other colonial nesting waterbirds...were extremely vulnerable to egg collecting and gunning for the millinery markets which peaked at the end of the nineteenth century. However, protective laws and changes in hat styles enabled the roseate tern and many other waterbird populations to recover by the 1930s. In recent decades, though, roseate terns have been harassed by herring and black-backed gulls. Gulls have been increasing in number because of an abundant supply of food: human garbage."—*U.S. Fish and Wildlife Service, "Roseate Tern Endangered Species Fact Sheet"*

"Historical records offer little insight into what type of habitat was preferred by the American Burying Beetle. Current information suggests that this species is a habitat generalist, ... with a slight preference for grasslands and open understory oak hickory forests. However, the beetles are carrion specialists in that they need carrion the size of a dove or a chipmunk in order to reproduce. Carrion availability may be the greatest factor determining where the species can survive."—*U.S. Fish and Wildlife Service, "American Burying Beetle Endangered Species Fact Sheet"*

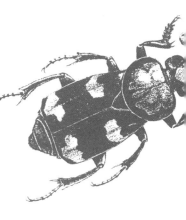

Title: Maine State Park and Historic Site Information Summary and Visitor News

Target Group: General audience

Available from: Maine Bureau of Parks and Recreation, Maine Department of Conservation, Station 22, Augusta, ME 04333-0022; telephone (207) 287-3821; fax (207) 287-3823

Cost: Free

COMMENT

Maine's Bureau of Parks and Recreation provides a brochure listing all Maine state parks and historic sites and the services provided at each park throughout the year. News items geared for park visitors are also available and can be requested for individual parks. The Bureau encourages and welcomes field trips, often providing park staff as speakers or leaders of special group programs. Call ahead to the park to make arrangements and to ensure that staff will be available to conduct programs. For further information about the Bureau's free outreach programs (which run from November through March), check pages 38.

EXCERPTS

"Maine Bureau of Parks and Recreation creates opportunities for people to enrich their lives through a wide range of quality, safe, outdoor recreational and educational experiences. As responsible stewards, we protect and provide access to examples of Maine's significant natural and historic resources for present and future generations."—*Maine Bureau of Parks and Recreation*

"The removal of a single species can set off a chain reaction effecting many others. It has been estimated, for example, that a disappearing plant can take with it up to 30 other species, including insects, higher animals, and even other plants."—U.S. Fish and Wildlife Service

Barry Van Dusen

Title: The Maine Naturalist

Target Group: General audience

Available from: Eagle Hill Field Research Station, PO Box 99, Steuben, ME 04680-0099; telephone (207) 546-2821; fax (207) 546-3042

Cost: $7.50 per quarterly issue or $30 for yearly subscription ($20 for students); back issues available

COMMENT

The Maine Naturalist is produced by Eagle Hill Field Station with a focus on issues pertaining to the bioregion that comprises the Gulf of Maine watershed and the rest of northern New England, the Adirondacks, and the Canadian Maritimes. Contributors include college and university faculty members and field biologists, undergraduate and graduate students, amateur naturalists, teachers, artists and writers. Topics are broad, providing a wide scope of natural history information. Articles include scientific research papers as well as general interest pieces, research summaries, photo essays, and other features. Book reviews are printed in the back of the book. Though tightly academic in appearance, this journal has a little bit of everything for anyone interested in the natural history of the bioregion encompassing the Gulf of Maine watershed. For information on seminars and workshops conducted at the Eagle Hill Field Station, see page 43.

EXCERPTS

> *"People in our bioregion have long hoped for a journal like* **The Maine Naturalist.** *It is finally here."—Editors,* The Maine Naturalist

"What steps can we take to make sure that our part of the world remains at least as diverse as it is now?...What scales and levels of protection make sense for the Acadian Bioregion? What is possible given the condition of the land, our financial resources and our political will?"—*Janet McMahon, "Saving All the Pieces— An Ecological Reserves Proposal from Maine," The Maine Naturalist, vol. 1, no. 4, p.213*

"Anecdotal reports received over the years by Maine Department of Inland Fisheries and Wildlife (MDIFW) biologists indicate that bobcats occasionally enter settled areas during winter....During February and March of 1993, a bobcat came to [author Sid] Bahrt's backyard in Pembroke, Maine...The bobcat was first seen in late February, but on 1 March was observed chasing a red squirrel...toward a bird feeder. It fell exhausted at the entrance to the squirrel's snow tunnel where it lay prostrate for some time. It was obviously in poor physical condition. Bahrt threw some frozen chicken breasts and fish onto the snow near his house. The bobcat was wary in approaching and taking the food, but when it did, it carried the food seven meters from the house to the edge of the nearby woods. It ate some of the meat, buried the rest of it, and then rested nearby within view of the house. Over a period of days, the bobcat spent hours lying in the same spot keeping watch over the squirrel tunnel. Eventually it caught the squirrel. After a week, Bahrt became concerned the bobcat was becoming too habituated and decided it was time to scare it away. Yelling and throwing logs at the bobcat were not effective. In a final effort, he threw out some bread instead of the usual chicken legs and breasts. The bobcat took the bread, then dropped it without eating it, and left Bahrt's yard. It was not seen again....Anecdotal observations such as those made by Bahrt add interesting pieces of information to the growing body of knowledge on the bobcat and are well worth reporting. Many questions, however, remain unanswered: what is the magnitude of bobcat winter mortality; do lynx increase when bobcats decline; how does the ten-year cycle influence lynx and bobcat numbers; and what coactions, if any, occur between the bobcat and the lynx?"— *Roger D. Applegate and Sid Bahrt, "Field Notes: Mortality of the Bobcat in Winter," The Maine Naturalist, vol.1, no.4 p. 227*

Sid Bahrt

Title: The Gulf of Maine Project: Building Partnerships to Protect Living Resources in the Gulf of Maine Watershed

Target Group: Land use decision-makers, general audience

Available from: Gulf of Maine Project, U.S. Fish and Wildlife Service, 4R Fundy Road, Falmouth, ME 04105; telephone (207) 781-8364; fax (207) 781-8369

Cost: Free

COMMENT

This two-page handout describes the U.S. Fish and Wildlife Service Gulf of Maine Project's innovative activities furthering habitat protection efforts in coastal regions of the watershed. In addition, the handout includes a map of the entire Gulf of Maine watershed and a description of important coastal habitats. The watershed map gives an accurate indication of the Gulf of Maine's expanse and is a great tool for students to use and reference individually—a lot easier than carrying an entire poster around. This handout should be part of any introductory curriculum package on the Gulf of Maine. For those interested in knowing more about specific activities at the Gulf of Maine Project, this handout references a series of additional fact sheets that describe habitat analysis, public outreach and habitat protection work being conducted.

EXCERPTS

The Gulf of Maine Project, established in 1991 as one of eleven U.S. Fish and Wildlife Service Coastal Ecosystem Programs, focuses on protecting economically, recreationally, and ecologically important coastal resources throughout the Gulf of Maine watershed. The Gulf of Maine Project compiles and shares biological data with many organizations. Using existing data along with biological expertise and state-of-the-art computer mapping and database management capabilities, the Gulf of Maine Project analyzes data and identifies important habitat. In addition, the Gulf of Maine Project offers technical assistance and directs interested organizations—including local conservation groups and land trusts—to funding opportunities that promote habitat protection...—*U.S. Fish and Wildlife Service, Gulf of Maine Project*

The Gulf of Maine watershed includes a variety of interconnected coastal habitats—salt marshes, mudflats, sandy beaches, intertidal and nearshore subtidal zones and islands. They all play a vital role in sustaining the natural environment and form the basis of human activity in the Gulf region...Cold, oxygen-laden waters subject to constant movement, mixing and upwelling create a nutrient-laden Gulf of Maine Marine environment—one of the world's most productive continental shelf communities. Many who live on the shores of the Gulf of Maine appreciate its biological wealth and have nourished themselves from its bounty. However, habitat loss, wetland and associated upland loss, over-harvesting, oil spills, pollution and other cumulative effects of development threaten the integrity of the Gulf ecosystem.—*U.S. Fish and Wildlife Service, Gulf of Maine Project*

Title: Minnow: The Children's Journal of the Gulf of Maine Aquarium/"A Drop of Water"

Target Group: Grades K-6, members

Available from: Gulf of Maine Aquarium, PO Box 7549, Portland, ME 04112; telephone (207) 772-2321; fax (207) 772-6855

Cost: Free to program participants and aquarium members

COMMENT

"One morning in Maine, a tiny drop of water squeezed out of a leaf. It rested there, reflecting the early morning sun. As the air warmed, the water drop felt itself rising into the atmosphere. No longer liquid, it was transformed into invisible water vapor. The water drifted upward. The leaf where it had lain seemed to grow smaller and smaller until it merged with the rest of the landscape into a patchwork quilt of brown and green and blue."

Thus begins the story of "A Drop of Water," as told in *Minnow*, the children's journal of the Gulf of Maine Aquarium that profiles selected educational and watershed-related issues. Available free of charge to participants in the Aquarium's classroom programs (and included in the newsletter for members), this issue of *Minnow* tells the story of a single drop of water as it turns from vapor back to water in a rain cloud, then falls into the Crooked River where it begins its long journey to Casco Bay through fish gills in Sebago Lake, down pipes that carry it to the bathroom of a Portland home, and on to a sewage treatment center before it reaches the sea. Additional pages describe water cycles and watersheds, the do's and don'ts of everyday water usage, and tactics for practicing water conservation. A clever educational tool for learning about water.

C. Michael Lewis

Title: **Annapolis River Issues**

Target Group: General audience

Available from: Clean Annapolis River Project (CARP), PO Box 395, Annapolis Royal, NS BOS 1AO Canada; telephone (902) 532-7533; fax (902) 678-1253

Cost: Free

COMMENT

Looking for some reading on worm digging in the Annapolis River? Or for information on the Atlantic Sturgeon? Or on the mammoth tides of the Annapolis River region? Currently, this series of fact sheets comprises 56 separate articles on a multitude of topics, all pertaining to the Annapolis River Basin. These articles clearly illustrate the importance of bringing together the expertise and perspectives of many organizations in order to tackle often difficult issues regarding our environment, its living resources, and our communities. More information on CARP is found on page 17.

EXCERPT

"It is to provide this public with information about the Annapolis River and Basin that CARP is sponsoring the preparation of a series of Annapolis River Issues. These articles are designed to present accounts of the state of knowledge about the Annapolis River and its watershed, and especially about issues that are important for its wise management. As far as humanly possible, the known facts will be summarized, or the current state of our ignorance noted—the latter so that attention may be drawn to matters that need to be better examined. It is not the intention that these articles should promote a single viewpoint, but, especially where controversy exists between people with different priorities, that all aspects of the issue may be reviewed so that residents of the Valley can make up their own minds." —*Clean Annapolis River Project*

"Harvesting worms began along with the sport fishery for striped bass and flounder. It is a multimillion dollar industry, especially in the United States. Worms are the most valuable (per pound) natural resource of any major North American marine species....The impact of worm harvesting in the Annapolis is difficult to assess. Because the worms take a long time to mature...it is very easy to overharvest by removing animals before they have a chance to reproduce. This has been the effect in Maine, where overharvesting has destroyed the resource and forced collectors up to the Bay of Fundy system." —*Clean Annapolis River Project, Annapolis River Issues, "Worm Digging in the Annapolis," Chap. 51*

Title: **The Casco Bay Watershed: From Bethel to the Bay poster**

Target: General audience/homeowners

Available from: The Casco Bay Estuary Project, 312 Canco Road, Portland, ME 04103; telephone (207) ~~828-1043~~ 207- 780-4820; fax (207) 828-4001

Cost: Free

COMMENT

This multicolored [14.5 x 20.5 inch] poster includes facts about the Casco Bay watershed and presents a map of the entire region, clearly designating counties, rivers, and lakes. It's a colorful example of the broad geographic scope of the watershed and would be a great illustration for any bulletin board or classroom. See page 115 for more information on the Casco Bay Estuary Project.

EXCERPTS *(taken from map)*

- Approximately 271,000 people live in the Casco Bay watershed.
- There are 37 towns, 3 cities, and 1 township in the Casco Bay watershed.
- There are 1,356 miles of rivers and streams in the Casco Bay watershed.
- There are 1,396 ponds and lakes in the Casco Bay watershed.
- Casco Bay covers 229 square miles.
- There are 578 miles of coastline along Casco Bay.
- There are 785 islands or ledges above mean high water in Casco Bay.
- The mission of the Casco Bay Estuary Project is to preserve the ecological integrity of Casco Bay and ensure the compatible human uses of the Bay's resources through public stewardship and effective management. —*Casco Bay Estuary Project*

23

Title: Getting Started—A Guide to Bringing Environmental Education Into Your Classroom

Target Group: Educators K-12, inservice providers

Available from: The National Consortium for Environmental Education and Training (NCEET), School of Natural Resources & Environment, University of Michigan, Dana Building 430 E. University, Ann Arbor, MI 48109-1115; telephone (313) 998-6726; fax (313) 936-2195

Cost: Single copy, $9.95; bulk rates available

COMMENT

Participating teachers' tales are interspersed with sections that provide practical information on how to start teaching environmental education—whom to call, what to read, and where to get more training. *Getting Started*, an integral piece of NCEET's EE-Toolbox, lists state, federal, nonprofit agencies, and organizations that provide a host of EE resources and general ideas on where to look in your own communities. It includes discussions of how to find funding for projects; networking with other educators; grantwriting tips; and extensive and easy-to-use resource indices and appendices. This guide offers an outstanding combination of practical information and anecdotal inspiration for more than just science educators.

EXCERPTS

"A 138-page guide written for teachers K-12, *Getting Started* uses personal stories about 35 real teachers, in a variety of disciplines, to convey concrete imagery on how to proceed in any classroom and to spotlight innovative ways teachers have integrated environmental education into their classrooms. Resource lists provide teachers with contacts at over 100 governmental, private, and nonprofit organizations that can help you find information on classroom activities, curricula, funding and inservice training opportunities."
—*NCEET*

"Throughout each section, success stories, in the words of the teachers who made them happen, create a web of positive examples illustrating how EE has an exciting role to play in all subject areas and for all grades. The multidisciplinary approach featured in *Getting Started* and the diversity of success stories provided are important strengths of this publication. *Getting Started* should be a valuable inspiration for teachers just beginning to include environmental education in their overall education efforts. The lists of resources contained in *Getting Started* should be a handy reference for the old hands in the field, too. —*Ed McCrea, President, North American Association of Environmental Education. Review*, The Environmental Communicator, *March 1994*

What teachers have to say about Getting Started:
"Where does all the trash go?" Bernice asked the busy students. "In the wastebasket," came the response. "And what happens to it after that?" Student shrugs all around: "It just goes away...."
—*NCEET Bernice Hauser*, Getting Started, *p.69*

"Young kids look at these [small shoots uncurling from the soil] and see some magical element of growth showing itself. By giving them hands-on knowledge about how seeds germinate, stages of growth, soil nutrition, decomposition, and so on, you might take away a bit of the mystery, but you give them an everlasting appreciation of the complexity and the interdependence of the earth's ecosystems."—*NCEET Debra Mullinnix*, Getting Started, *p.100*

"I began to look at myself as more of a facilitator of resources and much less as a source of information."
—*NCEET Karen Kenna*, Getting Started, *p.79*

TERRESTRIAL SYSTEMS

The Gulf of Maine's vast watershed extends far beyond the saltwater and tidal cycles of its 5,200-mile-long coast and extends across the political boundaries of two countries, from Cape Sable in Nova Scotia to Cape Cod, Massachusetts. The watershed's boundary is itself a topographic dividing line—inside this line, surface water flows into the Gulf of Maine; outside the line, water drains into the Gulf of St. Lawrence and other parts of the Atlantic ocean. Everything that happens to the living resources, habitats, and diverse terrestrial systems within the Gulf of Maine watershed ultimately has an impact on the coastal and marine systems of the Gulf of Maine itself.

Far away from the coast, in the northern forests, all facets of natural and human life between "the mountains and the sea" are connected by a web of freshwater flowing through streams, rivers, lakes, ponds, and wetlands, providing terrestrial and aquatic habitat for a diversity of wildlife, birds and plants. The composition of living communities and the interaction of natural systems throughout the entire watershed begins with the terrestrial systems and habitats that are fed by these waters.

We cannot understand coastal and near-shore systems without an awareness of their connection to these terrestrial systems. To do this, we need a general understanding of systems as the basic functioning units in the natural environment. The materials in this chapter present information about ecosystems in general, and about a variety of terrestrial habitats and species in the Gulf of Maine watershed.

Ecosystems: Natural Building Blocks

Biologists define natural ecosystems as distinct ecological units consisting of living communities of plants and animals interacting with the surrounding physical environment of soil, water, and air. Ecosystems are generally classified according to the structure of these components, such as specific plant or animal communities (*e.g.*, coniferous forest ecosystem), or by physical components which can be identified by land forms and water systems (*e.g.*, alpine, meadow, specific river basins). The living communities and structural components of an ecosystem are sustained by a series of interactions with climate, energy and nutrient cycles, and with other, adjacent ecosystems.

...an ecosystem must be managed using ecological principles which "see" no political boundaries... sustained use of the Gulf's resources, not only by ourselves but by future generations, will depend upon our wise stewardship of the Gulf environment...
—*"Sustaining Our Common Heritage," Gulf of Maine Council on the Marine Environment*

Ecosystems exist on a variety of scales, and can be described—depending upon the degree of detail—as everything from a continent to a small pond, or even puddle. The "hierarchy of scales" that we selected for the *Almanac* can be illustrated as follows:

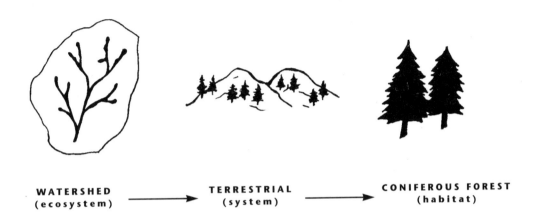

WATERSHED → **TERRESTRIAL** → **CONIFEROUS FOREST**
(ecosystem)   **(system)**   **(habitat)**

Adapted from H. Salwasser, "Conserving Biological Diversity: A Perspective on Scope and Approaches," *Forest Ecology and Management*, vol.35 (1990)

Terrestrial Systems in the Gulf of Maine Watershed

Terrestrial systems in the Gulf of Maine watershed predominate on soil not saturated with water. Human land uses in these upland areas typically include industrial and residential development and agriculture. Both *forest* and *nonforest* habitats are found in dry, upland areas.

The forests of the Gulf of Maine watershed are part of more than 26 million acres of forested lands called the Northern Forest Eco-region, which also includes the Adirondacks, the Berkshires in western Massachusetts, and parts of New Hampshire, Vermont, and southern Quebec. Twice the size of the Greater Yellowstone Eco-region in the western United States, the Northern Forest is currently the largest remaining wildland in the northeast.

Two major forest types—softwood forests (red spruce-balsam fir) and northern hardwoods (yellow birch, American beech, and sugar maple)—exist and mix throughout this region. This forested and mountainous region also supports and sustains a diversity of alpine, wetland and aquatic plant and wildlife communities. Among them are summer breeding grounds for more than 150 species of birds—known as neotropical migrants—that migrate every year to winter in the tropics.

Human impacts on the northern forests in the Gulf of Maine watershed are increasing, largely as a result of timber harvest and a growing demand for residential and recreational development. Intensive logging and development result in habitat fragmentation, disrupting the stabilizing ecological processes within the forest's diverse communities. Long-term sustainable forest-management practices and careful planning for recreational development are at the forefront of discussion and debate about human use of the northern forests.

Non-forest terrestrial systems in the watershed are found in scrub, field, and open or barren lands. Scrub vegetation consists of woody plants that are usually between half a meter and five meters high, with additional grass and other vegetation on the ground. Fields contain annual and perennial nonwoody plants, grasses, and sedges up to 2 meters in height. Exposed rocky surfaces and sandy soils are considered barren land, with little vegetation, with the exception of moss or lichen under one-tenth of a meter high.

Birds and land mammals are the most visible inhabitants of these terrestrial systems, utilizing them for food, shelter, breeding, and raising young. Countless insects and invertebrates live on, in, and over the land as well. Different soils provide habitat for microscopic organisms, insects, worms, and burrowing rodents. They, in turn, contribute to the nutrient cycles of larger systems by helping to aerate the soil and decompose organic material.

The land area and terrestrial systems within the Gulf of Maine watershed are inextricably intertwined in the overall story of the Gulf of Maine environment. Part of that story is told in the materials described in this chapter.

There is a pleasure in the pathless woods.

There is a rapture in the lonely shore,

There is society where none intrudes...

I love not man less, but nature more.

—George Gordon, Lord Byron

Title: **The Northern Forest Forum, Working for Sustainable Natural and Human Communities**

Target Group: General audience

Available from: The Northern Forest Forum, PO Box 6, Lancaster, NH 03584

Cost: $15 subscription (six issues per year)

COMMENT

Read this paper and you'll know the hot topics relating to the Northern Forest, what's politically correct and what's not, and who the players are. More importantly, you'll find out that there is a voice representing people concerned for the future of our Northern Forest and its livings things. This paper is FULL of information, views, opinions, reports, notices, statistics, and charts—which pertain to the Northern Forest. The paper serves as a forum for a host of views—many controversial, some contradictory, and most compelling. To give you a sense of what's here, the *Forum* has covered the proceedings of the Northern Forest Land Council extensively, presented proposals for the Maine Woods National Park (by RESTORE: The North Woods) and the Thoreau Regional Wilderness Reserve, and reported on the debate over the proposed development of the Sears Island Cargoport. The paper regularly features discussions about timber industries, clear-cutting, preservation of endangered species in the Northern Forest areas, restoration of the wolf to the Northern Forest, landowner rights and responsibilities, and more.

EXCERPTS

"The Northern Forest Forum was established two years ago to chronicle the momentous events now re-shaping our region, to inform and empower citizens inside and outside the region, and to promote the creative, bold exchange of ideas. The free and open exchange of ideas is the most critical part of any political, social or environmental movement. Ideas do not spontaneously generate in a vacuum." — *Jamie Sayen, Editor,* The Northern Forest Forum, *vol. 2, no. 6*

Forgotten Language: Giving Voice to the Northern Forest

"We are asking the public to see the Northern Forest in a new way, to make decisions about its future from a new perspective. If we wish this to happen we must first allow the change to occur within us. It is not enough for us to engage in the set rhythms, patterns, and parameters of the current debate. We must lead by going beyond them to introduce a more expansive way of dealing with our relationship to this forest—we must begin to speak in a forgotten language, one that has the power to convey our science and economics as well as our emotions, intuitions and intimate connections to the land....

This forgotten language fosters major change. It allows everyone to move into new frontiers of collaboration because it speaks from a place that is most meaningful to us all.

What is our responsibility to future generations, to people in other regions and countries of this planet, and to nonhuman life which shares the planet with us? Our existing social, economic, and political systems do not help us in accepting these responsibilities. These systems constrain us, and we must move beyond them in order to expand them. These systems that dictate the debate must be informed and then expanded through our own personal experiences with the land. The questions regarding our responsibilities will become real only to the extent that each of us sustains them in all our communications and interactions regarding the Northern Forest."— *Robert Perschel,* The Northern Forest Forum, *vol. 2, no. 3*

28

Title: New Hampshire Conservation Institute Courses, Workshops and Special Events

Target Group: Forest landowners, general audience

Available from: Society for the Protection of New Hampshire Forests, 54 Portsmouth Street, Concord, NH 03301-5400; telephone (603) 224-9945; fax (603) 228-0423

Cost: $10-15 for individual sessions; $50-120 for entire course or session; workshops range from no charge to $30; field trips and special events are anywhere from $3 to $6 for children and $5 to $10 for adults.

COMMENT

"Empowering and educating citizens to monitor and assess the health of their local environment...is a primary goal of the New Hampshire Conservation Institute." Moving into their third year of providing educational programming for forest landowners, professional foresters, teachers, state and federal personnel, and the general public, the New Hampshire Conservation Institute—the educational and research arm of the Society for Protection of New Hampshire Forests (SPNHF)—offers a substantial, affordable year-round program of courses, workshops, and special events. Designed to "foster greater awareness of New Hampshire's natural history and understanding of forest ecology," courses and events include "Nature's Year: A Seasonal Survey" in which participants observe and record nature's cycles in a variety of mediums (sketching, writing, photographing) for six months or in individual sessions if preferred. "Caring for the Land," trains individuals as Land Stewards to monitor and care for state conservation lands. The "Community Tree Stewardship Series" teaches participants to take care of trees—wherever they are— "whether in backyards, along city streets, or in community parks." One day workshops on timely topics like Geographic Information Systems (GIS) and its uses in land conservation have also been presented. Maple sugaring trips, wildflower festivals, and field trips to over 90 SPNHF-owned reservations provide learning opportunities for the entire family. So if you want a limb up—pardon the pun—on your knowledge and appreciation of forests and their value to the Gulf of Maine watershed, this is a mother lode of a source.

EXCERPTS

"The New Hampshire Conservation Institute has something for every interest. You can explore the world of the naturalist, learn how to improve your land for wildlife, or try out the latest in conservation computer technology. Or you could just take a relaxing canoe ride on beautiful Grafton Pond."

"More than 2500 professionals, volunteers, and landowners attended Institute courses and workshops on natural history, forest management, and land protection. In all, expert faculty from the Society and its cooperators held more than 120 individual classes in Concord, Bethlehem, Peterborough and other locations."— *Society for the Preservation of New Hampshire Forests*, Forest Notes, *Autumn 1994, p. 10*

"What will New Hampshire look like in the next century? The Society envisions a living landscape, where working woodlands and protected natural areas are woven into the fabric of life. We envsion large tracts of forestland growing high value wood products, providing jobs and recreation for our people, protecting habitat for native flora and fauna. We see wildlife, river, and trail corridors connecting natural areas with carefully managed forests. We see new partnerships promoting economic incentives, enlightened public policies, and responsible private action."— *from "A Vision and Agenda for the Society's Second Century,"* Forest Notes, *Autumn 1994, p. 9*

Title: **Video Programs by The Society for the Protection of New Hampshire Forests:** *Land in Trust* **(1989) and** *The Careful Timber Harvest: A Guide to Logging Aesthetics* **(1994)**

Target Group: General audience

Available from: Society for the Protection of New Hampshire Forests, 54 Portsmouth Street, Concord, NH 03301-5400; telephone (603) 224-9945; fax (603) 228-0423

Cost: *Land in Trust*, $25; *Logging Aesthetics*, $14; book and video, $20. Prices include shipping and handling.

COMMENT

Two noteworthy videos concerning forest and land conservation practices (each about twenty-minutes long) are available from the Society for the Protection of New Hampshire Forests (SPNHF). *Land in Trust*, a joint program cosponsored by the Vermont Land Trust, The Trustees of Reservations in Massachusetts and SPNHF, is about land protection techniques for landowners, local land trusts, and conservation groups—and anyone else interested in land protection issues. If you don't want to purchase the film, you can borrow it for $4 by contacting the Land Protection Department. Either way, viewing this video is worthwhile.

The second video, *The Careful Timber Harvest: A Guide to Logging Aesthetics* (1994), illustrates a "step-by-step overview of good forest practices," and is available with the accompanying book (*Guide to Logging Aesthetics*, by Geoffrey T. Jones). For more information on SPNHF or their educational and research offerings, see additional information on SPNHF's courses, workshops, and special events on the previous page.

EXCERPT

"The Society is a steward not only of a conservation ethic but of 90 forest reservations where we demonstrate that ethic every day. For decades, we have integrated economically productive timber management with the protection of wildlife habitat, watershed protection, recreation, and aesthetics. As demand for environmentally sensitive, economically sustainable forest management grows, these model woodlots will become ever more important for education and demonstration."— *Society for the Preservation of New Hampshire Forests*, Forest Notes, *Autumn 1994, p. 14.*

Title: **'Bart' the Eagle Presentation, Refuge Tours, and Interpretive Exhibits, Moosehorn National Wildlife Refuge**

Target Group: General audience

Available from: Moosehorn National Wildlife Refuge, P.O. Box 1077, Calais, Maine 04619; telephone (207) 454-3521; fax (207) 454-2550

Cost: Free of charge; contributions appreciated. All contributions towards 'Bart' the Eagle programs are earmarked specifically for Bart's care and upkeep.

COMMENT

On-site and off-site presentations are offered by the staff at Moosehorn National Wildlife refuge to schools, civic groups, and other interested groups. With advance reservations, groups of 20 or 30 can take a guided tour through refuge wildlife areas. Bart, the reserve's captive, flightless bald eagle is a star attraction; in 1993, Bart took part in 25 presentations on endangered species which reached 1,208 people. (Go, Bart!) For further information on Moosehorn NWR programs and presentations, refuge tours, or to make reservations for Bart the Eagle, call or write the refuge.

EXCERPT

"The ... bald eagle frequents both units of the Refuge. In recent years, as many as three pairs of eagles have nested at Moosehorn. Eagles are frequently sighted in the area around the Magurrewock Marshes near Route 1 on the Baring Unit and around the tidal waters of Dennys Bay on the Edmunds Unit."—*Moosehorn NWR*

Title: Yankee Woodlot Forestry Camp

Target Group: General audience/woodland owners

Available from: Tanglewood 4-H Camp and Learning Center, 375 Main Street, Rockland, ME 04841-3304; telephone (207) 596-0063, or 1-800-244-2104 (office); or Tanglewood 4-H Camp and Learning Center, RR2 Box 670, Lincolnville, ME 04849; telephone (207) 789-5868 (camp)

Cost: $190 Maine residents; $240 all others (includes accommodations, meals, and materials)

COMMENT

Offered each fall during the second or third week of September, Tanglewood's Forestry Camp for woodland owners is a short hands-on course in woodland management using a designated woodlot as an outdoor classroom. Learn to read a compass, make a map, read aerial photographs, identify trees and shrubs, evaluate soil conditions, and identify wildlife habitat during five days of hands-on participation. If you're familiar with public television's ten-part series, "Yankee Woodlot," this experience should have particular appeal; Forestry Camp expands on the series which has made scores of people aware of the value of our forests. The forestry camp is located in a remote part of Camden Hills State Park alongside the Ducktrap River which flows into Penobscot Bay just a few minutes away. The setting couldn't get much better than this.

EXCERPTS

A week at Forestry Camp might look something like this:

Monday
Registration & Orientation
Aerial Photo Interpretation
Basic Mapping

Tuesday
Dendrology
Stand Mapping

Wednesday
Ecology & Forest Management

Thursday
Timber Volumes and Values
Visit a Logging Business

Friday
The Management Plan: Putting it all together

Tanglewood: Why do we exist?
"The Tanglewood 4-H Camp was established in 1982 as a project of the Knox-Lincoln County Extension Association and the University of Maine Cooperative Extension to create an affordable, environmentally focused summer camp for Maine youth and to establish a natural resource learning center for people of all ages. Since that time it has become a learning and enrichment center where all ages can develop effective leadership skill, accept and celebrate diversity of culture, develop valuable life skills, and gain a global perspective through local identity."
-Tanglewood 4H Camp and Learning Center

Title: The Coverts Project in Maine

Target Group: General audience/wildlife ecology specialists

Available from: University of Maine (Attention: Cooperative Extension Specialist), 234 Nutting Hall, Orono, ME 04469; telephone (207) 581-2902

Cost: Free including lodging, meals, materials, and transportation

COMMENT

The Coverts Project in Maine is an extensive four-day hands-on training session in wildlife ecology and management designed to teach you about wildlife management in backyards, woodlots, or communities. What's interesting about this program is its commitment to educating entire communities in addition to program participants. Upon being accepted to the program (only twenty are accepted), participants agree to spend at least twenty-five hours in the next year "sharing what you have learned with your friends, neighbors, and community." And as it states in the Coverts literature, this required "payback" (because the program is free, after all) can take the form of just about anything: "You may do a tour of your own woodlot, or give a talk to a local civic group. You may work with a school helping children build bird boxes or conduct an evening class for adults. It's up to you." Whatever the service performed, beneficiaries of this program are not only those lucky enough to attend; our landscapes, our wildlife, our communities, and our children reap the rewards. Global environmental responsibility begins with ourselves and is attainable—an inspiring and promising concept.

EXCERPT

What will you learn about?
- wildlife and forest ecology
- wildlife habitat management
- developing a plan to reach out to your friends and community
- cost-share and incentive program
- wetlands
- many other topics
—compiled from Coverts brochure

A Covert is a thicket that provides shelter for wildlife.

We abuse the land because we regard it as a commodity belonging to us. Only when we see land as a community to which we belong will we treat it with love and respect.
—Aldo Leopold

Title: 4-H Earth Connections

Target Group: Grades K-8

Available from: Tanglewood 4-H Camp and Learning Center, 375 Main Street, Rockland, ME 04841-3304, telephone (207) 596-0063, or 1-800-244-2104 (office); or Tanglewood 4-H Camp and Learning Center, RR2 Box 670, Lincolnville, ME 04849; telephone (207) 789-5868 (camp)

Cost: Day-long program, $8/student; two-day program, $40/student

COMMENT

Earth Connections, one of Tanglewood's youth programs in environmental education, aims at heightening young people's awareness of the natural world and their role in it. Held during spring and fall, Earth Connections offers one- or two-day field trips for school classes from kindergarten through eighth grade. Earth Connections is organized into four topic areas—Yankee Woodlot Expedition, Forest Ecology Adventure, Freshwater Exploration, and Intertidal Discovery. Presentations can be adapted to suit particular grade levels. If a daylong adventure doesn't provide enough time at the woodlot or in the forest examining what lives there, overnight adventures are available for grades 4-8. Groups of eight to ten students sleep in cabins (accompanied by teacher or parent chaperones), and participants can expect to learn as much about themselves and cooperation as they do about ecology and their environment. Whether you opt for the one- or two-day experience, both hands-on, discovery-oriented expeditions are memorable for kids and grownups.

Other Tanglewood youth programs include a residential summer camp program (ages 8-14) and a day camp for younger campers (ages 6-8). All are environmentally focused with the goal of developing life-long skills, a sense of community spirit, and an awareness of the natural world among participants.

EXCERPTS

Yankee Woodlot Expedition

"This new educational experience is available to fourth graders or older students. Participants will spend a day learning the basic concepts of ecology along with lessons of sustainable forestry and woodlot management in a recently harvested demonstration area. Earthkeeping activities, such as creating habitats for small mammals and birds will be a part of the process. The day will also include an understanding of where wood and paper products come from, along with an emphasis on recycling paper."—*Tanglewood 4-H Camp and Learning Center*

Forest Ecology Adventure

"Students will be led on an expedition deep into the forest on all fours and with all senses, looking for signs of the many wild animals that live together with the trees, plants, and fungi in a mixed coniferous/deciduous forest. Through hands-on scientific methods students will discover the interconnected world of the forest "from the ground up", investigating soils, trees, and the wildlife that depend on these for their food and shelter."
—*Tanglewood 4-H Camp and Learning Center*

What will Tanglewood's 4-H Earth Connections program offer for those who participate?

Each day is designed to lead students through activities that will:

•Heighten Sensitivity

•Increase Awareness

•Improve Understanding

•Awaken Appreciation

•Encourage Commitment

•Invite Action

In addition, teachers will be provided with specific school-site ideas and activities for follow-up of the day's events. —*Tanglewood 4-H Camp and Learning Center*

Wilderness is the raw material out of which man has hammered the artifact called civilization.
—*Aldo Leopold*

Title: Project WILD Activity Guide

Target Group: Grades K-12

Available from: Maine Department of Inland Fisheries and Wildlife, Station 41, Augusta, ME 04333-0041; telephone, (207) 287-3371; fax (207) 287-6395. Project Wild, 5430 Grosvenor Lane, Bethesa, MD 20814; telephone (301) 493-5447; fax (301) 493-5627

Cost: Activity guides free *upon completion of six-hour workshop.* Workshop fee, $5. Workshops are arranged on a by-request basis. For more information contact Lisa Kane, Project Wild, (207) 287-3303.

COMMENT

Developed by the Western Association of Fish and Wildlife Agencies and the Western Regional Environmental Education Council, *Project WILD* has a steadily growing list of sponsors and contributors including the U.S. Environmental Protection Agency (EPA), National Wildlife Federation, U.S. Fish and Wildlife Service, National Audubon, International Association of Fish and Wildlife Agencies, and other prominent environmental organizations—all of which goes to say that this program in environmental education has a proven track record.

Organized into seven different sections, each activity in the *Project WILD* guide can be used independently or to supplement existing curriculums. Sections include: "Awareness and Appreciation"; "Diversity of Wildlife Values"; "Ecological Principles"; "Management and Conservation"; "People, Culture and Wildlife"; "Trends, Issues, and Consequences"; "Responsible Human Actions"; and a hefty section of appendices. *Project WILD* and its partner, *Project WILD Aquatic* (see page 50), is thorough and engaging in its approach, encouraging experiential learning about the environment. This guide should be a staple in any environmental education curriculum.

EXCERPTS

"Project WILD is based on the premise that young people and their teachers have a vital interest in learning about the earth as home for people and wildlife. The program emphasizes wildlife—because of its intrinsic, ecological and other values, as well as its importance as a basis for understanding the fragile grounds upon which all life rests. *Project WILD* is designed to prepare young people for decisions affecting people, wildlife and their shared home, Earth. In the face of pressures of all kinds affecting the quality and sustainability of life on earth as we know it,

Project WILD addresses the need for human beings to develop as responsible members of the ecosystem.

The goal of *Project WILD* is to assist learners of any age in developing awareness, knowledge, skills, and commitment to result in informed decisions, responsible behavior, and constructive actions concerning wildlife and the environment upon which all life depends."—*Project WILD*

"Some might say that *Project WILD* is an excellent set of teaching materials bound in an attractive format. Professional educators could describe these materials as a supplementary, interdisciplinary, educational program directed at providing learning experiences for students in kindergarten through grade twelve.

Project WILD is these things and more. These descriptions fall short of capturing the essence of the program. Quite simply, *Project WILD* is people—educators, resource managers, citizen conservationists and others—doing something together that they believe is important for children, and for the land and its resources, now and for the future."—*Project WILD*

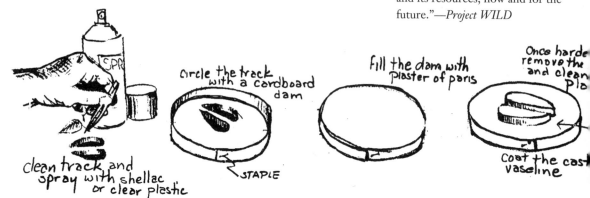

clean track and spray with shellac or clear plastic

circle the track with a cardboard dam

STAPLE

fill the dam with plaster of paris

Once harde remove the and clean Pla

coat the cast vaseline

Title: Mast Landing Camp

Target Group: Grades 2-9

Available from: Maine Audubon Society, Environmental Education Department, 118 Route One, P.O. Box 6009, Falmouth, ME 04105-6009; telephone (207) 781-2330; fax (207) 781-6185

Cost: Day Camp—$140-220 members, $155-240 nonmembers; Adventure Camp—$220-295 members, $245-320 nonmembers. Partial scholarships are available.

COMMENT

Maine Audubon Summer Camp programs at the Mast Landing Camp are divided into two age groups: a day camp for grades 2-6 and an adventure camp for grades 5-6. Sessions for both camps are either one or two weeks long. Day Camp programs range from studying art in nature through weaving, papermaking, and sculpture to learning about Native American life by building shelters and studying about village life. The adventure camp for older campers offers trips to Maine islands, backpacking expeditions in the White Mountains, or canoeing on rivers and lakes. All trips are staffed by state-certified leaders. Kids who want a fun and unique camp experience should join one of these Audubon experiences.

EXCERPTS

"Exploration and discovery are the heart of Mast Landing Nature Day Camp. A staff-to-camper ratio of one-to-seven provides exceptional educational opportunities and personal attention. Campers participate in a variety of nature-related activities that are challenging and fun. Each session has a theme that is expressed through experiential activities. These include structured group activities, solo experiences, and a choice time. Swimming, mudflat exploration, and all-camp games are traditional highlights at camp. Two sessions offer overnight adventures on the sanctuary. Camp meets Monday through Friday from 9:30 a.m. until 3:00 p.m."
—*Maine Audubon Society*

"Our Adventure Camp [offers] three canoe trips throughout the summer. One or two days of each session will introduce campers to trip preparation procedures such as gear review, packing, safety, fire-building, and logistics. Campers will also participate in team-building activities on our new challenge course. Adventure Camp trips are three to four days in length. Trips are led by the Adventure Camp director and a trip leader/naturalist…Group limit: twelve participants."—*Maine Audubon Society*

Our Goals

- **To introduce nature in a way that inspires imagination and appreciation.**

- **To create positive outdoor experiences for the campers.**

- **To increase camper's knowledge of their surroundings.**

- **To instill a sense of individual responsibility for the environment.** —*Maine Audubon Society*

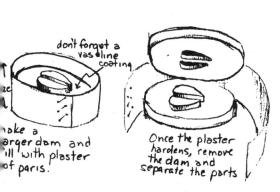

don't forget a vaseline coating

...ake a ...arger dam and ...ll with plaster of paris.

Once the plaster hardens, remove the dam and separate the parts

Paint the finished track so it looks realistic

34

Title: Maine Audubon Nature Programs and Nature Talks

Target Group: All ages

Available from: Maine Audubon Society, Gilsland Farm, 118 U.S. Route One, PO Box 6009, Falmouth, ME 04105-6009; telephone (207) 781-2330; fax (207) 781-6185

Cost: Weekend programs, $3 members; $4 nonmembers; special programs and trips vary in price. Contact Maine Audubon for schedule, information and/or reservations.

COMMENT

Maine Audubon Society operates an impressive number of programs and events year-round out of its headquarters at Gilsland Farm Environmental Center. During the summer (June, July and August,) weekend programs such as "What's Wrong with Maine's Bald Eagles?", "Wolves, Coyotes and Us," and "Hands-On Rocks" are offered in addition to art classes, nature walks around the farm, and evening programs to learn about constellations. Winter programs include winter camping seminars, an "Introduction to Snowshoeing," "Winter Tracking," and nature walks to study winter ecology, look at animal tracks around the farm, or simply enjoy the pristine surroundings of Gilsland Farm in its winter attire. Unless otherwise noted, most programs take place on Saturday or Sunday afternoons and last about an hour and a half.

Maine Audubon's extensive programs aren't limited to Gilsland Farm itself. (Contact MAS headquarters to find out what's happening near you.) Scarborough Marsh Nature Center, Mast Landing Sanctuary, and Fore River Sanctuary provide additional sites for natural history programs, canoe tours, marsh walks, or just traipsing around trails open to the public. The Discovery Center, located behind the visitor center at Gilsland Farm, is a great place for parents to introduce their young ones to the natural world. Hands-on activities and displays in the center provide interesting interactive learning. For more information on activities at Scarborough Marsh Nature Center, see pages 62; for other educational Audubon programs and materials see pages 33, 42, 43 and 55.

> "Now I see the secret of the making of the best persons. It is to grow in the open air, and to eat and sleep with the earth."
> —*Walt Whitman*

EXCERPT

"Gilsland Farm is the headquarters of the Maine Audubon Society, an independent environmental organization dedicated to the protection, conservation, and enhancement of Maine's ecosystems through the promotion of individual understanding and actions.

Gilsland Farm Environmental Center offers public programs throughout the year on 60 acres of rolling fields, woods and marshland alongside the Presumpscot Estuary in Falmouth. Two miles of trails are ideal for walking, cross-country skiing, and nature study. Indoor programs are held in the visitor center building. The Gilsland Farm grounds are open to the public, free of charge, every day from dawn until dusk."—*Maine Audubon Society*

Past Special Programs and Events hosted by Audubon:

Buzzing Bees: Preschool Discovery—Buzzing Bees is a fun and exciting 90 minutes of stories and activities for preschoolers.

Winter Bird Seed Sale—Maine Audubon's midwinter seed sale is an excellent time to replenish your supply of bird feed.

Seminar: Paths of Beauty in a Time of Despair—This seminar focuses on developing one's understanding of self and nature as a means of balancing the pain of current environmental reality.

Mushroom Hunter's Day—This daylong program...will include a combination of outdoor and indoor sessions, covering the beauty and ecological importance of fungi and their adaptations, identification techniques to distinguish edible from poisonous varieties, and field observation. —*Sample programs from Maine Audubon brochure*

Title: **National Audubon Society Expedition Institute Program Catalog and Video**

Target Group: College, undergraduate and graduate students

Available from: Audubon Expedition Institute, 155 High Street, PO Box 365, Department WG, Belfast, ME 04915; telephone (207) 338-5859; fax (207) 338-1037

Cost: Contact AEI/Lesley Degree Program for more information on tuition, application fees and financial aid.

COMMENT

If you're a high school senior, college undergraduate, or graduate student and if you're looking for an environmental education experience that gets you into the field, Audubon Expedition Institute (AEI) in affiliation with Lesley College, in Cambridge, Massachusetts, has a degree program for you. AEI carries you across North America studying environmental, community, and cultural issues in a variety of settings and contexts. For up to four semesters, students travel by bus, in groups of 20, to different regions of the country while studying a curriculum that conforms to high academic standards and is also specifically geared to the needs and benefits of a classroom on the road. By experiencing community living; developing individual programs and initiatives; leading seminars; conducting extensive research; meeting with authors, politicians, activists, environmental leaders along the way; student experiences become a vast collection of personal journeys. The program motto, "Our Campus is North America," illustrates the enormity of opportunity with AEI. Each semester focuses on travel in a particular region: Pacific Northwest Semester, Southwest Semester, Mountain/Plains Semester, Canadian Maritime/New England Semester, and a Southeast Semester. Courses are taught in communication, education, environmental studies, humanities, natural sciences, and psychology. While both a master's and a bachelor's degree in environmental education and environmental studies, respectively, can be earned from AEI and Lesley College, there are other options. Undergraduates, for instance, can transfer credits to a college of their choice. High school seniors can earn college credit while finishing their high school credits through Lesley's Advanced Placement Program. In other words, if there's a will to get on board, there's a way.

EXCERPTS

"Nature has always been and continues to be our best teacher. The places we have visited, and the people who inhabit them, have guided our thoughts. We have changed and grown as environmental and student needs have changed. Our lessons have been transforming, and through our experiences we have created an academic program that speaks to the environmental and educational needs of today.

We offer an opportunity to actively experience nature and people as parts of a whole. Our program fosters a thorough understanding of the world of plant, animal, air, earth, and spirit—the world where community, relationships, and life are of primary importance."—*AEI*

"AEI alumni hold key positions in education, industry, health care, law, and political and social activism. Graduates leave AEI with more than facts and figures—they leave with the skills and motivation to create change. With minds open to creative solutions, the expertise to investigate diverse viewpoints, and an ability to facilitate critical decision-making in the face of conflict, AEI alumni are affecting the conservation of all life."—*AEI*

What Alumni are saying:

"Living in a close-knit community for months at a time brings on feelings and situations that can never be gained from anything other than experience. My years at AEI were a time of accelerated growth, and occasionally I pat myself on the back for having had the courage to grab that much maturity all at one time. I need to climb the rocks, smell the flowers, canoe the rivers, or sleep on the moss to really fall passionately in love with a place. I learned this at AEI. Traveling to wild and beautiful places connected my thoughts to my feelings and instilled in me an appreciation that I could not have found anywhere else."
—*Jim Peterson;*
AEI Program Brochure

"If an environmental education means anything it must activate our connections with nature. It must energize our hearts and minds so that we care as much about the Earth as a favorite loved one...AEI provided such a unique educational process for me."—Dennis Paige; AEI Program Brochure

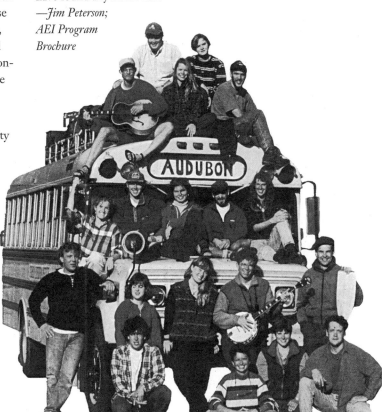

36

Sample activity, from Class #1:

Identify basic facts about migratory bird journeys:

A. Ask students to take out a quarter; hand out quarters to each student who doesn't have one. (Expect the students to toss and flip their quarters.)

B. Hand out a copy of the blackpoll warbler page to each student.

C. Focus attention on the over 2,000 mile journey of this quarter-weight bird, which doesn't carry any suitcase or backpack, but which finds ways to survive.

D. Ask the class to think about how the bird survives and how the bird gets basic necessities such as water, food, shelter, and warmth, without bringing anything with it, or carrying a suitcase. Explain that these are the kind of questions we will try to explore in this course.

E. Suggest that, each time they handle a quarter, the students think about the amazing journey of the blackpoll warbler and other migratory birds.—*U.S. Environmental Protection Agency, "Partners in a Paradise"*

Title: Partners in a Paradise: Migratory Birds and Our Habitat/ A Secondary School Curriculum Providing a Focused Introduction to Ecosystem Protection and Biodiversity

Target: Middle school, high school students

Available from: United States Environmental Protection Agency, 841 Chestnut Building, Philadelphia, PA 19107; telephone (215) 597-0376; fax (215) 597-3235

Cost: Currently available free of charge

COMMENT

This is a big curriculum—and not just in the number of pages and length of lessons. It's big in scope, meaning, and intent. *Partners in a Paradise* is a unique program structured around the study of migratory birds, biodiversity and ecosystem protection. Besides presenting environmental and scientific information, it is a curriculum intent on instilling values and appreciation for the natural world. It invites students—and teachers—to experience the joys of discovering birds and to understand the threats birds face from environmental hazards. Highly structured and well organized, the curriculum is arranged in units: "The Wonder of Birds, Migration and Survival in Natural Ecosystems"; "Flight to New World Habitats"; "Discovering Birds First-Hand"; and "Problems and Partnership in Biodiversity." Each unit includes several lesson plans—amounting to 22 lesson plans in the entire curriculum. Field trips, class activities, discussions about migration, mapping migratory routes, and bird identification are just a few of the activities suggested. Students are encouraged to begin a "life-list" to record every bird they encounter. Several additional sources for information are suggested, including audio-visual materials, books and relevant periodicals, and class-by-class outlines summarizing each unit to be presented. This innovative approach to studying and sustaining biodiversity is worth considering. Fewer and fewer songbirds are singing; it's time we listened.

EXCERPTS

"The study of migratory birds can be extraordinary...because in addition to its novelty, it has the potential to: 1) provide an interesting and focused introduction to the important topic of biodiversity and ecosystem protection; and 2) meaningfully interrelate a variety of school subjects that are usually packaged separately and taught in isolation....Learning about migratory birds provides a focused introduction to the crucially important planetary matters of biodiversity and ecosystem protection, and of sustainable survival for us all."
—*U.S. Environmental Protection Agency, "Partners in a Paradise"*

"This curriculum focuses on the students' own experiences and ideas, and attempts to personalize the topic of migratory birds in a way that will have long-term meaning for each student. The in-depth and integrated study of birds is important, but the overriding goal of the course is to develop in each student a curiosity for, a delight and intrigue in, and a respect for, the topics of migratory birds, biodiversity, and human relationships to natural systems that will last a lifetime...."—*U.S. Environmental Protection Agency, "Partners in a Paradise"*

From Segment Overview section:

Class #4 is set up to be an immersion into the South American rain forest. The lush rain forest is looked at as a total habitat, of which birds are an important piece. The rich and colorful beauty of the rain forest is a treasure to explore, even in second-hand pictures. It leads into a mystery to which no one really knows the complete answer...why would birds ever leave that warm paradise, to come to North America? These and similar questions are posed and considered in Class #5....

Appreciating the magnitude, length and difference of these journeys, and locating the islands, continents and... countries along the way is the focus of Classes #5, 6, and 7....In addition to opportunities to discuss and investigate the political and social conditions in the various countries, it is an excellent opportunity to focus on comparative land use and sociological patterns, examining which types of land use and culture provide habitat in which the birds, and other wildlife, can survive and biodiversity can flourish....

[Throughout classes #17-21] students [are encouraged] to think about broader issues concerning birds as important populations in the earth's natural systems, and to realize that migratory birds raise crucial issues at the local, national, and international levels, particularly regarding ecosystem protection. The final classes of the course are designed to be upbeat, focusing students on the existing tools humans have to protect migratory birds and biodiversity, and how the students can use these tools effectively."—*U.S. Environmental Protection Agency, "Partners in a Paradise"*

Title: The Chewonki Foundation Outreach Programs

Target: All ages

Available from: The Chewonki Foundation, RR2, Box 1200, Wiscasset, ME 04578; telephone (207) 882-7323; fax (207) 882-4074

Cost: One presentation $85; two presentations $170; three presentations $240; four presentations $300; each additional presentation $75; plus transportation costs at $.25 per mile from Wiscasset.

COMMENT

Several of Chewonki's programs on terrestrial ecosystems are described in detail below. Additional outreach units are available: "Endangered Species—Maine's Rare Creatures" (grades 4-adult); "Owls of Maine—The Habits and Adaptations of Maine's Native Owls" (all ages); "Scales and Tales— Amazing Reptiles!" (K-adult); "The Batmobile—Bats of the World" (all ages); "The Rain Forest—Diversity of Species" (grades 4-adult); and "The Bugmobile— Insects and their Relatives" (grades 2-8). "Fins & Flippers— The Ultimate Hands-on Experience!" is described on page 82; "Too Much Trash" and "The Rhythms of Farm Life" can be found on page 119. Contact Chewonki for an outreach program brochure and additional information on fees and reservations.

EXCERPTS

"Chewonki's Outreach Programs have been created to help students and teachers, parents and librarians, business executives and assembly-line operators discover and explore the lives of plants and animals and the world they inhabit. In 60 short minutes, students of all ages heft pilot whale vertebrae to assemble a skeletal puzzle; they handle paws, talons, teeth and beaks to understand the relationship between form and function; they scrutinize their own use of resources to find ways to conserve; and they sit quietly, enraptured, before a barred owl, American kestrel, iguana, big brown bat, or American alligator.

We believe that environmental ethics are *learned*, and that group problem-solving is central to the lesson. The programs presented here may help you as a parent, teacher, camp director, librarian or business manager to enhance the environmental literacy of your children, students, or peers."—*The Chewonki Foundation Natural History Outreach Program brochure*

The Balance of Nature—Predators (grades 3-8)

"Predators play important roles in nature yet they are commonly misunderstood and mistreated. We look at predators from around the world and examine predator-prey relationships. We explore attitudes toward predators and reasons for their persecution throughout history. Belle, our live American kestrel, shows the unique adaptations of birds of prey. A mounted coyote is the focus of discussion on current issues that relate to predators in Maine."

Fur, Feathers & Feet—Introduction to Birds and Mammals (grades pre–K-1)

"What makes a bird a bird and a mammal a mammal? How are they alike and how do they differ? This program, designed for grades pre-K-1 is an active discovery time using many hands-on materials and activities. We dress up two volunteers as a bird and a bear to illustrate how birds and mammals adapt. Our live black duck, Millie, and mounted mammal specimens provide a close look at animals and their special features."

From Mice to Moose—Mammals of Maine (grades 2-6, maximum group size of 25)

"Students participate in hands-on activities to develop an understanding of the mammals of Maine. Using an extensive collection of mounted mammals, tanned skins, skulls, and other specimens, we investigate specific adaptations and identify the important roles these animals play in the intricate food web."

Josephine W. Ewing

38

Title: Maine Bureau of Parks and Recreation/Department of Conservation Outreach Programs

Target Group: Grades 3-5

Available from: Maine Bureau of Parks and Recreation, Maine Department of Conservation, Station 22, Augusta, ME 04333-0022; telephone (207) 287-3821; fax (207) 287-3823

Cost: Free

COMMENT

Maine's Bureau of Parks and Recreation offers free outreach programs to schools and other interested groups around the state. "Earth Day Every Day" and "Parks in the Schools" are two subject areas represented, and though each is designated for grades 3-5, both clusters of lessons can be adapted for other age groups. Following the theme of *You can do a world of good. Every day is Earth Day*, the "Earth Day Every Day" program provides slide shows on current environmental problems, a hands-on activity on water pollution, an "Animal Jeopardy" game to teach appropriate behavior around animals, and a brainstorming session focusing on things children can do to improve their environment. Similarly, "Parks in the Schools" includes a short slide show, a recycling activity, a "Park Town Meeting," and role-playing. All activities aim to promote understanding and stewardship of our natural environment so that young people will want to take care of it. Make arrangements by contacting one of the Maine Bureau of Parks and Recreation offices listed below. Programs are offered primarily from November through March, when outdoor activity at the state parks dwindles.

EXCERPTS

"Earth Day Every Day" objectives:

"Participants will see the Earth as a beautiful and fragile place, exemplified by and connected with their nearby state parks. They will see themselves as responsible for their Earth and capable of helping to take care of it through their actions in their own communities.

Participants will be able to:
1. Show the way they think that the Earth's land, water, air, and living things should be;
2. Name some places where they can enjoy an unspoiled environment, including their state parks;
3. Discuss appropriate behavior around animals in their environment, especially in regard to the threat of rabies;
4. Demonstrate knowledge of some ways in which their environment is being degraded;
5. Explain that everything in the world is connected, and that the things that happen half a world away will affect participants and their favorite places;
6. See themselves as agents responsible for their Earth through actions on a local level that will make a difference on a global level.—*Maine Bureau of Parks and Recreation*

"Parks in the Schools" objectives:

"Our aim is to educate people who use the outdoors about the kinds of responsible behavior that will ensure the continuation of this environment in the future. We hope that people will apply what they learn from parks to other aspects of their own lives.

Participants in this program will be able to:
1. Name state parks and historic sites that offer various opportunities for enjoyment;
2. Hear about and see park resources that need their care;
3. Discuss appropriate behavior around the animals in their environment, especially regarding the threat of rabies;
4. Demonstrate understanding of the importance of separating trash as the basis of recycling;
5. Describe things that people should do to help care for the environment in the parks and elsewhere."—*Maine Bureau of Parks and Recreation*

Conservation is a state of harmony between men and land—*Aldo Leopold*

Offices of the Maine Bureau of Parks and Recreation:

Maine Bureau of Parks and Recreation (287-3821), State House Station 22, Augusta, ME 04333

Southern Region (693-6231), RR1, Box 101, Naples, ME 04055

Central Region (596-2253), RR1 Box 1070, Thomaston, ME 04861

Western Region (645-4217), PO Box 523, Wilton, ME 04294-0523

Northeast Region (764-2040), 1235 Central Drive, Presque Isle, ME 04769

Penobscot River Corridor (695-3721), PO Box 817, Greenville, ME 04441

Title: A Guide for Conserving Wild Plants of Maine

Target Group: General audience

Available from: The Maine Natural Areas Program, Maine Department of Conservation, Station 93, Augusta, ME 04333; telephone (207) 287-2211; fax (207) 287-8040

Cost: Free

COMMENT

As a tool for promoting voluntary conservation of Maine's natural areas, the Maine Natural Areas Program provides this comprehensive list of wild plants and conservation recommendations. "Natural areas" are defined as, "those lands in Maine that support rare and endangered plants and animals, exemplary natural communities, and unique geological, hydrological, or scenic features." *A Guide for Conserving Wild Plants of Maine* reflects the program's commitment to protect valuable scientific—and aesthetic—resources around the state by educating landowners and encouraging voluntary conservation actions. Inventorying and monitoring species, administering the official list of Maine's endangered and threatened plants, maintaining a register of natural areas, and promoting natural area conservation through education, publications, and presentations are some of the tasks of the Maine Natural Areas Program. The pamphlet offers guidelines in the following sections: "Good Manners for Conservation"; "Special Cautions"; "Pick Freely Where Abundant"; "Pick in Moderation Only Where Abundant" and "Leave Growing-Do Not Disturb." A key explains how species are categorized in each section and what special cautions should be noted. It's worth getting a copy of this leaflet. Keep it where you can refer to it easily; it's a handy source.

This guide was developed and compiled by the Garden Club Federation of Maine with technical assistance from the Josselyn Botanical Society and the Endangered Plant Technical Advisory Committee of the Maine Critical Areas Program.

EXCERPTS

Good Manners for Conservation

Obey No Trespassing signs. Ask owner's permission.

Before picking or digging wild plants:

—Use a camera. "It is better to take nothing but pictures and leave nothing but footprints."

—Ask yourself, "Do I really need this?"

—Identify the plants. Use this list with wild plant guides.

—Pick only common plants when and where abundant.

—Pick only what you need and can transport in good condition.

—Use clippers or knife when gathering flowers.

—After picking, keep flowers or plants fresh and moist.

—Always leave more than enough blossoms to develop seeds for future plants.

—Before disturbing any plant, consider its many values in nature. Is it a ground cover, protecting against soil erosion? Does it provide food or cover for wildlife? What are its relationships with nearby plants?

The greatest threat to our wild plants is destruction of habitat. When plants are about to be destroyed by road construction or building development, a plant rescue operation may be tried.

—Secure permission of the owner.

—If possible, transplant the threatened plants to a nature center, preserve, park, or other protected area open to the public.

—Take plenty of soil to protect the roots.

—Try to plant in the same kind of setting, habitat, and soil type.

—It's best to transplant in early spring or after the seeds ripen.

—*Maine Natural Areas Program,* A Guide to Conserving Wild Plants of Maine

Additional publications available from the Maine Natural Areas Program:

• *Elements of Natural Diversity: Rare, Threatened, and Endangered Plants*

• *Natural Landscapes of Maine: A Classification of Ecosystems and Natural Communities ($3.50)*

• *A Classification System of Marine and Estuarine Habitats in Maine: An Ecosystem Approach to Habitats*

Pick in Moderation Only Where Abundant

A	Arrowhead
S	Bayberry or Candleberry
	Black Alder or Winterberry
A	Blue Flag
F	Blue Vervain
W	Bunchberry
A	Buttonbush
W	Checkerberry or Wintergreen
W	Dogtooth Violet or Trout-Lily
S	Dusty Miller
W	Goldthread
W	Groundnut
A	Labrador Tea
A	Marsh Marigold or Cowslip
W	Partridgeberry#
F	Ragwort
F	Rose
W	Shadbush
F,W	Viburnum
F,W	Violet, White

Special Cautions

\# These plants are threatened by collection for holiday decoration and commercial use.

Special Habitats

F Fields, roadsides, cutover areas, disturbed areas

W Woodlands and edges of woods

A Wetlands and aquatic habitats

S Special habitats— bogs, mountaintops, cliffs, seashores, sand dunes, salt marshes

—*Maine Natural Areas Program,* A Guide to Conserving Wild Plants of Maine

Title: The Refuge Reporter

Target Group: General audience

Available from: National Wildlife Association, 10824 Fox Hunt Lane, Potomac, MD 20854; telephone (301) 983-9498

Cost: $12 for annual subscription; $22 for two-year subscription

COMMENT

The *Refuge Reporter* is a quarterly publication entering its third year of being "devoted exclusively to news and commentary about the National Wildlife Refuge (NWR) System managed by the Fish and Wildlife Service of the U.S. Department of the Interior." Reporting on news at the national and local levels from the 500 refuges in the current National Wildlife Refuge system, the *Reporter* communicates the need for public involvement in the establishment and ongoing care of wildlife refuges. In the 1994 summer issue, there was an article particularly pertinent to the Gulf of Maine entitled "Wildly Different Wildlife Habitat in Seven Down East Maine Refuges." A substantial piece of the article is devoted to Moosehorn NWR. (The article also includes Maine's other downeast refuges: Petit Manan, Pond Island, Cross Island, Franklin Island, Seal Island, and Sunkhaze Meadows.) For a general discussion of Moosehorn NWR, this is a good source of information on its management, the birds and mammals thriving there, and activities available to the public as well as a short sidebar about Moosehorn's ongoing research on the American woodcock. While you're at it, read the rest of the newspaper (just a few 8.5" x 11" pages) and learn about other issues. This informal little publication provides interesting insights into the workings and policy-making of the National Wildlife Refuge system.

"It is a country full of ever-green trees, of mossy silver birches and watery maples, the ground dotted with insipid, small, red berries, and strewn with damp and moss-grown rocks, a country diversified with innumerable lakes and rapid streams, peopled with trout and various species of leucisci, with salmon, shad, and pickerel, and other fishes; the forest resounding at rare intervals with the note of the chickadee, the blue-jay, and the wood-pecker, the scream of the fish-hawk and the eagle, the laugh of the loon, and the whistle of ducks along the solitary streams; at night, with the hooting of owls and howling of wolves; in summer, swarming with myriads of black flies and mosquitoes, more formidable than wolves to the white man. Such is the home of the moose, the bear, the caribou, the wolf, the beaver, and the Indian. Who shall describe the inexpressible tenderness and immortal life of the grim forest, where Nature, though it be mid-winter, is ever in her spring, where the moss-grown and decaying trees are not old, but seem to enjoy a perpetual youth; and blissful, innocent Nature, like a serene infant, is too happy to make a noise, except by a few tinkling, lisping birds and trickling rills?"
—Henry David Thoreau, The Maine Woods

EXCERPTS

"Moosehorn NWR is unrivaled in American woodcock research, a major reason for its establishment. These upland birds are intensely studied and managed at Moosehorn, where suitable nesting and feeding habitat is maintained.

This northeastern refuge is also outstanding for a number of other reasons: a wide variety of wildlife; large expanses of forested, water, and wetland areas; and spectacular coastal scenery. Visitors will find something to do at Moosehorn year-round, whether enjoying nature and viewing wildlife, hiking, or cross-country skiing and snowmobiling.

Moosehorn NWR was established in 1937 as the first in the chain of migratory bird refuges that stretch more than 2000 miles along the east coast to the Florida Keys. The refuge consists of two units totaling 24,000 acres (37.5 square miles), a third of which is designated wilderness."
— The Refuge Reporter, *vol. 2, no. 4, Summer 1994*

"There is a wealth of information that needs to be made available to people, whether they are seriously or only casually interested in national wildlife refuges. If subscriber renewal rates are any indicator, we think that *Refuge Reporter* is appreciated as an interesting and helpful information source."
—The Refuge Reporter, *vol. 2, no. 4, Summer 1994*

Painted by Nancy Howe

Title: Moosehorn National Wildlife Refuge Self-guided Walks and Trails

Target Group: General audience

Available from: Moosehorn National Wildlife Refuge, PO Box 1077, Calais, ME 04619; telephone (207) 454-3521; fax (207) 454-2550

Cost: Free

COMMENT

At the Baring Unit of the Moosehorn National Wildlife Refuge (covering 16,080 acres, located off U.S. Route 1 southwest of Calais) there are 50 miles of trails and roads open for hiking, cross-country skiing, and snowmobiling. The Woodcock Trail lends insights into the life and management of the American woodcock; the Bird Walk provides access to viewing many birds living in and migrating through the refuge (including bald eagles and great horned owls); and the Nature Trail, the newest trail, leads trekkers through a variety of habitats. Each trail is self-guided and has a corresponding leaflet describing the significance of particular stops along the way. (Other leaflets listing the birds and mammals of the refuge are also available.) A nice way to get outside, get healthy, and get smart, too.

Julien Beauregard

EXCERPTS

Stop 5—The Nature Trail

"You have entered a very important area for wildlife. Aspen (locally called popple) provides feeding areas for woodcock, nesting areas for songbirds, and food for grouse, deer, and moose. Therefore, the Moosehorn National Wildlife Refuge is managed to produce aspen in many areas. Aspen will not grow underneath other trees so areas are cut to allow them room to grow. They grow from seeds, or more often, sprout from the roots of cut trees, and may grow six feet in one year. The brush piles you see throughout the trail provide shelter and observation posts for birds, snowshoe hares, shrews and mice."—*United States Fish and Wildlife Service, Moosehorn NWR*

Stop 4— The Woodcock Trail

"Clearings are used as courting areas and as summer and fall night roosting areas. A few minutes after sunset each evening in the spring, the male walks or flies into a small opening called the singing ground to perform his spectacular courtship, buzzing "peent" every 4 or 5 seconds. After repeating himself about 20 times, the male takes flight.

The spiraling courtship flight lasts about one minute, during which time he emits a vocal chirping combined with a whistle of wings. During the final few seconds of flight he drops silently to his singing ground and starts the series over until darkness. A similar ritual takes place at dawn before the male returns to his daytime cover. These openings are also used in the summer. As soon as the young are able

to fly, woodcock move to these openings or to large fields each evening at dusk. The reason for this behavior is not clear, but current evidence shows that woodcock do not feed extensively in fields at night, except during migration. Perhaps the likelihood of encountering predators in fields is less than in daytime cover. (These areas are maintained as fields through controlled and mowing.)"
—*U. S. Fish and Wildlife Service, Moosehorn NWR*

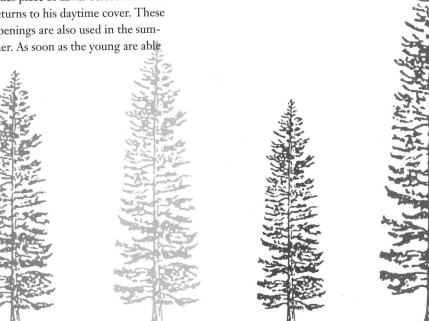

42

Title: Maine Audubon Classroom Outreach Programs

Target Group: Grades K-8

Available from: Maine Audubon Society, Gilsland Farm, 118 U.S. Route One, PO Box 6009, Falmouth, ME 04105-6009; telephone (207) 781-2330; fax (207) 781-6185

Cost: $50 per class plus $.24 per-mile charge for schools outside a 10-mile radius of Maine Audubon headquarters

COMMENT

Maine Audubon Society (MAS) offers an extensive educational outreach program of classroom natural history units. In order to accommodate the hands-on aspect of the curriculum, MAS asks that classes be no larger than 25 students. Schools can sponsor up to three presentations a day, and since programs are organized into three age-appropriate groupings (K-3, 4-8, and K-8), nobody has to miss out. Make a day of it for the whole school. MAS provides follow up activities for teachers. For more information on materials and programs from MAS, see pages 33, 43, 55 and 62.

EXCERPTS

Descriptions of sample lessons from MAS :

Hands-On Snow Science (Grades K-3)

"In small groups, students will explore how snow is formed by "Searching for Snow Seeds" in a hands-on science experiment. Each group will be given the materials to melt snow in search of the "seeds" and will compare the results. We will also look at snow as an insulator using taxidermy mounts and will explore the importance of snow cover in a winter landscape."

Hands-on Worms (Grades 4-8)

"In this program students will meet the performers of the Traveling Worm Show with whom they will examine the parts of a worm, have a dig for worm eggs, yearlings, and adults, and figure out why worms are said to be such vital parts of natural ecosystems. Through hands-on activities and "worming around," students will become acquainted with the processes that make worms tick. Students will also explore questions about how worms can be such efficient recycling machines and learn how to set up a classroom worm world!"

Hibernators and Migrators (Grades K-3)

"Have you ever wondered why the leaves on the trees change colors? How robins and geese know precisely when to head south? Students will be introduced to the fascinating processes of hibernation and migration and their meaning to the residents of the natural world. Meet some of Maine's migrators and hibernators through investigative games and hands-on activity."—*Maine Audubon Society*

I pray to the birds. I pray to the birds because I believe they will carry the messages of my heart upward. I pray to them because I believe in their existence, the way their songs begin and end each day—the invocations and benedictions of Earth. I pray to the birds because they remind me of what I love rather than what I fear. And at the end of my prayers they teach me how to listen.

—*Terry Tempest Williams,* Refuge. *New York, Vintage Press, 1991, p. 149*

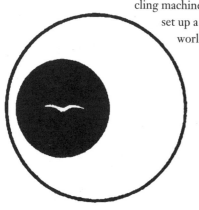

Title: Advanced, Professional and Specialty Field Seminars and Workshops on the Maine Coast

Target Group: Advanced/professional audience

Available from: Eagle Hill Field Research Station, PO Box 99, Steuben, ME 04680-0099; telephone, (207) 546-2821; fax (207) 546-3042

Cost: $295 per seminar, plus meals and accommodations. For information on graduate or undergraduate credit, teacher recertification credit, research grants, financial aid, and additional fees, contact the station

COMMENT

From May through September, Eagle Hill Field Research Station conducts a variety of week-long, intensive seminars taught by professionals and natural history experts. Fields of study include botany, entomology, geology, marine biology, and ornithology. Currently entering its eighth year conducting workshops, Eagle Hill enjoys an excellent reputation for its professional presentations, quality educational programs, setting, and informal atmosphere. Past participants have included independent scholars, university professors, museum personnel, federal and state agency personnel, teachers, and amateur naturalists. The application procedure is serious (two to five pages of a "well-written" and "well-reasoned" research proposal must be submitted by every applicant), but that should not deter the serious student of nature, no matter the professional affiliation. The "intellectually challenging and aesthetically pleasing setting" should be reason enough to attend. More on the station's publication, *The Maine Naturalist*, can be found on page 20.

EXCERPT

"Seminars meet all-day from Monday through Friday. They generally combine intensive field studies and follow-up work in the lab with lectures, discussions, and a review of the current literature. Meals are relaxed settings for informal discussions. Evenings are free for independent studies, slide presentations, or follow-up discussions by the fireplace in the dining hall's comfortable lounge.

Eagle Hill overlooks one of the most beautiful areas on the eastern seaboard, from the rocky evergreen coast of Maine from Acadia National Park to Petit Manan National Wildlife Refuge and beyond. For the study of natural history, the unusual variety of essentially pristine habitats in the immediate area offers many outstanding opportunities."—*Eagle Hill Field Research Station*

Title: Maine Audubon Society Teacher's Resource Center

Target Group: Educators (all levels)

Available from: Maine Audubon Society, Environmental Education Department, 118 Route One, PO Box 6009, Falmouth, ME 04105-6009; telephone (207) 781-2330; fax (207) 781-6185

Cost: Borrower's Card for individuals, $10 members, $12 nonmembers; $25 for schools and organizations. Photocopies, $.10 per page.

COMMENT

A resource well worth considering, the Teacher's Resource Center is open to the public as long as you obtain a MAS Borrower's Card. (See above for details or call Maine Audubon.) The card will entitle you to borrow print and audiovisual materials—of which there are plenty.

EXCERPT

"The Teacher's Resource Center is a lending library which provides educators with environmental materials for classroom and outdoor use. The materials may be borrowed in person or through the mail, and are appropriate for teachers, parents, Scout or 4-H leaders, camp educators, recreation specialists, and environmental educators. Maine Audubon staff is available to consult with anyone who needs assistance finding information and materials for specific projects.

The Teacher's Resource Center is made up of:
- current environmental education curricula and supplements
- background information books, field guides and children's books
- videos and slideshows
- posters depicting natural history subjects
- periodicals and newsletters about science teaching and environmental education
- vertical files containing articles, pamphlets, and lesson plans."
—*Maine Audubon Society*

Sample course offerings from Eagle Hill WRS:

Quantitative Sampling of Vegetation

Introduction to Field Ornithology

The Northern Forest: Soil/Site Relationships

Field Ornithology: Autumn Migration I & II

Fall Mushroom Foray

Technical Editing of Scientific Writings

Field Ethnobotany

Geomorphology

Advanced Natural History Illustration Workshop

FRESHWATER SYSTEMS

Almost all of the water on our planet is in the oceans that cover three-quarters of the Earth's surface. Less than 3 percent of the global water supply is freshwater, and more than three-quarters of that is frozen in glaciers and polar ice. The rest, found in ground-water reserves and aquifers, lakes, streams, and rivers, provides aquatic habitat for a host of plant and animal species, and supplies water for all the living systems on land. People use water for drinking, washing, agriculture, industry, transportation, recreation, waste disposal, and energy production. Water is a basic and essential element for all living resources.

Throughout the world, population growth and increased demand for freshwater is resulting in more and more use of available freshwater supplies. In the Gulf of Maine watershed, the supply of freshwater comes from an annual average rain and snowfall of about 44 inches. Every year, over 250 billion gallons (946 billion liters) of freshwater flow through rivers, basins, lakes, and wetlands to estuaries—and finally to the Gulf itself. All along the path—from the headwaters hundreds of miles away from the coast to the sea—there are abundant aquatic ecosystems, providing habitat for a diversity of living resources.

Aquatic Habitats in the Gulf of Maine Watershed

Freshwater habitats in the Gulf of Maine watershed can be found in streams, ponds, rivers, lakes, and in freshwater wetlands. Freshwater habitats shelter and sustain living resources that are adapted to the specific characteristics found there—species in streams are adapted to one set of conditions; species in ponds have quite different lives.

Freshwater wetlands—including bogs, peatlands, fens, swamps and marshes—are defined as places "flooded all or part of the time with freshwater," and are a vital interface between land and water, helping control floodwaters, filtering pollutants, and providing nesting, breeding, feeding, and nursery grounds for resident and migratory birds and wildlife.

In general terms, biologists categorize freshwater ecosystems in the Gulf of Maine watershed in two ways: by the amount of current passing through them, and by the kinds of material found in and under the water.

Freshwater systems can be:
- *intermittent*, with flowing water only part of the time, such as a seasonal creek;
- *upper perennial*, characterized by continuously flowing water typical of streams, with steep gradients that result in rapid water flow (a waterfall is the steepest gradient of all, for example), and little flood plain development (a *flood plain* is the area of normally dry shore created by stream deposits vulnerable to flooding during storms);
- and *lower perennial*, with continuously flowing water, low gradients, and a well-developed flood plain, usually found in rivers closer to the coast.

The Hydrologic Cycle

The Hydrologic Cycle (also called the Water Cycle) is the process that moves water around the earth. It can change the form of water from liquid to water vapor to ice, and even clean it along the way, but it can't make more water. The water you drink today may have been lapped up by dinosaurs millions of years ago! The Water Cycle is powered by the sun, which evaporates water from oceans, rivers, lakes, and even trees. As the water vapor rises, it cools, condensing into clouds. Winds blow some of the clouds over land. The water falls to earth as precipitation. Runoff flows on the surface into streams, river, or ponds. Water that sinks into the soil flows through underground reservoirs, or aquifers, as groundwater. Water passes through many different aquatic habitats before gravity pulls it back to earth's lowest point, the ocean. —*Katahdin To The Sea (Wild Gulf Poster Series)*

Within each of these categories, freshwater systems can also be described according to the material under water:

- *rock bottom* (consisting of boulders or bedrock);
- *unconsolidated bottom* (mud, sand, or cobble and gravel);
- *aquatic beds* (floating or submerged plants); and
- *emergent wetland* (plants rooted in water, but only partially submerged).

Ingredients of Freshwater

Runoff from precipitation and erosion carries nutrients from land such as potassium, nitrogen and phosphorus into freshwater systems. These particles are gradually broken down and released by bacteria. Other key ingredients carried by the runoff are dissolved oxygen and carbon dioxide. These important gases directly affect the number of organisms that can live and breathe in the water. Generally, oxygen supply in the water drops at night, when photosynthesis by aquatic plants cannot take place.

The presence of too many nutrients in an aquatic ecosystem often results from sewage discharge, food-processing wastes, and nonpoint source pollution (from agricultural runoff, roads and other paved surfaces, storm sewers, etc.). This oversupply of organic material leads to premature or accelerated *eutrophication* of freshwater systems, often called *cultural eutrophication*, since it is largely the result of human activities. (*Natural eutrophication*, which is part of the gradual successional change that occurs in aquatic ecosystems, takes place on a much slower, geologic time scale.)

Cultural eutrophication causes a rapid overgrowth of algae and other plant life, modifying the entire habitat and eliminating or replacing many of the original inhabitants (sometimes even causing dramatic events such as fish kills.) Examples of cultural eutrophication that have occurred in the Gulf of Maine watershed can be found in the Sebasticook and Cobbossee River drainage basins, both of which have disproportionately high levels of nitrate, phosphorus and ammonium.

Fish in rivers have been classified by zone based primarily on current speed and slope of the stream. In the Gulf of Maine watershed, these zones can be characterized by trout, sculpin, chub, or dace in fast flowing streams; suckers and shiners in medium flow water; and finally, sunfish and catfish.
—*adapted from* An Ecological Characterization of Maine's Coast North and East of Cape Elizabeth, *U.S. Fish and Wildlife Service*

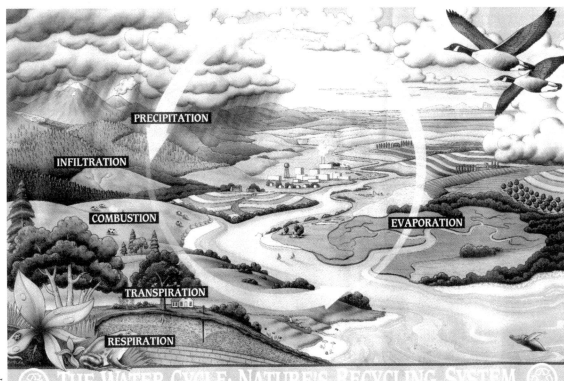

PRECIPITATION

INFILTRATION

COMBUSTION

EVAPORATION

TRANSPIRATION

RESPIRATION

Ketler

THE WATER CYCLE: NATURE'S RECYCLING SYSTEM

46

Living in Freshwater

Sunlight is the primary source of energy in freshwater systems, just as it is in all ecosystems. Phytoplankton and other algae are the primary producers of food in freshwater habitats. Zooplankton are the primary consumers, who themselves become food for secondary consumers such as crustaceans, insects and other invertebrates. These, in turn, are food for fish, amphibians, birds and mammals. Many birds and mammals inhabit freshwater systems only for certain portions of the year, primarily as predators when the water is not frozen. Many fish, on the other hand, stay within the ecosystem for their entire lives.

Near the headwaters of a river, fast-flowing streams fed by melting snow make ideal habitats for aquatic creatures that prefer swift, dynamic conditions. Brook trout and Atlantic salmon spawn and grow in these cold, oxygen-rich waters. Algae and aquatic plants adapted to constant water movement also live in these places. Trees and other vegetation on the stream's shore (known as the *riparian zone*) are essential for shade to keep the water cold. By comparison, rivers found farther downstream provide a quieter, calmer environment. Muddy bottoms, gentler currents, and warmer water create habitats for fish and wildlife species that need a less rambunctious environment to thrive.

Lakes in the Gulf of Maine watershed contain habitats similar to those in ponds, particularly close to shore, but—unlike ponds—they are usually too deep to have rooted plants on the bottom. The still waters of lakes, ponds, and freshwater marshes support a diversity of habitats, providing places for species to hibernate through the winter, to hatch their eggs in spring and to protect and nurture their young. Largemouth bass, perch and brown bullhead; salamanders, turtles, frogs and other amphibians; and mosquitoes and other aquatic insect larvae all depend upon these still waters.

Vast numbers of aquatic insects function as consumers in freshwater ecosystems. They are usually described according to the way they eat—their *feeding strategies*—which, at various times in their life cycles, separates them into different parts of the habitat. *Collectors* (black flies and caddisflies are good examples) are passive feeders who strain their food as it moves through the passing current. *Scrapers* or *grazers* can literally scrape their food (usually algae or plant material) from surfaces in either still or moving water. *Shredders* depend on decaying matter for sustenance, and help keep the system functioning by reducing organic material for further breakdown by bacteria. *Predators* are those insects that aggressively pursue other organisms to eat (the all-too-familiar mosquito, for example).

Bogs are an unusual kind of freshwater wetland habitat, with a different mix of species. The water is low in oxygen and is also acidic from the sphagnum moss (peat moss) that often completely covers the surface. Consequently, very few fish are able to live in bogs. Bogs do, however, support snapping turtles, frogs, and many insects, along with an amazing diversity of vegetation—from orchids to cranberries.

In summer, ponds and freshwater wetlands create habitats for a variety of birds, including red-winged blackbirds and kingfishers, and for mammals such as moose, muskrats, and beavers. In the fall, these same habitats provide feeding and resting grounds for many species of migrating birds, including Canada geese and black ducks.

Vital Connections

The Gulf of Maine watershed is part of a vast network of freshwater wetlands that provide habitat for more than one-third of all the bird species in North America. Nearly a third of the endangered and threatened plants and animals in North America need wetlands to survive. The natural processes occurring in freshwater wetlands also are important to peoples' lives—recharging groundwater supplies, filtering pollutants, providing irrigation water, and reducing the destructive effects of storm water.

Throughout history, freshwater habitats in the Gulf of Maine watershed have also been used—at times very intensively—by people. It is not difficult to think of the impact that human activities have had on natural processes. Vegetation has been removed from riparian zones to promote water transportation. Dams have been constructed across rivers and streams for hydroelectric power. Houses have been built on the edge of ponds and lakes used for recreational boating, water-skiing and sport fishing. Bogs and marshes have been filled to make surface area for parking lots, shopping centers, industrial buildings and residential housing. Peat from bogs is being mined for fuel and garden use. And, all the while, more people need more drinking water. Many freshwater habitats for fish and wildlife in the watershed have been fragmented or eliminated to make room for human "habitat."

Government, agencies, organizations, and private citizens have undertaken a variety of actions to restore freshwater habitats in the Gulf of Maine watershed. As knowledge about freshwater ecology grows, and public support for habitat protection increases, federal, state, and provincial environmental programs are being implemented to protect freshwater ecosystems and habitats. Examples include the State of Maine's zoning restrictions on development on or near wetlands, numerous provisions in the United States' *Clean Water Act*, publicly driven efforts to remove or relocate dams, scientific advances such as fish ladders and other fish passageways, and the U.S. Fish and Wildlife Service Partners for Wildlife Program for wetland restoration (see inset). Supported by increasing public understanding of the importance of these dynamic systems in our lives, these efforts are bringing life back to freshwater systems throughout the Gulf of Maine watershed.

The Partners for Wildlife Program:
Three-quarters of the wetlands remaining in the United States are privately owned. The Partners for Wildlife program improves and protects fish and wildlife habitat on private lands through alliances between the U.S. Fish and Wildlife Service, other organizations, and individuals, while leaving the land in private ownership. The program has protected and restored thousands of acres of habitat for migratory birds and other wildlife. So far, over 9,000 landowners have teamed up with the U.S. Fish and Wildlife Service to restore thousands of acres of wetland habitat and associated uplands. Activities include restoring wetlands, setting land aside to provide food and cover, delaying haying to provide habitat for ducks and other wildlife during nesting and migration, and managing grazing to improve vegetation. Individual landowners in the Gulf of Maine watershed can become involved by contacting the U.S. Fish and Wildlife Service at (207) 827-5938. A biologist will discuss your needs, the opportunities available to you, and assist you in any way possible. If your property contains damaged or unused habitat that can be improved for wildlife, U.S. Fish and Wildlife Service biologists can help you plan and design a habitat management project. On the ground, we can help move dirt, establish vegetation, reseed upland areas to native vegetation, and much more. If your project meets our criteria, the U.S. Fish and Wildlife Service may share or pay all costs.—*adapted from* **Partners for Wildlife Brochure**, *U.S. Fish and Wildlife Service*

Title: All About Turtles

Target Group: Grades K-3

Available from: Gulf of Maine Aquarium, PO Box 7549, Portland, ME 04112; telephone (207) 772–2321; fax (207) 772–6855

Cost: $50 per program plus mileage

COMMENTS

All About Turtles, one of the Gulf of Maine Aquarium's in-school programs, teaches about turtles in a spirited and experiential way. Activities include role-playing, viewing slides, making turtle puppets and costumes, reading stories, exploring ponds and more. A few characters illustrated in a special edition of *Minnow* magazine (the children's newsletter of the Gulf of Maine Aquarium, see p. 21) will surely be familiar to fans of some other famous turtles ("How many words can you make from *cowabunga* in five minutes?"). For a book of its size (formatted like a greeting card with pages), this one contains lots to learn and do. It would be a fun handout as part of a classroom unit. See pages 83 and 101 for more from the Gulf of Maine Aquarium.

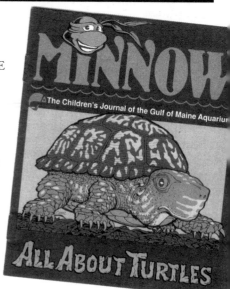

EXCERPT

"This forty-five-minute presentation will teach second-graders throughout the state about freshwater ecology through the eyes of turtles indigenous to Maine. Children will have an opportunity to dress up as a painted turtle, to learn about turtle body parts, and each child will have a role to play in a story about a day in the life of a painted turtle. The program is accompanied by a 16 page issue of *Minnow*, the children's journal of the Gulf of Maine Aquarium. *Minnow* includes stories and activities as well as background information, experiments, and craft projects.

The development of this program was funded by Kevin Eastman, co-creator of the Teenage Mutant Ninja Turtles™. In this program, the Ninja Turtles™ are armed with the tools of scientific inquiry, including dip nets, Secci disks, and magnifying glasses."
—*Gulf of Maine Aquarium*

Title: Habitat Values of New England Wetlands

Target: General audience

Available from: U.S. Fish and Wildlife Service New England Field Offices, 22 Bridge Street, Concord, NH 03301; telephone (603) 225–1411; fax (603) 225–1467

Cost: Free

COMMENT

A guide to wetlands in the New England region, this publication explains the diversity of wetland habitats and their inhabitants. The book is divided into sections on coastal and inland wetlands and on habitat enhancement. Different categories of wetland systems—palustrine, lacustrine, and riverine—are discussed and described. Species lists of specific inland wetland regions are included for reference at the back of the book.

EXCERPT

"Several different types of inland wetlands are found in the Northeast. *Palustrine Forested, Palustrine scrub shrub* and *Palustrine Emergent* habitats are the most common. Palustrine is the term used to describe nontidal wetlands dominated by trees, shrubs, and persistent emergent vegetation (Cowardin *et al.* 1979). These wetlands were traditionally referred to as marshes, swamps, bogs and fens. Lacustrine wetlands are inland systems that include permanently flooded lakes and reservoirs. Riverine systems consist of streams, rivers and riparian zones.

Federal, state, and local regulations for inland wetlands has only recently become a reality. Many of these ecosystems have either been lost to development or severely fragmented, reducing habitat value. Protection of these valuable systems is important in maintaining regional, national, and global biological diversity."—*U.S. Fish and Wildlife Service*

Title: Fish Friends, A Curriculum Supplement for Grades 4 to 6

Target Group: Grades 4-6

Available from: Atlantic Salmon Federation, Fort Andross, 14 Maine Street, Suite 400 Brunswick, ME 04011; telephone (207) 725-2833; Atlantic Salmon Federation, PO Box 807, Calais, ME 04619; telephone (506) 529-4581; fax (506) 529-4438. Atlantic Salmon Federation, PO Box 429, St. Andrews, NB, CANADA EOG 2XO

Cost: $19.95 CAN., plus $4 CAN. postage ($800 covers the cost of an incubator to raise salmon eggs in the classroom.)

COMMENT

Fish Friends is a project of the Atlantic Salmon Federation's Education and Public Awareness Program. It comprises a series of twelve lessons for the classroom and, after a thorough period of field-testing, has been distributed to schools throughout Canada's Atlantic provinces. The 106 page curriculum is available in English and French. The program has expanded into the United States too, where 30 schools are currently engaged in the program.

Beginning with habitat, this packet of lessons addresses issues of biodiversity, freshwater ecosystems, sustainability, stewardship and more. Each lesson builds on the section prior to it, and uses a variety of activities and resources to challenge students experientially and intellectually. *Fish Friends* also incorporates a host of exercises to develop language, art and math skills. Each section is marked with icons (representing art, writing, reflective thinking, measuring, hands on) to indicate which skill areas are being addressed in each exercise. Ending with a unit on stewardship, *Fish Friends* allows students to role-play, encouraging them to apply what they have learned and to experience the dilemmas of environmental decision-making firsthand. Background information is included in each unit from a variety of outside sources like E. O. Wilson's *Diversity of Life*, the World Resources Institute, the National Round Table on the Environment and the Economy, and the Nova Scotia Department of Fisheries. The curriculum progresses from fish eggs to community values, creating an interactive series of lessons that inspire the teaching and learning of science, habitat values, and environmental ethics.

EXCERPT

What Would You Do? You are fishing at a secluded lake and have caught seven fish during your first day at the lake. Now, on the second day, the fishing has been great and you have caught five fish in the first hour, all of which are bigger than yesterday's fish. The law allows you to possess twelve fish. Should you:

- continue to fish and keep all the fish

- get rid of the smaller fish you caught yesterday and keep the big ones to stay within your limit

- have fish for lunch

- quit fishing and go for a hike

- other

—sample activity from Fish Friends

Title: Natural Resources Highlights: The Penobscot River Watershed

Target Group: General audience

Available from: Penobscot River and Bay Institute, Box 2147, Brooksville, ME 04617; telephone (207) 326–4822

Cost: Contact the above for information

COMMENT

Produced by the Water Resources Program at the University of Maine in association with the Penobscot Riverkeepers 2000, *Natural Resources Highlights* is a collection of fact sheets featuring specific information on the Penobscot River watershed area. Topics include: *A Bird's Eye View, Hydrology of the Watershed, 300 Years on the Penobscot, Human Influences, Water Quality, and Decisions to be Made.* The information serves as an accessible and organized summary of important habitat characteristics in the Penobscot River watershed. A useful introductory teaching or research tool.

EXCERPTS

"Fisheries—The watershed's lakes and rivers host more than eighty-four anadromous, catadromous, and freshwater species. They include commonly recognized fish such as brook trout, small mouth bass, and the Atlantic salmon. Other species include eels, shad, whitefish, and sturgeon. Early settlers took alewives, shad, smelt, striped bass, and salmon for food as well as commercial markets. Dams and pollution have reduced or destroyed most of these populations."—*Penobscot River and Bay Institute*

> "To understand the interaction among organisms in the environment, it is useful to draw boundaries around certain groups of organisms which interact in a relatively direct way, such as a community or neighbourhood grouping. Within these biological neighbourhoods, it is possible to assign organisms an 'address', describing their typical location. An organism's address is its habitat."
> —*Atlantic Salmon Federation*

Joe Eaton –
Old Town
827-0369

Natural Resources Highlights:
Penobscot River Watershed

Water Resources Program
University of Maine

C. Michael Lewis

"It's not easy to maintain your grip in a frigid, fast-moving mountain stream. Performing everyday functions like eating, moving, or holding on as the water cascades over rocks and waterfalls is like a mountain climber maneuvering across a rock face in a gale-force wind. The creatures of the headwaters have evolved their own versions of grappling hooks, rappelling ropes, and crampons."—Gulf of Maine Aquarium

Title: Streams

Target Group: General public

Available from: Maine Department of Environmental Protection, Bureau of Land and Water Quality, Station 17, Augusta, ME 04333; telephone (207) 287-3901

Cost: Free

COMMENT

A small, thorough, brochure-size booklet, *Streams* describes the different components of freshwater stream habitats, their occupants, and neighbors (including the two-legged ones). Appropriately, the booklet includes a section encouraging us to consider what we use in and near streams and to recognize that our actions directly affect these habitats and our own water supply. A brief bibliography and suggested reading list, along with telephone numbers and names of agencies to contact for further information, are listed at the back. *Streams* was produced for the Gulf of Maine Aquarium by the State of Maine Department of Environmental Protection. See pages 21, 48, 83 and 101 for more from the Gulf of Maine Aquarium.

EXCERPTS

"What could be more dynamic than a stream? It is constantly changing its flow, its depth, even its bed, as anyone knows who has observed a stream in different seasons or at different places along its course. It scours, shifts channels, meanders, floods, erodes, carries and deposits silt. Squeeze a stream in one place, and it bulges in another. Where it is restricted, the stream speeds up to compensate, eroding downstream banks or spreading out to flood adjacent property."—*Gulf of Maine Aquarium*

"From the air, the edges of a stream appear as bright green tracks furrowed into the forest floor...This is the riparian zone, a protective margin of vegetation that keeps the water clear and cool for the creatures of the stream. It is also important to almost all of our forest animals, which come not only to drink, but to find food, shelter and hiding places. In summer, shade from the water's edge moderates temperature, humidity and light. In winter, thickets of trees and vines buffer the area from harsh winds. This provides a protected habitat for many woodland animals."—*Gulf of Maine Aquarium*

Title: Project WILD Aquatic: Aquatic Education Activity Guide

Target Group: Grades K-12

Available from: Maine Department of Inland Fisheries and Wildlife, Station 41, Augusta, ME 04333-0041; telephone (207) 287–3303; fax (207) 287–6395; Project Wild, 5430 Grosvenor Lane, Bethesa, MD 20814; telephone (301) 493-5447; fax (301) 493-5627

Cost: Free and available only to workshop participants (see below)

COMMENT

This is a comprehensive, multidisciplinary curriculum for K-12 students, dealing with freshwater and saltwater habitats. Lessons for older and younger students are identified and adapted for each target group. A lengthy list of appendices serves as a guide for teachers or leaders and contains a "Metric Conversion Chart," a section on "Field Ethics," "Hints for Using Simulated Field Trips," "Evaluating and Assessing Student Learning," "Guidelines for Responsible Use of Animals in the Classroom." Developed as a sequel to *Project WILD*, this version suggests that *Project WILD* materials be introduced first to teach students about habitats. (See p. 32.)

Materials and lessons are organized into seven sections: "Awareness and Appreciation"; "Diversity of Wildlife Values"; "Ecological Principles"; "Management and Conservation"; "People, Culture and Wildlife"; "Trends, Issues and Consequences"; "Responsible Human Actions." All activity descriptions provide substantial background information; a statement of objective; a description of methods; a list of needed materials; and suggested procedures. For each section, a box summarizes the activity in a quick thumbnail

Aquatic

sketch, notes key vocabulary, identifies subject areas, lists skills the activity emphasizes, estimates duration, and suggests appropriate appendices for further reading. For more information on Maine Department of Inland Fisheries and Wildlife offerings, see pages 15 and 32.

EXCERPTS

"From wetlands to whales, and puddles to ponds, *Project WILD Aquatic* can help you incorporate stimulating activities into your lesson plans. Each workshop participant will receive an Aquatic activity guide, along with handouts, posters, prizes, and background information. Workshops are offered in three- to six-hour segments."—*Project WILD*

Field Ethics

The question of whether to collect some objects from natural settings—either temporarily or permanently—is difficult to answer. Such decisions are left to individual teachers and their students. We do, however, urge thoughtful decision-making about the process. We urge caution and respect for the living environment. In most cases, we urge no collecting at all—and recommend instead simply leaving the natural environment as it is found, with as little impact from students in the process of learning as possible. There are times, however, when it may seem appropriate and so instructionally powerful that some limited forms of collecting are desired. If so, we recommend involving students in the process of deciding whether, what, and how to collect...they are more likely to develop an ethic that

considers their impact on ecosystems. This kind of thoughtful decision-making about the consequences of our actions is an important, life-long skill.

We also need to consider an ethic that goes beyond the collecting issue. We can affect living things in other ways, too. For example, just by walking over fragile areas outdoors or observing animals under certain conditions, we can destroy or disturb organisms. When we leave a trail, we can kill plants and animals. When we walk on rocks, we can remove new soil and crush mosses and lichens if they are present. When we walk along the banks of a pond or stream, vegetation can be affected. When we leave traces of aquatic vegetation on a shore, they can change the beauty and ecology of an area.

The following ethic was developed by a class of sixth graders:

1. We should obey all laws protecting plants and animals.
2. We should ask the owner before we take anything.
3. We should only collect an animal if we know we can keep it alive long enough to learn from it.
4. We should not collect things that will hurt us.
5. We should only collect something if there are a lot of them in that place.
6. We should only collect something if we can learn something very important about it.
—*excerpted from* Project WILD Aquatic

Project WILD Aquatic Activities:

Aqua Words
Water Wings
How Wet Is Our Planet?
Water Plant Art
Are You Me?
Designing a Habitat
Puddle Wonders
Water Canaries
Wetland Metaphors
Marsh Munchers
The Edge of Home
Hooks and Ladders
Where Does Water Run Off After School?
Fishy Who's Who
Migration Headache
Aquatic Roots
Net Gain, Net Effect
Watered Down History
Water We Eating?
Aquatic Times
The Glass Menagerie
To Dam or Not to Dam
Dragonfly Pond
Turtle Hurdles
Plastic Jellyfish
Something's Fishy Here!
Alice in Waterland

52

Title: **Green Lake National Fish Hatchery Visitor's Guide**

Target: General audience

Available from: U.S. Fish and Wildlife Service Green Lake National Fish Hatchery, RFD 4, Box 135, Ellsworth, ME 04605; telephone (207) 667–9531; fax (207) 667–5559

Cost: Free

COMMENT

This brief and useful guide is available directly from the hatchery. It describes the life cycle of the Atlantic salmon and the process of rearing smolts (adolescent salmon); how and where salmon eggs are incubated and hatched; how an accelerated growth program of heating the water speeds up development, etc. The brochure also describes the hatchery's self-guided tour and contains a map and explanations of areas closed to the public. The hatchery is open from 8:00 a.m. to 4:00 p.m. every day. Group tours can be arranged by appointment.

EXCERPT

"Green Lake is one of several national fish hatcheries located in New England, operated by the U.S. Fish and Wildlife Service. It was authorized in 1967 to produce Atlantic salmon for restoration of annual runs in rivers where the native populations have been lost or severely reduced, and to augment depleted stocks in those rivers where wild salmon still exist....

Efforts at Green Lake are concentrated on rearing *smolts*, young salmon generally averaging seven to nine inches long which are ready to migrate to the ocean. Working in close cooperation with the Maine Atlantic Sea-Run Salmon Commission, the hatchery now annually releases over 600,000 smolts, plus a varying number of *fry* (one to two inches long) and *parr* (three to five inches long)....

Smolts are released into Maine rivers in May and migrate down river to the ocean. They spend two or three years at sea, traveling as far as the west coast of Greenland before returning to their home rivers as eight- to twenty-five-pound adults...

Captive populations of adult Atlantic salmon are also maintained at the hatchery. These fish, which have never been released from the hatchery, provide additional eggs for Atlantic salmon research and restoration programs throughout New England."—*USFWS Green Lake National Fish Hatchery*

Title: **Wicked Big Puddles, A Guide to the Study and Certification of Vernal Pools**

Target: General audience

Available from: Reading Memorial High School—Vernal Pool Association, 62 Oakland Road, Reading, MA 01867; telephone (617) 944–8200; fax (617) 942–9133

Cost: $10, plus $3 postage and handling

COMMENT

Wicked Big Puddles (*WBP*) will tell you what a vernal pool is, how to find one, how to identify this wetland habitat, and how to protect it as a certified wetland. The guide comes complete with photographs and a sample certification kit. The fact that this program is a student-run operation should not go unnoticed and should serve as a model and an impetus for other high-school groups to become involved in their own environmental education initiatives.

EXCERPT

"*WPB* guides the novice through vernal pool certification, from the finding of a vernal pool and identification of its organisms to the collection of evidence and the submission of the certification packet.

Wicked Big Puddles is written by Leo P. Kenney (Advisor) and produced and printed by members of the Vernal Pool Association. The Vernal Pool Association is a student group at Reading Memorial High School whose goal is to promote the identification, appreciation, study, and protection of vernal pools. To meet this goal, the Vernal Pool Association runs workshops, produces educational materials and studies and certifies vernal pools. The Vernal Pool Association is particularly interested in involving other high-school students in vernal pool activities."—*Vernal Pool Association*

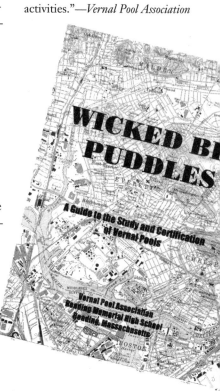

Title: A World in Our Backyard: A Wetlands Education and Stewardship Program

Target: Grades K-12

Available from: For Loan: The Environmental Protection Agency, Region 1 Library, John F. Kennedy Federal Building, One Congress Street, Boston, MA 02203-2211; telephone (617) 565-3300. New England Interstate Training Center, (207) 767-2539; New England Aquarium Teacher Resource Center, (617) 973-6590. For purchase: Environmental Media Corporation, PO Box 1016, Chapel Hill, NC 27514; telephone 1-(800) ENV-EDUC; fax (919) 942-8785

Cost: Guidebook, $12.95; videocassette, $29.95; complete package, $39.95. Shipping and handling: $3.75 for $30 purchase or less; $5.75 for purchase of $30-$60; shipping and handling charges only for loans.

COMMENT

This complete teaching package includes a 15-minute video about three different school wetland-education programs, a 7-minute video that serves as an introduction to wetlands for students, and an accompanying 140-page teacher's guide full of background information on wetland systems. The guide includes definitions, experiments, and activities, commenting on the importance of wetland stewardship activities; information on federal, state, and local regulatory programs; and suggestions for developing wetland protection programs in your own communities. In addition to teaching about wetlands and their functions, this multimedia package focuses on the influences threatening these valuable habitats, and offers ideas for initiating community and local protection programs. Teachers will find this program exceptionally thorough in teaching the value of wetlands and our relationship to them; nonteachers and community members will find useful background information and a substantial list of additional resources. Though designed for educators, this guide is in and of itself an education and should not be overlooked by anyone with an interest in protecting local wetlands.

EXCERPTS

"This guide and accompanying videocassette is a resource of information about wetlands in New England for educators. It suggests ways of studying wetland characteristics, why wetlands are important, and how students and teachers can help to protect a local wetland resource. This guide is unique in that it encourages students to go beyond learning about wetlands by 'adopting' one: to have them become familiar with a local wetland and advocate its protection through stewardship activities. This guide aims to help students get to know the complexities of wetlands, discover wildlife, enjoy the experience of being outdoors, and learn how necessary wetlands are to the health of our environment."—*New England Interstate Water Pollution Control Commission,* A World in our Backyard

"Some wetlands develop in low-lying areas in the landscape where water drains and collects. Others border salt or fresh bodies of water such as oceans, rivers or ponds, while still others are isolated in forests and urban areas. As transitional zones between upland and aquatic systems, wetlands often support both terrestrial and aquatic species, contributing to the diversity of plants and animals they support.

Wetlands also vary considerably in their appearance and size. Regional and local differences in vegetation, hydrology, water chemistry, soils, topography, and climate contribute to the variety of wetland types found around the world. Some wetlands are inundated with water year-round while others are only seasonally flooded, and the depth and duration of flooding can vary widely. Others are only saturated at or near the surface of the soil. Wetlands may occupy just a few hundred square feet or cover thousands of acres."
—*New England Interstate Water Pollution Control Commission,* A World in our Backyard

Fact: Long dismissed as foul, unprofitable places, wetlands are now prized as one of the richest ecosystems on earth.
Often referred to as 'nature's kidneys,' wetland plants and soils filter storm water runoff and protect our drinking water supplies.

Fact: We continue to lose an acre of wetland every minute.
Nearly half the wetlands that were once found across the United States have been filled or drained for land uses such as agriculture and development."
—*New England Interstate Water Pollution Control Commission,* A World in Our Backyard

Getting your students involved:
"To understand wetlands, your students need to know where the water in wetlands comes from and why it's important. Increasing their understanding of the many reasons water is important to people and wildlife will heighten their appreciation of a resource which is often taken for granted…. An important concept for students to know is that water is always moving from high to low due to gravity and that any piece of land belongs to a very small watershed which is part of a larger watershed, which is part of a still larger watershed, and so forth."—*New England Interstate Water Pollution Control Commission, "Chapter 1, Wetland Science," A World in Our Backyard*

54

Title: Great Meadows National Wildlife Refuge Brochure and Programs

Target: General audience

Available from: Great Meadows National Wildlife Refuge, Weir Hill Road, Sudbury, MA 01776; telephone (508) 443-4661; fax (508) 443-2898

Cost: Free admission to the Refuge. Most programs are free. For information, contact the Refuge.

COMMENT

Consisting of two units totaling 3,400 acres noted for rich wildlife habitat, Great Meadows National Wildlife Refuge has long been valued as a prime spot for birdwatching, hiking, snowshoeing and cross-country skiing, observing wildlife and plants, and learning natural history. The Refuge is located along 12 miles of the Concord and Sudbury rivers, not far from Thoreau's beloved Walden Pond. A U.S. Fish and Wildlife Service visitor center with exhibits and information about wildlife and endangered species management programs, is located at the Weir Hill unit in Sudbury, where there is also a hiking trail and educational facilities. The Concord unit offers 3 miles of trails around an impoundment pool and through woodlands, providing prime opportunities for viewing wildlife. Educational programs and materials available from Great Meadows are numerous. (See below for a list of refuge-specific teaching materials and other publications.) School groups are welcome year-round and are able to participate in a variety of outdoor activities, films and slide presentations. A classroom laboratory for wetlands study is available for teachers who participate in the refuge-sponsored teacher workshop, and a host of programs are open to the public as well. Great Meadows National Wildlife Refuge offers magnificent teaching opportunities, rich in the ecology and history of the region—to say nothing of its poetry.

EXCERPTS
Lesson Plans and Materials available from Great Meadows NWR:

A Closer Look…Microscopic Life in the Wetlands, by Barbara Munkres. A survey of microscopic life found

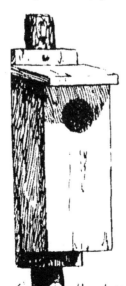

in Great Meadows wetlands, how to use the Wetlands Laboratory in the Visitor Center, microscope techniques and troubleshooting. For teachers of elementary grades, scout leaders, etc. Includes bibliography. 14 pages, photocopied.

A Walk at Weir Hill Through Three Habitats. An introduction to the Weir Hill Unit of Great Meadows NWR, this guide describes the Refuge, pond habitat, red maple swamp, and upland woodland habitat with a few thought-provoking or discussion-provoking questions and answers at each site. Elementary grades. 5 pages, photocopied.

Wetlands Packet. A packet of educational materials for use on-site and in the classroom, it includes an introduction to the values of wetlands, flora and fauna sketches, wetlands activities, Wildlife Assistance Certificate information, and a wetlands bibliography. Activities and the bibliography are keyed to grade level. 16 pages, photocopied.

The Elbanobscot Environmental Education Manual, edited by Barbara Robinson. A handbook for environmental educators for programs to be used in schools, communities or the region. References, handout materials, activities and ideas on outdoor education workshops. Mimeographed, 141 pages.

"Many relics of early people found in the vicinity date back to 5500 B. C. …Indians named the Concord River 'Musketahquid,' their word for grassy banks. Settlers named the grasslands left in summer by the river's retreat from its floodplain the 'Great River Meadows.' Hay was harvested annually and provided an important income for early white settlers. With the advent of industrialization in the early nineteenth century, a mill dam was built in Billerica. The dam caused the river's level to rise and to extend into the meadows; the resulting wetland environment was too moist to support the prized hay crop, and thus was considered useless. The newly created habitat was attractive to waterfowl, which increasingly used the area. In fact, the wetlands became highly valued for hunting and fishing."
—*U.S. Fish and Wildlife Service Great Meadows National Wildlife Refuge*

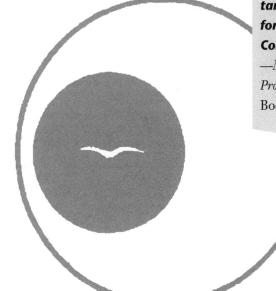

A Bibliography of Books and Materials for the Study of Wetlands and Ponds, prepared by Barbara Munkres, Refuge Volunteer.

Bedford Environmental Education Program, by Becky Ritchie. A series of eight booklets of indoor and outdoor activities and field trips for environmental educators of grades K-6, including special needs groups.

The Meadows Messenger. Free quarterly newsletter by Great Meadows staff, featuring articles by area naturalists, management activities at Great Meadows NWR and a schedule of activities.

National Wildlife Week Teacher Kits. Each spring, the National Wildlife Federation supplies Great Meadows NWR with free kits that include posters, lesson plans, and student activities based on the current year's theme.

BIRDS of Great Meadows National Wildlife Refuge. A checklist of the 221 species of birds recorded at Great Meadows in the last ten years, prepared in cooperation with the Massachusetts Audubon Society.

Title: Learn About Loons

Target: Grades K-8, general public

Available From: Maine Audubon Society, Gilsland Farm, PO Box 6009, Falmouth, ME 04105-6009; telephone (207) 781-2330; fax (207) 781-6185

Cost: $50 refundable deposit for teacher's guide; $15 suggested user fee

COMMENT

The Maine Audubon Society maintains a Teacher's Resource Center (see page 43) at its headquarters in Falmouth, and during the past two decades it has collected a wide variety of environmental educational materials. *Learn about Loons* is a good example of Maine Audubon's work. Teachers and students are introduced to the unique physical adaptations of the loon, its habitat, and the important relationship between loons and people. The teacher's guide includes lesson plans, resource information, color photographs and illustrations, audio-and videotapes, and taxidermy specimens including feet, eggs, feathers, wings, and bones. A mounted loon in a display case is available for a loan. Guides may be borrowed for up to three weeks at a time from the Teacher's Resource Center.

In addition to their headquarters in Falmouth, Maine Audubon maintains a number of other centers. Their Scarborough Marsh Nature Center (page 62) provides a schedule of field trips throughout the spring, summer, and early fall.

The 1989 Coast Week Cleanup in Maine covered 176 miles of shorefront and collected an average 102.6 pounds of debris per mile. (Data compiled by the Maine Coastal Program with assistance from the Center for Marine Conservation.)
—Maine Coastal Program, The Estuary Book

ESTUARINE SYSTEMS

Estuaries in the Gulf of Maine watershed are ancient river valleys drowned as a result of rising sea levels after the last Ice Age. Estuaries, located where rivers run into the sea, represent the areas where freshwater mingles with saltwater. Estuaries are characterized by slow currents and sedimentation that leads to the formation of extensive mudflats, visible at low tide. As mudflats accumulate sediment, the soil gets deeper and the land builds upward, allowing grasses that survive in saltwater to establish themselves. Over time, the salt marsh continues to grow upward, creating soil from decaying grass. Eventually, fully developed salt marshes may only be inundated with saltwater at high tide.

Differences in winds, local topography, and tidal exchange affect the way saltwater and freshwater mix in an estuary, making it difficult to draw precise boundaries for them. The Maine Department of Marine Resources describes estuaries as "not constrained by geography," and points out that "the entire Gulf of Maine can be considered an estuary…" (See *Estuarine Studies: An Activities Text for Maine Schools*, p. 68.)

The U.S. Fish and Wildlife Service defines estuaries as "deep water tidal habitats and adjacent wetlands which are usually semi-enclosed by land, but have open, partially obstructed, or sporadic access to the open ocean, and in which ocean water is at least occasionally diluted by freshwater runoff from the land" (Cowardin, *et al.* 1979).

When despair for the world grows in me
and I wake in the night at the least sound
in fear of what my life and my children's lives may be,
I go and lie down where the wood drake
rests in his beauty on the water, and the great heron feeds.
I come into the peace of wild things
who do not tax their lives with forethought
of grief. I come into the presence of still water.
And I feel above me the day-blind stars
waiting with their light. For a time
I rest in the grace of the world, and am free.
—*Wendell Berry*

Combinations of Fresh and Saltwater

Estuaries are generally classified into three basic categories: salt wedge, partially mixed, and fully mixed. *Salt wedge* estuaries occur in rivers in which the bottom, depth, and slope of the river creates highly stratified layers of fresh-and saltwater. Freshwater floats on top of the heavier saltwater from the ocean, creating two separate layers of water that do not mix readily.

Partially mixed estuaries occur along the Gulf of Maine coast in places where the tides can move farther upriver—usually in an estuary with parallel sides and uniform depth, resulting in partial mixing of the saltwater layer with the upper layer of freshwater, creating a layer of brackish water along the estuary floor.

Fully mixed estuaries progress from salt to brackish to freshwater, without the vertical layering that occurs in salt wedges or in partially mixed brackish/freshwater estuaries.

Estuaries function as the last step in the natural purification system through which river water flows before reaching the ocean. They are the final physical and chemical filters in the watershed. As river water slows and spreads through an estuary, sediments carried in the water are no longer buoyed by swift river currents, and settle into the bottom or are trapped by marsh vegetation. Marshes act like sponges during periods of high water, and can absorb as much as 30,000 gallons of water per acre, an important natural flood control system for surrounding land areas.

One acre of salt marsh can absorb 30,000 gallons of water.
—*Maine Coastal Program*, The Estuary Book

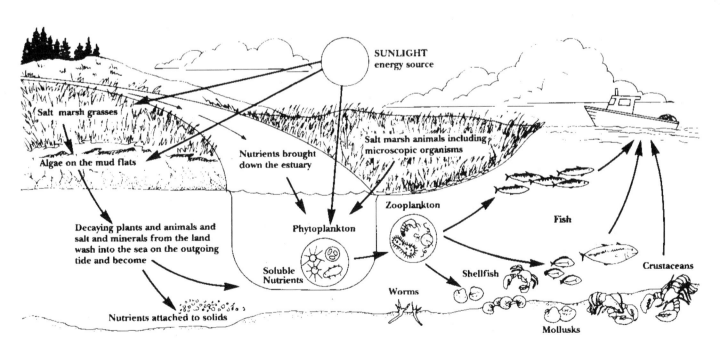

An estuary at work. Reprinted with permission from the Maine State Planning Office.

Estuarine Habitat: A Critical Nutrient Source

The thirteen major estuaries in the Gulf of Maine watershed include over 3,000 miles of Gulf of Maine shoreline, with a combined drainage area of 22,417 square miles. Many forms of marine life—including fish and crustaceans—reside at least temporarily in estuarine habitat. Sediments that accumulate at the bottom of estuaries are rich in nutrients, and nourish large populations of worms, fish, and shellfish. These animals depend on estuaries for food and shelter during juvenile and larval stages of their growth, often moving in and out of the area with the tides in order to feed. Plants in estuaries fall into two basic types: rooted species (such as cord grass and marsh hay) and microscopic phytoplankton that serve as the primary food source for the estuary.

Over two-thirds of commercially important marine species in the Gulf—including alewives, striped bass, salmon, shad, flounder, shrimp and clams—spend part or all of their life cycles in estuaries. Thus estuaries have long been considered the "nurseries" of near-ocean fisheries. Estuaries also offer vital feeding and resting grounds for migratory birds along the North Atlantic Flyway, and provide habitat for a diversity of waterbirds. Terrestrial mammals, including raccoons, foxes and other furbearers, often feed in salt marshes in the upper reaches of an estuary, or even on exposed mudflats.

The following topics included in the coastal policies of the State of Maine are within the scope of estuary planning:

1. **Port and Harbor Development**
2. **Marine Resource Management**
3. **Shoreline Management and Access**
4. **Hazard Area Development**
5. **State and Local Cooperative Management**
6. **Scenic and Natural Areas Protection**
7. **Recreation and Tourism**
8. **Water Quality**
9. **Air Quality**

—*Maine Coastal Program*, The Estuary Book

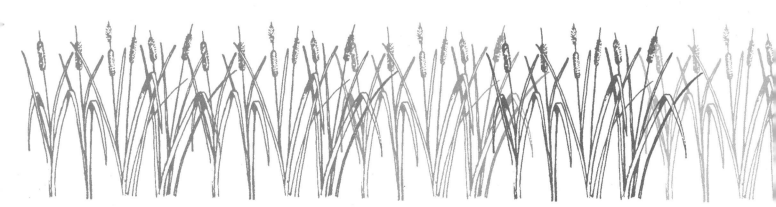

A Vulnerable World

Since estuarine sediments tend to accumulate on the bottom, any pollutants captured in those sediments remain in the area much longer than pollutants in the water itself. As a result, activities such as dredging in harbors stir up sediments and create a chemical soup that is reintroduced into the aquatic habitat.

A less obvious threat to the health of estuarine habitats and its living resources is the cumulative loss of wetlands and habitat degradation that is occurring up and down the Gulf of Maine coast. Development to accommodate human population growth has disrupted natural processes in estuaries. Consequently, their value as habitat—both to plant and animal communities, and to ourselves—has been seriously compromised.

Estuarine habitats in all their variety, and in all their dynamic forms, are critical components of the Gulf of Maine ecosystem. They dominate the coastal region of the watershed and are essential to the lives of many species essential to us. Changing quietly with the seasons and the tides, estuaries are so much a part of our lives that it is quite possible to take them for granted. The materials in this chapter reinforce the importance of estuaries and offer tools with which to teach one another about their value.

Specific information for this introduction was drawn from the recent publications of the Gulf of Maine Council on the Environment (Sustaining our Common Heritage), the Maine Department of Marine Resources, and the U.S. Fish and Wildlife Service, Gulf of Maine Project.

Loss of Eel Grass Beds Affects Productivity in Great Bay
The loss of eel grass beds in New Hampshire's Great Bay has been linked to pollution from the surrounding areas, and to a natural wasting disease. Without the eel grass to trap soil particles and anchor the estuarine substrate, many acres of shellfish beds have been buried by shifting sediments. The populations of small fish and other organisms that form the bottom of the aquatic food chain have declined, resulting in a less diverse and productive estuarine ecosystem.
—Gulf of Maine Council on the Marine Environment, 1989, excerpted from "Sustaining Our Common Heritage"

Title: The Wells Reserve Discovery Program

Target: Grades K-6

Available from: The Wells National Estuarine Research Reserve, 342 Laudholm Farm Road, Wells, ME 04090-9988; telephone (207) 646-1555; fax (207) 646-2930

Cost: $5 per booklet, loan of backpack free

COMMENT

Discovery Tours at the Wells National Estuarine Research Reserve are an innovative opportunity for children to increase their understanding of various aspects of the coastal environment through direct observation and experimentation within the Reserve. Ten Discovery Guides have been developed, each illustrated with a cartoon character that makes science and discovery fun and accessible. With these booklets, each designated for a certain part of the Reserve's multifaceted environment, children and their families can explore a variety of trails and habitats using a backpack filled with self-guided experiments and learning activities. These experiments show the many ways animals and plants adapt to the challenges of life in and around the estuary. The series of Discovery Guides were written for two levels: Level I guides are for grades K-2; Level II guides are for grades 3-6. Booklets and backpacks are available at the Visitor Center. With these discovery tools in hand, children are sure to enjoy the independent and inventive nature of this program.

EXCERPTS

"Hi, my name is Tess Tern. I'm a least tern, one of the smallest varieties of terns. I visit the Wells Reserve every summer to live on the beach. There used to be hundreds of other least terns that formed a colony and settled on these sandy beaches to raise their young, but our colony is getting smaller and smaller. I would like to show you an area near where I live. You'll have to use your binoculars to look for me because if you come too close you will disturb our colony and I will not be able to nest here. Perhaps you can help us by sharing my story with others."
—*Wells Research Reserve, "Life on the Edge," Discovery Booklet*

"The estuary presents certain dangers to those that feed here. The rivers that flow down out of the hills of the uplands often carry hazardous chemicals to the estuary. These toxic materials cling to the sediment carried by rivers and settle on the river bottom or around the stems of the marsh grasses. Small creatures that consume these sediments often absorb the harmful chemicals. This is how dangerous chemicals enter the food chain and eventually reach us—or you."
—*Wells Research Reserve, "Life on the Edge," Discovery Booklet*

Sidebar

Discovery Booklets available from The Wells National Estuarine Research Reserve:

Level I

Mountains to Sand - Wanda Worm teaches you about the wonders of the soil.

Raindrops to the Sea - Annie Otter tells you about the journey water takes as it flows out to sea.

Searching through the Seaweed - Randy Raccoon takes you through the uplands, marsh, and beach.

Nature's Quiet Song - Dan Deer teaches you the quiet ways of looking for wildlife.

Life at Laudholm Farm - Grandpa Lester takes you on a tour of Laudholm Farm where he grew up.

Level II

In Living Soil - Scooper Mole takes you on a tour through the soils of Wells Reserve.

Home is My Favorite Habitat - Mitchell Mummichog teaches you about his home in the estuary.

Life on the Edge - Tess Tern tells you how plants and animals survive in their habitats.

A Wild Family - Callie Coyote helps you train your senses to watch nature.

A Trip to Long Ago - Bright Star guides you back to the time when Native American people lived here.

Patricia Smith

61

Title: The Wells National Estuarine Research Reserve Junior Researchers and Advanced Junior Researchers Program

Target: Ages 9-11 and 11-13

Available from: The Wells National Estuarine Research Reserve, 342 Laudholm Farm Road, Wells, ME 04090-9988; telephone (207) 646-1555; fax (207) 646-2930

Cost: Jr. Researchers $100; Advance Jr. Researchers $260

COMMENT

Junior Researchers, Wells Reserve's summer program for 9-11-year olds, is in its fifth season of providing hands-on field experiences that focus on the structure and importance of estuaries. A maximum of 20 children meet for a 2-week session to investigate various aspects of the natural world. Topics such as estuarine habitats, food webs, adaptations, animals of the estuary, and stewardship are introduced and discussed with the final objective being to link the plants, animals, their habitats, and their food webs with the local environment.

The Advanced Researcher program was developed for 11-13-year olds and for those who have finished the Junior Researcher program. This advanced program provides a unique opportunity for a creative educational experience using the natural surroundings of the Reserve. A two-week session with a maximum of 15 participants per session meets from 9 a.m. to 3 p.m. for an in-depth investigation of estuarine concepts. Estuarine ecology and field sampling methods are introduced through activities that also emphasize personal inquiry about natural environments. Hiking and exploration of the Reserve, investigation of animal and plant life, studying the weather and its effects on the Reserve's inhabitants, examining animal signs, tidal influences, plankton and the food web are important parts of the program. To cap off their Researcher experience, students complete their own research project and enjoy an "owl prowl" and the wonders of astronomy during a sleep-over in the Reserve's barn.

EXCERPT

"The Wells National Estuarine Research Reserve at Laudholm Farm preserves 1,600 acres of fields, forest, wetlands and beach on the coast of southern Maine. Laudholm Farm is a historic salt-water farm. The preserved buildings of the farm are centrally located for the ongoing research, education and visitor programs. The varied habitats of the Reserve are home to a variety of wildlife. Endangered and threatened species survive in the protection of the estuary.

The Reserve features a fully equipped modern research facility. Scientists at the Reserve are actively engaged in studying the impacts of pollution and climactic changes on the estuarine environment.

The Education Department's mission is to inform the public about the importance of the estuarine environment and the proper stewardship of this vital resource."—*The Wells National Estuarine Research Reserve*

Title: The Wells Reserve Fourth Grade Program

Target: Grade 4

Available from: The Wells National Estuarine Research Reserve, 342 Laudholm Farm Road, Wells, ME 04090-9988; telephone (207) 646-1555; fax (207) 646-2930

Cost: $2 per student

COMMENT

Fourth graders from Maine and New Hampshire have the opportunity to be introduced to estuarine ecology, learn the importance of an estuary, and begin to understand their responsibility for the environment by participating in Wells Reserve's Fourth Grade Program, now in its fifth successful year. Students first become aware of their natural surroundings, then develop a curiosity and appreciation for those surroundings, followed by an understanding of natural processes, and finally they develop a sense of the need for stewardship action.

In addition to investigating the estuary and its bordering habitats, games are regularly included as a teaching method to reach program objectives. Students in small groups of no more than ten study selected topics in depth. Areas for reflection and/or games are designated and student journals are introduced.

The three-hour morning program begins in May or October and is run on Tuesdays and Thursdays for seven weeks. Teachers receive packets including an introduction to the program, pre-trip guidelines, program timetable, pre-trip check-off, Reserve rules and regulations, trail etiquette, general information on estuarine ecology, vocabulary list, field guide sheets, pre- and post- activities, a trail map, and a Reserve brochure. Packets for parents and/or chaperones are also available.

"After completing their visit to the Wells Reserve, students will be more aware, curious and appreciative of the intricacies of nature; will have a better understanding of the interdependence of all life forms; and will have a sense of the need for personal action that will contribute to wise stewardship of the earth."
— *The Wells National Estuarine Research Reserve*

Activity 1: Energy and You

Part A: Sail Away!

Students are guided through a journey, sailing down a river to the sea. Attention will be focused on the energy from the sun, the wind, and the water. Using this imagery students will then brainstorm the concept of energy.

Part B: It's Electric

Students conduct an experiment to determine their families' electrical energy consumption. How efficient are the systems? How efficient are the students in their use of electricity?

Activity 2: Energy Basics

Part A: What is Energy?

Students view and discuss concepts presented in "Energy," a video that introduces them to broader concepts.

Part B: Estuarine Energy Flow

An overview is given of the energy flow within an estuarine system by an introduction to wave energy, light energy, and the transfer of energy through organisms.

— *The Wells National Reserve, "Activity Overview," DEPTHS Discovering Ecology: Pathways to Science*

Title: DEPTHS Discovering Ecology: Pathways to Science

Target: Grades K-8

Available from: The Wells National Estuarine Research Reserve, 342 Laudholm Farm Road, Wells, ME 04090-9988; telephone (207) 646-1555; fax (207) 646-2930

Cost: Based on program needs. Call for more information.

COMMENT

The DEPTHS program focuses on estuaries as an introduction to ecology. It has been successfully piloted in schools around Maine and New Hampshire for several years. The program is a three-week-long curriculum for grades K-8. Teacher workshops for participating schools are led by the Wells Reserve as part of the program to illustrate use of materials. *Estuarine Ecology: An Introduction to Ecology* accompanies the materials and provides necessary background information.

Activities for each grade level are based on a theme, which aids students in understanding the principles of estuarine ecology. Kindergarten classes study the estuary by making observations, while Grade 1 uses similarities and differences as their theme; Grade 2 studies relationships in the estuarine ecosystem and Grade 3 focuses on change; Grade 4 examines communities; Grades 5 considers watersheds; Grade 6 participates in the study of adaptations. Grade 7 studies energy and Grade 8 examines global changes. Each unit contains activities that integrate life science, earth science, and physical science.

Initially, each grade level considers examples from their own familiar world of experience that represent their "theme." Subsequent lessons build upon the established themes and address a variety of learning styles while teaching about different aspects of the estuary (such as flora, fauna, types of soil, and the effect of being in a tidal zone.) Each activity has clearly stated student objectives, material lists, and time frames. The Wells Reserve provides all materials needed for completing the activities, and it holds workshops to train teachers in using the curriculum and evaluating its effectiveness. Blueprints and directions are available for schools interested in building the materials themselves.

EXCERPT

"Seventh graders will be introduced to the various forms of energy most apparent in the estuary on an imaginary boat ride, and then record their personal use of energy at home. They will discuss energy forms, and learn about wave energy, energy transfer in organisms, and solar energy. Then they will perform hands-on activities that reinforce and enhance this knowledge. Finally students will look at alternative energy sources and will evaluate their own energy conservation practices.

After studying energy in the seventh grade, students are ready to look at the interaction and relationships between the concepts and to see how energy systems affect global environmental changes."—*The Wells National Reserve, "Seventh Grade: Energy" unit, DEPTHS Discovering Ecology: Pathways to Science*

Title: The Scarborough Marsh Nature Center

Target: Grades K-8, general public

Available From: Maine Audubon Society, Gilsland Farm, PO Box 6009, Falmouth, ME 04105-6009; telephone (207) 781-2330; fax (207) 781-6185

Cost: $50 refundable deposit for teacher's guide; $15 suggested user fee

COMMENT

In addition to their headquarters in Falmouth, Maine Audubon maintains a number of other centers. Their Scarborough Marsh Nature Center provides a schedule of field trips throughout the spring, summer, and early fall.

Regular Spring Ecology Walks offer hands-on exploration in Maine's largest salt marsh. The walks are scheduled between 9:00 a.m. and 3:00 p.m., Tuesdays through Fridays from late April to mid-June. With the guidance of a trained volunteer naturalist, groups of all ages can experience the wonders of spring in the marsh.

EXCERPT

"This walk affords an ideal opportunity to greet the glossy ibis and the snowy egret, to discover mummichogs and to hold a stickleback, to observe plants, and to experience the beauty and excitement of the marsh as it comes to life after a Maine winter. You will also be able to see some of the common residents of the marsh in our indoor mount presentation…

So put on your mud boots and go catch a scud! We look forward to sharing the wonders of spring with you at the Scarborough Marsh Nature Center."—*Maine Audubon Society, "Spring Ecology Walk" announcement*

Title: The Wells National Estuarine Research Reserve Self-Guided Programs

Target: Grades K-12, teachers, informal groups

Available from: The Wells National Estuarine Research Reserve, 342 Laudholm Farm Road, Wells, ME 04090-9988; telephone (207) 646-1555; fax (207) 646-2930

Cost: $30 consultation fee; $1 per student

COMMENT

Wells Reserve's Self-Guided Program at Laudholm Farm provides educators who wish to use the Reserve with a resource that supports their science curriculum. Prior to the on-site visit, educators are asked to develop a field-trip plan which must include a statement of goals and objectives, a description of activities at the Reserve, and pre- and post-visit activities.

To help prepare this plan, field-trip leaders meet with the Reserve education staff to explore possible activities and to become familiar with the Reserve's trail system. Educators will receive a packet that includes guidelines for developing a field-trip plan; suggestions for pre-trip preparation; rules and regulations of the Reserve; trail etiquette; general information on estuaries; field guide sheets, activities; a bibliography, trail map and calendar; and an informational brochure. To support field-trip preparation, the Reserve also includes a chaperone's packet. The library is available for use if additional information is desired, and a backpack containing a magnifier, binoculars, hydrometer, soil and air thermometers, and field guides is available for loan on the day of the field trip.

EXCERPT

"You'll find a wide range of educational opportunities at the Wells National Estuarine Research Reserve. Each is designed to be enjoyable, challenging, and above all, to provide crucial knowledge of this rich environment where the rivers meet the sea. Whether you're a bird-watcher or a graduate student, a family on a summer outing or a lifelong naturalist, the Wells Reserve has created an educational program specifically designed to give you a higher level of appreciation for our environment.

As you participate in any program at the Reserve, you'll find your increased knowledge will lead you to become a steward of estuaries and the web of life to which they are connected."—*The Wells National Estuarine Research Reserve*

© June Henshaw

Title: Sunkhaze Meadows National Wildlife Refuge visitor pamphlet

Target: General audience

Available from: U.S. Fish and Wildlife Service Sunkhaze Meadows National Wildlife Refuge, 1033 South Main Street, Old Town, ME 04468-2023; telephone (207) 827-6138; fax (207) 827-6099

Cost: Free

COMMENT

This visitor brochure and map contains information on history, wildlife, habitat management, and visitor opportunities. The refuge is open year-round with opportunities for hiking, canoeing, cross-country skiing and snowshoeing. The area was designated a national wildlife refuge shortly after a failed attempt to harvest its peatland, the second largest in the state. Future educational facilities are planned for this site. Purchase of refuge lands were supported in part by royalties from offshore oil-drilling collected through the federal Land and Water Conservation Fund.

EXCERPT

"Sunkhaze Meadows National Wildlife Refuge, established in 1988, is located on Sunkhaze Stream in the town of Milford, Maine, just a few miles north of Bangor. The name Sunkhaze is derived from the Abenaki phrase Wetchi-sam-kassek which, roughly translated, means 'concealing outlet,' referring to the stream's well-disguised confluence with the Penobscot River. The 9,337-acre refuge surrounds nearly 5 miles of Sunkhaze Stream and another 12 miles of tributary streams. Major habitats include forested uplands, alder/willow riparian zones, and cedar swamps, as well as the bog for which the refuge is named.

Since Sunkhaze Meadows NWR is already blessed with a wide variety of habitats within its boundaries, managers have little need to change or create habitat favoring one species over another. It is the intention of the refuge staff to maintain this great diversity of habitats."—*U.S. Fish and Wildlife Service, Sunkhaze Meadows National Wildlife Refuge*

Other opportunities at the Reserve include:

- Seven miles of trails which are open daily throughout the year
- Tours conducted by trained docent volunteers
- Visitor Center exhibits
- Lectures and workshops
- Teacher workshops
- Outreach programs (See the DEPTHS curriculum, page 62)
- College level courses on coastal ecology
- Library

Title: **The Estuary Book: A Guide to Promoting Understanding and Regional Management of Maine's Estuaries and Embayments**

Target: General audience

Available from: Maine Coastal Program, Maine State Planning Office, Station 38, 184 State Street, Augusta, ME 04333-0038; telephone (207) 287-3261; fax (207) 287-5756

Cost: Free

COMMENT

This 48 page guide book provides a thorough education on estuaries—what defines them, what influences them, and what is needed to protect them. Discussions of natural features of estuarine environments, the consequences of development on estuarine areas and habitat, and estuarine planning and management strategies are covered in three chapters which are highly instructional and informative without being unwieldy in scientific jargon. Readable and interesting, the information here should be considered by community members, educators, or any concerned individuals with an interest in protecting unique local resources. With ample illustrations, graphs, maps, and charts, source and reading lists, summaries of successful community plans, community regulatory and nonregulatory measures, lists of management issues, and much more, this book offers a comprehensive look at estuarine systems and our necessary involvement with them.

"An estuary management program is designed to protect, sustain, and improve the resources of an estuary watershed....Ideally, estuary management involves all the communities bordering an estuary or within the same coastal watershed working together to define common goals and strategies to sustain the quality of coastal waters and other natural resources that they share."
—*Maine Coastal Program,* The Estuary Book

EXCERPTS

"Estuaries are among the most precious resources of our coast. As productive environments where fresh- and saltwaters meet, estuaries provide valuable habitat for an abundance of marine life, birds, and other creatures as well as pathways to inland waters for migratory fish. The vistas of undisturbed marsh and clean tidewaters are treasured scenic resources and visually define a quality of life cherished by coastal residents and visitors to Maine. . .

In December of 1989, the Maine Coastal Program initiated the Estuary Project to focus on the management needs of these productive coastal systems. While investigating the problems of Maine estuaries and developing a state strategy for estuarine management, the project identified a need for informational materials on Maine estuaries and on the environmental problems associated with estuarine resource use...*The Estuary Book* was created to pull together basic information on

estuarine systems and coastal pollution as well as to provide ideas for communities and citizens concerned with the future of our estuaries.

The objective of *The Estuary Book* is to provide information about estuaries, the impact of uses on the environmental health of an estuary, and what communities and concerned individuals can do to successfully manage and protect their local estuarine resources."
—*Maine Coastal Program,*
"Introduction," The Estuary Book

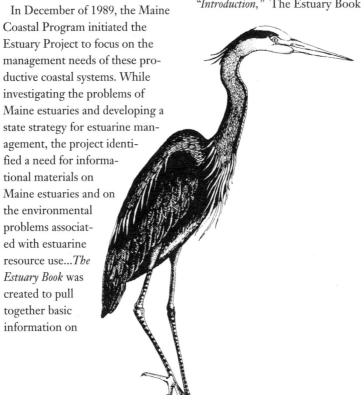

"Marshes are important to the maintenance of a balanced coastal ecosystem. In the spring and fall, when coastal rivers swell from snow melt and rains, marsh grasses along rivers and tidal creeks slow the rush of waters, which allow sediment to settle and protect the shore from erosion. Spongy wetland soils absorb and gradually release waters thus moderating flood conditions and storm surges. The grasses and soils of coastal marshes trap pollutants, nutrients, and sediments from land run-off, thereby improving water quality.

Each winter, ice rafts and tides break up decaying marsh grasses and wash the plant bits into estuary waters. Decaying particles of marsh grasses, algae, seaweed, and other plants are the cornerstone of the estuarine food chain and contribute to the productivity of estuarine waters. Many commercial seafood species such as lobster, herring, menhaden (pogies), alewife, crab, oyster and clam rely on the rich food supply of estuaries during some part of their life cycle. Small fish seek shelter in marsh grasses at high tide from great blue herons and other birds that stalk the shallows to feed. Bald eagles and ospreys also hunt in the marshes and occasionally nest in tall trees along the estuary shore."—*Maine Coastal Program, "Introduction,"* The Estuary Book

Principle characteristics of Maine coast estuaries

1. Estuaries have three subsystems—the riverine, estuarine, and marine.
2. The flow of freshwater into Maine estuaries varies greatly with the season.
3. Mixing between the fresh- and saltwater layers, and estuarine water circulation depend on the shape of the estuary, the volume of river flow, the height of tide and [velocity of] winds.
4. Estuaries collect pollutants from the entire watershed.

—*adapted from Maine Coastal Program*, The Estuary Book

"Good water quality sustains life. At the heart of estuary planning is a concern for water quality. Water quality affects fish, shellfish, and other natural resources as well as the available uses of the estuary by people."
—*Maine Coastal Program*, The Estuary Book

Title: Fundy Salt Marshes...Ours To Protect Poster

Target Group: Grades K-12

Available from: Huntsman Marine Science Centre, Public Education Programs, Brandy Cove Road, St. Andrews, NB, Canada E0G 2X0; telephone (506) 529–1200; fax (506) 529–1212

Cost: Free

COMMENT

A joint product of the Conservation Council of New Brunswick, the World Wildlife Fund, and the Endangered Spaces Local Action Fund, this color poster is a welcome addition to the estuary "story." It features a background photo of a salt marsh, with insets about their importance and what people can do to protect them. Simple, straightforward, easy-to-read, important to think about.

EXCERPT

"Salt marshes are one of the earth's most productive ecosystems. As they decay, the plants found growing on the marshes act as fertilizer for the sea, sending rich nutrients to marine life with every tide. Many fish, shellfish, birds and mammals at some point in their life cycle depend on salt marshes for feeding and spawning, resting or nesting.

Most of the original salt marshes along New Brunswick's Fundy coast have already been altered or destroyed. Can we afford any additional losses of this important natural habitat, which will reduce populations of wildlife that depend on it and further threaten commercial fisheries?" —*Conservation Council of New Brunswick*

Other materials from Huntsman Marine Science Centre:

Huntsman Marine Science Centre has an extensive collection of marine science materials and programs available for purchase or loan including:
• HMSC Lab Manual for upper-elementary, and high-school students
• Whale, shark, seal and oceanography kits
• On-site and off-site education programs
• Salt marsh education kit
• Fishery kit
• *Voices of the Bay*—Reflections on Changing Times Along Fundy Shores, and *Tidal Life*—A Natural History of the Bay of Fundy
• Coastal Discovery Cards
• Sea Trek Information Series

66

The Salmon Times

Title: Adopt-A-Salmon Family Multidisciplinary Watershed Education Program

Target Group: Grades 5-8

Available from: U.S. Fish and Wildlife Service, Central New England Anadromous Fish Program, 151 Broad Street, Nashua, NH 03063; telephone (603) 598–4392; fax (603) 598–3478

Cost: Curriculum package is provided to participating schools at no charge. However, cost of the salmon egg incubator is the school's responsibilty.

COMMENT

Adopt-A-Salmon Family is a hands-on, multidisciplinary watershed education program for middle school students. Throughout the year-long program, students learn about the biological and cultural dynamics of watersheds by focusing on anadromous fish restoration. By raising and releasing a "salmon family" into a local river, students experience ownership in their watershed, an important first step toward the development of a stewardship ethic.

Program elements include field trips to a fish hatchery and local river, school visits by U. S. Fish and Wildlife Service employees or other facilitators, teacher-led classroom instruction, and in-classroom incubation of Atlantic salmon eggs. Through a monthly newsletter, *The Salmon Times*, students explore a variety of watershed themes, including the water cycle, ecosystems, biodiversity, habitat protection, endangered species management, water quality and pollution, anadromous fish restoration and environmental-cultural linkages. The program involves students in science, math, social studies, history, and language arts studies.

The U.S. Fish and Wildlife Service, in partnership with University of New Hampshire Sea Grant Extension and New England Salmon Association, has developed a formal "Adopt-A-Salmon Family" program package that consists of a teacher's guide, newsletter templates and poster series. Eventually, the program will be offered to middle schools throughout New England.

EXCERPTS

"The *Adopt-A-Salmon Family* program promotes awareness of the Atlantic Salmon Restoration Program and fosters watershed stewardship in fun and innovative ways. Through a variety of classroom and field exercises, students examine the complexities of the watershed and gain an understanding of the impacts of human existence on that system. They come to view the relative success of the anadromous fish restoration program as a reflection of overall watershed health...

As the culminating program event, student will stock fry in a stream. This 'citizen-action' event will afford the students a real opportunity to contribute to the restoration of Atlantic salmon and will underscore the program's watershed stewardship theme. All students will receive a certificate of program completion.

The flexibility inherent in the Adopt-A-Salmon Family program allows for optimal teacher creative input and involvement. The true multidisciplinary nature of the program promotes student proficiency in geography, science, mathematics, language arts, sociology and art. The teacher may elect to incorporate computer science skills and other disciplines as well."
—*U.S. Fish and Wildlife Service, Central New England Anadromous Fish Program*

Free At Last!

"Many of the salmon you saw last fall at the Nashua National Fish Hatchery are about to begin a journey, one that will take them far from the concrete raceways they have come to call home. As you might remember from your hatchery tour, once the fish have been spawned, they become surplus to the restoration program. In past years, these fish were stocked into lakes and ponds. Starting last spring, 1,500 of the surplus fish were released into the Merrimack and Pemigewasset rivers in New Hampshire. This stocking will be repeated again this spring. The Purpose of the new program, called the Brood Stock Fishery, is to provide fishing opportunities for anglers.
—*U.S. Fish and Wildlife Service, Central New England Anadromous Fish Program*, The Salmon Times, *vol. 1, no. 7, p.1*

A Historic Effort to Restore Atlantic Salmon

In 1886, the states of Massachusetts and New Hampshire joined forces to restore the salmon to the watershed. They did many of the same things that are done today. Fish were raised in hatcheries for release into rivers, and ladders were built to provide migrating salmon with passage over dams. Using a variety of designs, fish ladders were constructed from wood. They all amounted to watery 'staircases' and were surprisingly effective.

Since there were no longer any wild fish in the watershed, salmon eggs were obtained from Canada, and later, from the Penobscot River in Maine. During the first stocking in 1867, 15,000 salmon eggs were deposited directly into the Pemigewasset and upper reaches of the Merrimack Rivers. Fry, raised in state and private 'hatch houses' were stocked out in future years. Eventually a salmon hatchery, built specifically for the Merrimack River program, was established at Livermore Falls, in Plymouth, New Hampshire.

The restoration program was successful for two decades. 3,600 returning Atlantic salmon were counted at the Essex Dam in Lawrence in the spring of 1893. Misfortune struck in 1896 when a spring flood destroyed the fish ladder at the Essex Dam. This event spelled the end of the restoration effort. Salmon would not reappear in the river for almost a century.
—The Salmon Times, *April, 1994*

Title: **Massachusetts Bay Program Newsletter, Bays Connections**

Target: Teachers, general public

Available From: Massachusetts Bays Education Alliance, 100 Cambridge Street, Room 2006, Boston, MA 02202; telephone 1-800-447-BAYS

Cost: Contact for information and membership rates

COMMENT

The concept of the local watershed as one's environmental address is one of the many ideas promoted by *Bays Connections*, the educational newsletter of the Massachusetts Bays Program. This piece is tightly edited—fine print in three columns—in order to condense a large amount of information on both sides of a sheet of (recycled) paper. Each issue focuses on a particular issue; fish and the fishing crisis, watersheds and wetlands, for example. Teachers and others are advised of specific curriculum materials, of the availability of resources, of upcoming meetings and even important legislation.

Involvement of teachers and students in hands-on work in the watershed also appears to be a central tenet of *Bays Connections*. Connections to the Internet, connections to the Department of Fisheries, connections to special purpose libraries—*Bays Connections* does a good job of bringing readers pertinent and timely information, schedules of events, addresses, telephone numbers and a dose of encouragement.

The Mass. Bays program is a regional effort, though tied actively to coastal programs throughout the larger Gulf of Maine region. Ideas and suggestions for teachers in Massachusetts will be helpful to others in New Hampshire, Maine, Nova Scotia or New Brunswick.

EXCERPTS

Stream Watchers Sought

"A wonderful way to engage student interest in fisheries is by forming a Fishway Stewardship Team through the Fishway Stewardship Program of the Massachusetts Division of Marine Fisheries (DMF) and Riverways Programs. There are over 200 fishways on some 100 coastal streams in Massachusetts, and your students' help is greatly needed to provide passageways for the migratory fish as they search for their spawning grounds.

With so many fishways, the State and communities cannot possibly oversee the maintenance and operation of them all, so school participation is welcomed. The DMF and Riverways Programs will provide on-site instruction which includes management plans and operating protocol for your students to follow."—*Mass. Bays Program*, Bays Connections Newsletter, *Summer, 1994*

"The watershed concept has environmental agencies and advocates abuzz these days. Why? Because planning and acting at the watershed level is often the best way to reduce nonpoint source water-quality problems. As our abundant winter snow melts this spring and flows into storm drains and streams throughout the watershed of the bays, the water carries downstream with it a cocktail of dissolved and particle-bound heavy metals, organic chemicals, and pathogens. Reduction of pollution introduced through nonpoint source stormwater runoff often means fixing the upstream sources."
—*Mass. Bays Program*, Bays Connections Newsletter, *Spring 1994*

68

Title: **Estuarine Studies: An Activities Text for Maine Schools, Department of Marine Resources, Fisheries Education Unit #16**

Target Group: Grades 9-adult

Available from: Maine Department of Marine Resources, Education Division, Station 21, Augusta, ME 04333-0021; telephone (207) 624–6578; fax (207) 624-6024

Cost: Free

COMMENT

This thorough, information-packed unit is part of the Education Division's larger "Fisheries Education" curriculum. Packaged in a 40-page 8.5" x 11" booklet, "Estuarine Studies" presents an amazing array of facts, ideas, activities, and topics for further research to challenge teachers and their students (high school level and beyond) to think and work like scientists. Many of the activities are hands-on projects (*e.g.*, wave machines, data collection and measurement techniques and beach transects.) This no-frills, serious examination of estuarine habitat and the dynamics of estuarine ecosystems will take commitment on the part of students and teachers, but the knowledge gained is well worth it.

Ask questions and note trends

Are clam flats closed due to bacterial pollution? Is water quality getting better or worse? Are there more applications for shoreland building permits than there used to be? Are the shorelands of the estuary "hardened" with parking lots, riprap, seawalls, and other modifications? Are there old dumps at the shores of the estuary or in nearby marshes and small wetlands? Where were the old mills and industries located, what did they produce and discard? Are the estuary shores and inlets littered with plastic trash and other debris? What has been the overall effect of incremental development along the estuary and in the estuary watershed?—*Maine Coastal Program*, The Estuary Book

---

EXCERPTS

"The study of an estuarine area is a study in 'change.' The estuary is an ecosystem in motion obedient to its masters: the force of the tides, the push of the wind, the gravity of the earth and the biological demand of all the creatures living in it. From moment to moment these forces are at work changing the chemical, physical and biological make-up of the estuary.

Estuaries are fragile boundaries between marine and freshwater habitats. Their value to the commercial fisheries, recreation and shipping make them economically important. Their value to the thousands of aquatic animals and plants that live in these areas remain uncalculable."—*Maine Department of Marine Resources, Education Division*, Estuarine Studies: An Activities Text for Maine Schools

"An estuarine system is dependent upon nutrients supplied by chemical, geological, and biological processes. These nutrients affect the primary production of the systems. Photosynthesis is the fundamental process by which energy and essential nutrients enter the estuarine food chain. Plant growth continues until some basic requirement limits that growth. Nitrogen availability tends to be a limiting factor on primary production in estuarine and marine environments. Sources of nitrogen are complex and may vary among estuaries. The supply of nitrogen in any estuary depends on the circulation.

Three major external sources of inorganic nitrogen to an estuary are: 1) inorganic nitrate nitrogen introduced in the bottom flow of saline water from the ocean; 2) nitrate (and possibly ammonia) that enters from agricultural use in runoff; and 3) sewerage-derived nitrogen (both nitrate and ammonia). Regenerated nitrogen from within the estuary can also be an important source for plant growth.

Nitrogen leaves the estuary with surface outflow in the form of inorganic nitrogen, detritus, phytoplankton, zooplankton, and migration of fish and birds.

…Circulation patterns, mixing and upwellings are extremely important to the nutrient revitalization of the estuaries. These soluble and solid organics are recycled and kept within the estuary primarily because of the circulation pattern driven by the tides."—*Maine Department of Marine Resources, Education Division*, Estuarine Studies: An Activities Text for Maine Schools

---

Sample activities excerpted from Estuarine Studies: An Activities Text for Maine Schools, *Maine Department of Marine Resources, Education Division:*

(1) Heating and Cooling Comparison between Fresh- and Saltwater

The time it takes to heat up an equal amount of fresh and saltwater to an equal temperature is a simple measure of the amount of heat needed to alter the system.

Materials:

2 shallow pans, 2 thermometers and a timer, fresh- and saltwater.

Procedure:

1. Select 2 shallow pans. Fill one with freshwater and the other with an equal volume of saltwater.
2. Place a thermometer in each pan and *record the temperature of each*.
3. Place the pans outside and *record the time*. (In the winter, the water will cool quickly, in other seasons the temperature will rise if you place the pans in the sun.)
4. *Record the temperature every five minutes from the start*. Let the water in the pans warm or cool 10° F.

Data Analysis:

1. Which pan of water cooled or warmed the fastest?
2. What do you think makes the difference?
3. In the spring of the year, which area would warm the fastest, a river, an estuary, or open ocean? Explain your answer.

Research Topic:

Does the Gulf of Maine freeze? Explain your ideas.

(2) Salt Marsh Transect

A salt marsh transect can be an effective method of gaining information about the relationships and influence of elevation and salinity on a wet area.

Materials required:

2 five-foot poles; 25 feet of string; graph paper, pail, fine-mesh dip-net or pole with strainer attached to one end, meter stick, and a carpenter's line level.

Procedure:

1. Divide students into groups of five and assign the following duties:

Team members: two pole attendants; person to measure height of string above the surface; two persons to graph the flora and fauna in conjunction with elevation.

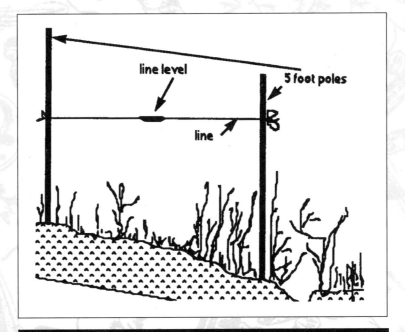

Title: **Field Trip in the Classroom: A Teacher's Guide and Student Activities Text Based on Actual Field Data Collected on the Kennebec Estuary**

Target Group: Grades 9-Adult

Available from: Maine Department of Marine Resources Education Division, Station 21, Augusta, ME 04333-0021; telephone (207) 624–6578; fax (207) 624-6024

Cost: Free

COMMENT

A companion to the _Estuarine Studies: An Activities Text for Maine Schools_ book, _Field Trip in the Classroom_ is a teacher guide and student activities text based on actual field data collected on the Kennebec estuary. Similar in style, presentation, and scope to _Estuarine Studies_, these activities extend the scientific approach to estuarine ecology by bringing data from a real estuary directly into the classroom, along with a first-hand look at the Kennebec estuary through a scripted slideshow. Although many of the principles examined build on the previous Estuarine Studies unit, _Field Trip in the Classroom_ can easily stand alone.

EXCERPT

"These activities were designed to permit students to make scientific evaluations using actual estuarine study sites and data in as nearly an ideal situation as a field trip would provide. The package is built around the scientific studies being conducted currently on the tidal segment of the Kennebec River and its estuary.

There are several parts to this field trip. A slide program will show the river and its estuary to help students 'see' the area under study. A video shows a typical Maine marsh that might be found in the estuary. The data collection and field testing are also shown on slides. Data table and 'paper' samples are all directly from the scientists' logs. All activities portrayed in the manual are based on actual research activities currently being conducted."
—_Maine Department of Marine Resources, Education Division, Fisheries Education Unit #17,_ Field Trip in the Classroom

"Plankton samples collected in the estuary reflect both the plant and animals in the lower base of the food chain that utilize these areas. These samples are influenced by the season, weather, tides, amount of sunlight, salinity and numerous other factors. Because of these variables, every sample taken with a plankton net will be different, but the statistical dominance will be the same. These samples provide information on the health of the estuary, the diversity of life within this environment, and the potential utilization of the estuarine resources."
—_excerpted from_ Field Trip in the Classroom, _"Biological Samples— Plankton," Maine Department of Marine Resources_

Title: Birds of Parker River National Wildlife Refuge and Refuge Brochure

Target Group: General public

Available from: U.S. Fish and Wildlife Service, Parker River National Wildlife Refuge, Northern Boulevard, Plum Island, Newburyport, MA 01950–4315; telephone (508) 465–5753; fax (508) 465-2807

Cost: Free

COMMENT

These brochures in the set of National Wildlife Refuge (NWR) publications are indispensable if you plan to visit the 4,662 acres of beach, dunes, bogs, freshwater impoundments and tidal marshes of the Parker River National Wildlife Refuge. Located on the southern two-thirds of Plum Island near Newburyport, Massachusetts, this refuge is unique in that it is one of the few natural barrier "beach-dune-salt marsh complexes" left in the northeast—and a stunning one at that. The refuge strongly focuses on habitat management activities and wildlife population studies. The general brochure provides background about the refuge, maps, and suggestions for activities while the bird brochure lists the 303 species that have been seen on the Refuge in the past decade.
Carry it with you and see how many you can check off.

EXCERPTS

"Bird activity at the Refuge is highlighted by shorebird migrations and flocks of swallows in late summer and large flocks of waterfowl in the fall and early spring.

Most birds are migratory. The peak migration periods at Parker River are usually March 1 - June 7; and August 1 - October 31. Bird activity on the Refuge is highlighted by shorebird migrations and flocks of swallows in late summer and large flocks of waterfowl in the fall and early spring."

"Due to an ever-growing world, places that provide the necessary food and shelter… for wildlife are at a premium. At Parker River Refuge, like other national wildlife refuges, we strive to provide the best natural habitat possible for wildlife. Some habitat management activities conducted at the refuge include salt marsh restoration, controlled burning of vegetation, pest plant control, installation of artificial nesting structures and water level manipulations."—*excerpted from Parker River NWR brochure*

© June Henshaw

These additional 39 species have been recorded no more than several times in the last 20 years.

Pacific loon
Eared grebe
Western grebe
Cory's shearwater
American white pelican
Little egret
White ibis
White-faced ibis
Fulvous whistling duck
Garganey
Sandhill crane
Wilson's plover
Black-necked stilt
Spotted redshank
Terek sandpiper
Bar-tailed godwit
Little stint
Long-tailed jaeger
Franklin's gull
Thayer's gull

Ross' gull
Sabine's gull
Ivory gull
Gull-billed tern
Sooty tern
Black guillemot
Atlantic puffin
Barn owl
Chuck-will's widow
Black-backed woodpecker
Say's phoebe
Scissor-tailed flycatcher
Common raven
Carolina wren
Sedge wren
Bohemian waxwing
Grasshopper sparrow
Henslow's sparrow
LeConte's sparrow

Title: The Salt Marsh: A Complete Guide to Conducting Successful Field Trips for Grades K-12

Target: Grades K-12

Available from: The Seacoast Science Center, Odiorne Point State Park, 570 Ocean Blvd., Rye, NH 03870; telephone (603) 436–8043; fax (603) 433–2235

Cost: $11.95

COMMENT

Like *The Rocky Shore* (mentioned in the chapter on marine ecosystems), *The Salt Marsh* teacher guide helps teachers plan for field trips and suggests appropriate activities and ideas for particular age levels and facets of the estuary experience. Guidelines for chaperones; helpful logistical information and checklists; safety measures (even a "What to Wear" section); key to plants and animals; a glossary and bibliography, and various "salt-marsh specific" worksheets, games, and experiments are included. Either in tandem with other Seacoast Science Center guides or taught as an independent unit on marsh ecology, *The Salt Marsh* will provide teachers and their students with valuable and memorable hands-on and feet-in-the-mud learning opportunities.

EXCERPTS

The field of environmental education has increasingly moved away from the identification approach to learning. Concept learning allows participants to think and explore for themselves and is adaptable to any environment from the salt marsh to your backyard. It connects a student to the natural world by making them a part of that world, not an outsider observing the life within. This personalized approach to 'scientific' learning makes students aware of the vital role they play in any habitat, from the salt marsh, to the rain forests, to their own backyard."—*Seacoast Science Center, "Concept Learning,"* The Salt Marsh

"Today, the value of salt marshes is better understood than it was 30 years ago. We now know that marshes are vital for clean water, healthy fish populations, and sound economics. Citizens understand that [marshes] are an important stop-over point for migrating birds and waterfowl. Fishermen know that a high percentage of the marine fish they depend on for their living use the salt marsh as a nursery or feeding ground. Ecologists know that marshes are important exporters of nutrients in the form of detritus to the marine ecosystem...Today, salt marshes are again recognized as valuable resources. Teaching students about the importance of salt marshes, the roles they have played in our history, and the functions they serve for us today is the first step in promoting salt marsh stewardship."
—*Seacoast Science Center*

"The Seacoast Science Center is a public/private partnership. It is managed by the Audubon Society of New Hampshire under contract with the State of New Hampshire, in affiliation with the Friends of Odiorne Point, Inc., and the University of New Hampshire Cooperative Extension/Sea Grant Program...

We have a full complement of programming available from naturalist-led walks throughout the park to slideshows on marine and natural and cultural history. Most groups prefer to have a combination of organized and free time so that they can explore the exhibits and park at their own pace. We specialize in marine programs for families and senior citizens."
—*Seacoast Science Center*

Sample "Questions for the Field"

- How can an animal's behavioral adaptations increase its chances for survival?
- What changes may take place in the salt marsh on a daily, seasonal, or geological basis? (Don't forget ice!)
- What are the basic ingredients of a salt marsh ecosystem?
- What is the significance of the sun to the salt marsh ecosystem?
- Identify two or three salt marsh 'mini' habitats and explain how they differ from each other.
- What are examples of positive and negative human impact on a salt marsh?
- What is an example of plant/animal interdependence?

—*excerpted from Seacoast Science Center, "Concept Learning,"* The Salt Marsh

COASTAL AND MARINE SYSTEMS

Nearly two million years ago, during the last Ice Age, glaciers cut through massive North American landscapes, carving what is now the 5,200-mile-long shore of the Gulf of Maine. The last of the great ice swaths retreated from our area about 12,000 years ago after forming the shallow basins and banks of the Gulf floor and shaping more than 4,500 islands in the Gulf. The Gulf of Maine coast is legendary for its beauty and history, and for the abundance of life it sustains. It has been celebrated in song and literature, and has become part of the essential image of "wildness" that Henry David Thoreau described as central to the human spirit. To many of us, the ocean begins somewhere beyond the salty ledges and pine covered cliffs of the Gulf's coast. Here in the coastal and marine systems—and the plant and animal communities that live there—are the basis of our connection with the sea; the bridge between our terrestrial lives and the vast, marine world that makes up three-quarters of the planet.

The link between the Gulf of Maine and the open Atlantic is the Northeast Channel, a deep underwater passage dividing Georges and Brown banks. This channel brings cold ocean water from the northeast into the Gulf of Maine, where it mixes with freshwater from numerous rivers draining into the Gulf. River runoff and strong tides drive swirling patterns of counter-clockwise currents that mix nutrients and sustain the plankton that is the basis of the Gulf's food chain. It takes approximately three months for currents to circulate water once around the Gulf; that water moves and mixes nutrients throughout the Gulf, nourishing invertebrates, fish, marine mammals, and birds.

Energy for a Different Way of Life

In biological terms, one of the biggest differences between terrestrial and marine systems is the means by which energy is converted to food—the source of biological productivity. In both cases, on land and on sea, the process begins with photosynthesis and sunlight, and depends on plants, which are the first link in the food chain.

On land, plants provide direct food energy to herbivores, who eat parts of plants or its products (e.g., seeds and fruit). But most of the organic matter that makes up a typical land plant is consumed by bacteria and fungi when the plant decays.

In the sea, however, phytoplankton—tiny aquatic plants—perform the essential process of photosynthesis while suspended in the upper layers of the water—and they are quickly and often completely consumed by an almost equal volume of zooplankton (tiny aquatic animals) resulting in a very active, rapid turnover of energy and marine biomass. This "plankton ecosystem" is a dynamic, mobile, and fluid energy source that forms the basis of most of the marine habitats in the Gulf of Maine.

The greatest concentrations of biological productivity in the Gulf occur during phytoplankton "blooms" in the summer months, particularly over the sunlit waters of Georges Bank, where the sea floor is so high in places that the water is less than 9 feet (1.8 meters) deep.

"Our attitude toward the ocean must change. We must stop considering it such an invulnerable immensity that any human interference will go unnoticed. After thousands of years of ignorance and superstition, we must now learn to understand, love, and respect the sea. Because the ocean, where all creatures come from, is life itself."
—*Jacques-Yves Cousteau*

73

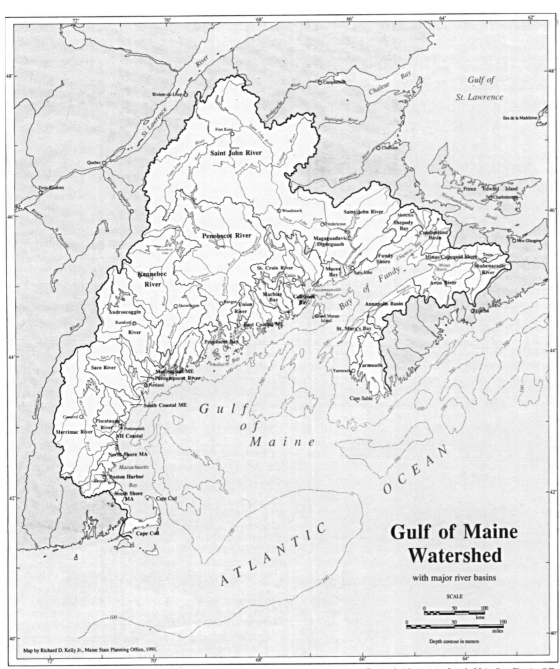

Gulf of Maine Watershed

with major river basins

SCALE

Map by Richard D. Kelly Jr., Maine State Planning Office, 1991.

As the Gulf of Maine shaped our past, so will it shape our future. We can no longer afford to manage only the resources we see. If we restrict our focus to the stretch of coast that is visible, we limit our understanding of the vital role the Gulf plays in defining and enriching our lives. Our vision of environmental and economic issues must be expanded to include our neighboring sea.
—*excerpted from* Charting our Course: An Activity Guide for Grades 6-12 on Water Quality in the Gulf of Maine, *Maine Coastal Program, 1989*

Reprinted with permission from the Maine State Planning Office

Habitats in the Gulf of Maine

The Gulf of Maine provides marine habitat for an abundant variety of marine life; it is recognized as having one of the highest levels of biological productivity that exists anywhere in world. Habitats range from island cliffs, ledges and mudflats—vital for colonial nesting seabirds, seals, and shorebirds—to boulders, cobbles and mud on the ocean floor sheltering over 1,600 species of bottom-dwelling creatures. In between, the water column sustains its own array of living things, from microscopic plankton to immense whales that feed in the Gulf. Intertidal ledges, eel grass beds, muddy and sandy sediments, and salt marshes all contribute to the diversity of fish, marine mammals, and birds that depend upon the Gulf.

Perhaps the most characteristic habitat in the Gulf of Maine ecosystem is the rocky intertidal shore, which provides home to all kinds of marine life. The large tidal range that occurs every day in the Gulf of Maine creates a fascinating array of adaptations in coastal and marine plants and animals. Most species living in rocky intertidal habitats are invertebrates (animals without backbones). Species such as barnacles, dog whelks, periwinkles, starfish and mussels cling to rocks and live in tidepools. Plants like sea lettuce thrive in very salty water. Brown rockweeds have air bladders that give them buoyancy and keep them floating close to the sunlit surface. Irish moss and kelp provide shelter for crabs and young lobsters.

Other familiar coastal habitats include mud, sand, gravel and cobble beaches of the Gulf shore. These also require special adaptations by the plants and animals living there. From microorganisms to razor clams and sandworms to shorebirds, beach inhabitants must be tolerant of a high-energy environment with extremes in temperature, wind, and water conditions; and many species literally "dig in" to maintain permanent residence. On sandy beaches above the high-tide mark, long grasses anchor sand dunes and provide shelter, breeding and nesting areas for shorebirds.

"We are taught by sophisticated people that regionalism is passé. Let us not participate in that and let us not permit our children to participate in it. Let us take the emotional and intellectual chance of saying that this is not the leftover sector of our nation; that, rather, this is the true soul of the country, the place that cries out loudest to the human spirit; that this place is exalted, that it is sacred. Use that word, sacred, and whatever kind of ethic it is, use the word ethic, because the word properly connotes rigor and high aspirations. Last, let us be sure to say this to all of the people, for the contentiousness really can wane when we realize, and act upon, our common melded past and future."
—*Charles Wilkinson*, Eagle Bird. *New York: Vintage Press, 1993. p. 161*

The Gulf of Maine provides critical habitat for the northern right whale, the most endangered of all the marine mammals found in the region. Between April and July, these animals concentrate around Nantucket Shoals and the Great South Channel, west of Georges Bank, and they are found at the mouth of the Bay of Fundy from late summer into the fall. Females winter and give birth to young off the coast of Georgia, but the males' wintering areas are uncertain.
—*excerpted from* Sustaining Our Common Heritage, *Gulf of Maine Council on the Marine Environment, 1989*

Ocean Residents

More than 100 different species of fish live in the waters of the Gulf of Maine. They are usually grouped into three major categories: *pelagic* (those fish that usually swim and stay within the open ocean), *demersal* (those that live on or near the ocean floor), and *anadromous* (those that feed and grow in the ocean, but travel upriver to freshwater to spawn. Until recently, familiar demersal fish species such as cod, haddock, and pollock maintained a productive and profitable groundfishing industry in the Gulf of Maine (see "Human Systems, Issues and Impacts," p. 98). Well-known pelagic species include yellowfin and bluefin tuna, swordfish, and herring. Anadromous fish include striped bass, alewive, rare Atlantic salmon and endangered Atlantic sturgeon.

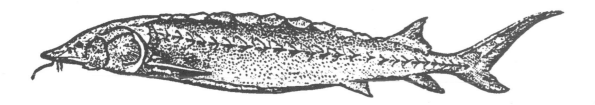

Marine mammals are present in greatest numbers during the summer months, when nutrient upwellings provide the greatest supply of food for dolphins, porpoises, and migrating whales. Finback and humpback whales, the most commonly sighted whales in the Gulf, filter plankton from ocean water for their food. Smaller marine mammals in the Gulf of Maine include saddleback or common dolphins, white-sided dolphins and harbor porpoises. Harbor seals are year-round Gulf residents, using the open ocean, rocky ledges and undeveloped islands for their homes. Once nearly hunted to extinction, harbor seals are now abundant, and can be seen sunning themselves or swimming around many a rocky ledge or island shoreline.

Major groups of birds in the Gulf of Maine include petrels, waterfowl, gulls, terns, alcids, herons, cormorants, plovers and neotropical migrants. They cross back and forth between coastal and open-ocean habitats—in search of food, rest and nesting sites to raise their young. Though gulls and herons are currently abundant, other waterbirds such as the piping plover and roseate terns are so rare that they have been listed as threatened or endangered under the protection of the Endangered Species Act. And although most populations are still small today, the Atlantic puffin—a colonial nesting seabird—is making a comeback on some islands in the Gulf of Maine. Its small plump-bellied orange-beaked spectre has become a popular marketing gimmick around the region, and toy versions are sold in gift shops all along the coast.

Three basic laws of survival rule the tidepool:

- *Keep from being washed away at high tide*

- *Keep from drying out by the sun at low tide*

- *Keep from being eaten*

—*excerpted from* **Katahdin to the Sea: Aquatic Environments in Maine** *poster (see p. 14)*

A Bounty of Information

Nowhere in the course of compiling materials for this *Almanac* has it been more apparent that this is only the beginning of a truly comprehensive survey of educational resources available about the Gulf of Maine. The wealth of educational resources about the interface between land and sea, and about the marine environment beyond, is both encouraging and challenging to anyone wishing to learn about this vast and beautiful saltwater world. The entries described in this chapter are only a sampling of the human energy and creativity that has gone into exploring and explaining this environment.

The coastline of the Gulf of Maine reflects the geologic history of the region— smooth and sand-lined or indented and rockbound, depending on the hardness and texture of the bedrock, where the glaciers deposited their sediment loads, and how the sediments have been reworked. The southern coast of the Gulf of Maine, between Cape Cod, Massachusetts, and Cape Elizabeth, Maine, is characterized by long sandy beaches, soft cliffs and bluffs, and an occasional rocky headland. Here, numerous barrier beaches protect extensive salt marshes.

Between Cape Elizabeth and Passamaquoddy Bay at the mouth of the Bay of Fundy, the coast is extraordinarily rugged, indented, and rockbound with thousands of islands and ledges. Sediment needed to form sand beaches and salt marshes is limited, because the exposed bedrock is primarily granite and erodes very slowly. Often referred to as a drowned coastline, the present-day shoreline evolved as rising sea levels flooded prehistoric river valleys.

The Bay of Fundy was shaped primarily by faulting and subsequent erosion by glaciers. The Bay is famous for the highest tides in the world, which can range up to fifty feet (fifteen meters). The shore of the Bay is characterized by red sandstone cliffs and hard volcanic rocks. Swift tidal currents erode the softer headlands, creating immense mudflats that provide spectacular stopover areas for thousands of migrating shorebirds each fall.

—Gulf of Maine Council on the Marine Environment, 1989, Sustaining Our Common Heritage

GUIDELINES FOR VESSELS IN THE VICINITY OF WHALES IN THE GULF OF MAINE

When in sight of whales...

• avoid excessive speed or sudden changes in speed or direction

If you are less than 200 yards away...

• approach stationary whales at no more than idle or "no wake" speed
• parallel the course and speed of moving whales
• do not attempt a head-on approach to moving or resting whales

If you are less than 100 yards away...

• stay to the side or behind whales and do not cut off their path
• limit your time to fifteen minutes in close approach to whales
• do not approach within 100 feet of whales
• if whales approach within 100 feet of your vessel, put engine in neutral and do not re-engage props until whales are observed at the surface, clear of the vessel. Breaching, lobtailing, and flipper-slapping whales may endanger people and/or vessels. Feeding whales often emit subsurface bubbles before rising to feed at the surface. (Stand clear of light green bubble patches.)

In all cases...

• do not restrict the normal movement or behavior of whales, or take actions that may evoke a reaction from whales or result in physical contact with a whale. Diving on whales is considered to be an intentional approach of whales and a violation of federal laws.

For more information on what you can do to protect whales and their habitat contact:

National Marine Fisheries Service Northeast Region One Blackburn Drive Gloucester, MA 01930 tel. (508) 281–9254

—adapted from Protect the Whales, *a joint publication of the International Wildlife Coalition, Massachusetts Coastal Zone Management, Massachusetts Division of Fisheries and Wildlife, Massachusetts Division of Marine Fisheries, National Marine Fisheries Service, Stellwagen Bank National Marine Sanctuary, and the U.S. Environmental Protection Agency.*

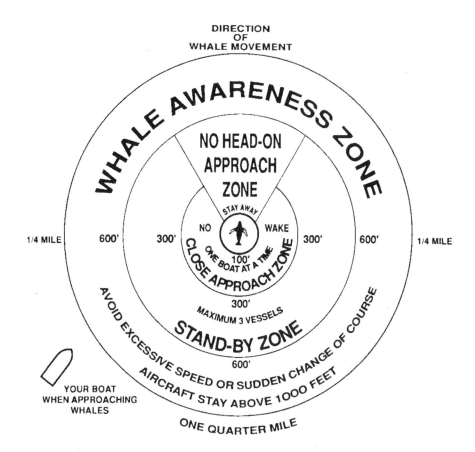

78

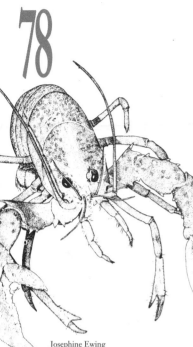

Josephine Ewing

Bluefin Tuna
(*Thunnus thynnus*) are visitors to the Gulf of Maine during summer months. They are the largest fish found in the Gulf, reaching up to 14 feet (4.3 meters) in length and weighing several hundred pounds. Tuna are pelagic, living in the deep waters of the Gulf and wandering the open Atlantic in schools. They prey on smaller schooling fish such as herring and mackerel.
—*Gulf of Maine Project*

Title: Gulf of Maine Species Fact Sheets

Target Group: General audience

Available from: Gulf of Maine Project, U.S. Fish and Wildlife Service, 4R Fundy Road, Falmouth, ME 04105; telephone (207) 781-8364; fax (207) 781-8369

Cost: Free

COMMENT

Single-page fact sheets describe eight coastal and marine species—bald eagle, great blue heron, striped bass, black duck, lobsters, Atlantic menhaden, piping plovers and harbor seals. Like a page out of a magazine, each fact sheet summarizes basic material about each species, its life cycle, its habitat needs, and its relationship to the human population. These eight coast-oriented sheets are particularly interesting to anyone who wants to discover particulars about these species. Beautifully illustrated, they will teach you some surprising facts. Get them while they last. (See page 19 for other fact sheets from USFWS).

EXCERPTS

"In the summer months, lobsters migrate to inshore waters, then return to deeper water as the temperature decreases. Migrations also take place prior to storms. The distance lobsters travel during migrations is a function of their size, age and location. Larger lobsters generally travel farther than the small, inshore lobsters; big lobsters can travel hundreds of miles in a summer..."—*USFWS*

"The menhaden's greatest predators are bluefish, which follow them around the Gulf of Maine throughout the summer months and are thought to contribute to the periodic, and at times overwhelmingly pungent, strandings of menhaden on the shores of numerous coves and bays along the coast..."—*USFWS*

"The piping plover's names comes from its call-notes, plaintive bell-like whistles that are often heard before the birds are seen. When sitting still, their buff-colored plumage, black necks, and black forehead bands make them virtually invisible in the sand..."—*USFWS*

"Harbor seals have large eyes, and, unlike the sea lions that are often in zoos and aquariums, they have no external ear part and do not use their hind flippers to move around on land..."—*USFWS*

Title: Wild Gulf Poster

Target Group: General audience

Available from: The Chewonki Foundation, RR2, Box 1200, Wiscasset, Maine 04578; telephone (207) 882–7323; fax (207) 882–4074

Cost: $15 (includes shipping and handling); $30 for the entire set of four Wild Gulf posters

COMMENT

This poster, commissioned by the National Fish and Wildlife Foundation, was the inspiration for the Wild Gulf educational initiative. Created by Nils Obel, a scientific illustrator whose work has been honored and exhibited in galleries on both sides of the Atlantic, the Wild Gulf poster reflects Obel's renown for artistry and scientific accuracy. His vivid depiction of marine life in this poster is both elegant and lifelike; the fish appear to swim off the paper. Text beneath the large, four-color print describes each of the seven species pictured, along with information about the fish, their habitat and their future. Once you see the poster, you won't forget it.

EXCERPT

"The waters off the northeast coast of North America are an extraordinary place. Currents and tides move through underwater banks and wash across the coast to form a network of estuaries and islands that stretches over 5,200 miles and nourishes marine life in all sizes and shapes. This part of the Atlantic Ocean is called the Gulf of Maine... Fish in the Gulf of Maine live in a variety of habitats. Those living in the open ocean are called *pelagic*. They are large, swift swimmers who eat smaller fish. Many fish in coastal waters travel in schools, feeding on plankton. Groundfish (*demersal*) live on shelves and banks in shallow water. Several species of fish in the Gulf of Maine are *anadromous*, feeding and growing in the ocean, but traveling upriver to freshwater to spawn."—*The Wild Gulf Project*

Josephine Ewing

Title: Island Ethics: Recognizing and Protecting Colonial Nesting Seabird and Waterbird Islands in the Gulf of Maine, A Guide for the Public

Target Group: General audience

Available from: Gulf of Maine Project, U.S. Fish and Wildlife Service, 4R Fundy Rd., Falmouth, ME 04105; telephone (207) 781-8364; fax (207) 781-8369

Cost: Free

COMMENT

This informative illustrated brochure (which folds out into a 17" x 22" poster) details the need for vigilance in caring for nesting colonies on islands in the Gulf of Maine. Sections include "Seabird and Waterbird Life," "Human Impacts," "How You Can Help," a list of general guidelines for proper ethics when visiting islands, and a listing of organizations throughout the Gulf of Maine providing additional information on islands. Schools, chambers of commerce, island touring businesses, boat charters, sea-kayaking outfitters or any group exploring near these islands should have these brochures available.

Josephine Ewing

"Disturbing nesting seabirds during the nesting season (April 1 through mid- to late-August throughout most of the Gulf of Maine) is extremely harmful to eggs and chicks. People should stay off these nesting islands during this time and direct their activities to the many suitable non-nesting islands."
—USFWS

EXCERPT

"This brochure provides information about the lives of colonial nesting seabirds and wading birds and explains why your help is needed to ensure that they continue to prosper in the Gulf of Maine. With information, consideration and restraint during their nesting season—a critical part of the year—we can all help protect these birds and the habitat they need to survive."
—USFWS, *Gulf of Maine Project*

"For hundreds of years, seabirds and waterbirds in the Gulf of Maine were exploited for meat, eggs and feathers; later, nesting sites along the coast and on islands were disrupted by residential developments, pastures, quarries and timber harvesting. The great auk, a flightless colonial nesting seabird once present by the hundreds of thousands in the North Atlantic region, was harvested to extinction in the early 1800s.

There were almost no marine birds left nesting in the coastal region of the Gulf of Maine by the beginning of the twentieth century. Concern about the loss of these birds contributed to the passage of the Migratory Bird Treaty Act of 1918. The act enabled a gradual process of recovery among the populations of colonial nesting seabirds in the Gulf. At the same time, the changing economy forced people to abandon many islands, allowing seabirds to recolonize their former sites. Today, Maine's Penobscot Bay alone supports more than 26,000 pairs of nesting seabirds on more than 120 islands and ledges."—USFWS, *Gulf of Maine Project*

BIRD NESTING AREA

PLEASE: DO NOT PROCEED BEYOND THIS SIGN.

We need your help to avoid disturbance to nesting birds occupying this area.

THANK YOU

"Human disturbance can frighten birds, make them abandon their nests, or leave eggs and chicks vulnerable to predators."
—USFWS

Title: BIOS News, the Newsletter of the Brier Island Ocean Study

Target Group: General audience

Available from: The Brier Island Ocean Study, Westport, Digby County, NS, Canada B0V 1HO; telephone (902) 839-2960; fax (902) 839-2075

Cost: Free

COMMENT

Mailed free regularly to members (or upon request to nonmembers), the Brier Island Ocean Study (BIOS) newsletter includes information on current happenings at the organization: research trip findings, summaries, and short articles; updates on the field season, a BIOS fact sheet which presents thorough information on particular species; and updates on the Adopt-a-Fundy-Whale project that provide known locations or sightings of specific adopted whales.

A brochure on the Adopt-a-Fundy-Whale Program (with introductions to ten humpback adoptees, a photograph—or "flukeprint"—of each, a brief history of the Brier Island Ocean Study and a general discussion of the flukeprint of humpback whales demonstrates the progress being made by this group in understanding and caring for these giant mammals. For $25, become a member, adopt a humpback whale, and recieve the BIOS newsletter.

EXCERPTS

"BIOS, an acronym for the Brier Island Ocean study has its roots in the Greek language and means, appropriately—life. Appropriate because it is life we are studying, specifically the marine wild-life surrounding Brier Island. Located at the southwestern tip of Nova Scotia in the lower Bay of Fundy, the Brier Island area is a seasonal home for numerous cetacean (whales, dolphin, and porpoise) species...BIOS founders, Carl Haycock and Harold Graham began conducting vessel surveys in the lower Bay of Fundy in 1984 and found the waters surrounding Brier Island ideal for studying cetaceans and other marine life including seabirds. BIOS research programs have contributed important information about several endangered species including the Humpback, Finback and Right whales which inhabit these waters."—BIOS, *Adopt-a-Fundy-Whale Project brochure*

Foggy

Foggy is a special whale to us, as we have watched her grow since she was a calf in 1987. We have seen her every year since, and were delighted that she was the first humpback to return this year. She is five years old now. When we first saw her, she was in companionship with another young humpback who we call Blanco. Blanco is a three year-old male. On June 24 we were very excited to see Foggy reunite with Muddy. These two whales have been close companions many times over the past four years and have spent a lot of time together. On one occasion we saw Foggy in close association with her mother, Bermuda, and her new calf! We also saw Foggy and Blanco get together with Lacey, Foggy's sister! When that happened, the three of them seemed to be having a lot of fun rolling, flippering, coming around the boat, unusual behavior for Foggy and Blanco as they are usually not as exuberant, but that's not the case for Foggy's sister, Lacey, who is very active and appears to be very friendly. One sad note in August we saw Foggy trailing a long piece of orange rope. It appeared to be trailing out of her mouth, around one of her flippers, and behind her several hundred feet. We tried but were unable to grasp the rope, however another, smaller whale-watching boat was able to grab the line, make it fast to the boat, pulling the line through and free of Foggy. Everyone cheered, and we have seen her many times since, with no apparent marks or injury from the entanglement."—*The Brier Island Ocean Study,* "Adopt-A-Whale Updates," BIOS News, *issue 4, January 1993*

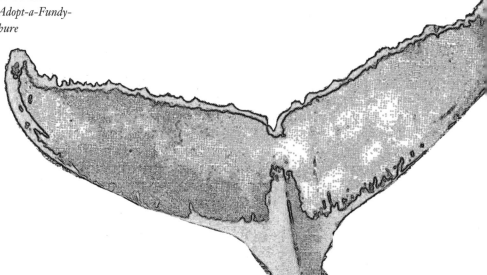

Title: The Gulf of Maine Environmental Atlas

Target Group: General audience, high school and adult

Available from: Island Institute, 60 Ocean Street, Rockland, ME 04841; telephone (207) 594-9209; fax (207) 594–9314

Cost: Softcover $29.95; hardcover $50 plus shipping and handling; special discounts will be available for purchase by schools and libraries.

COMMENT

Look at the table of contents for this comprehensive and timely publication is enough to make us expect that this *Atlas* will become a welcome and important resource for, as the Island Institute puts it, "Gulf of Maine citizens concerned with the regional landscape, its ecology and issues."

Topics covered include coastal geology, biological oceanography, marine resources, plant and animal communities in the watershed, and human interaction with the landscape and biological systems. Chapters, authored by researchers from a variety of institutions and organizations, include special sections on migration, climate and sea-level changes, aquaculture, and many other issues. The atlas is generously illustrated with color photographs, many of which are satellite views from space, giving us a unique glimpse of the Gulf. This is both a book to learn from and enjoy looking at again and again. (For more information about the Island Institute, see pages 110 and 111 in the "Human Systems" chapter.)

EXCERPT

"The Gulf of Maine, from Cape Cod to the Bay of Fundy, is a unique regional ecosystem: an almost enclosed sea bounded by an international watershed; shaped by volcanoes, glaciation, and geologic forces; rich in marine resources; diverse in terrestrial systems; and occupied by indigenous people for 6,000 years. Through *The Gulf of Maine Environmental Atlas*, we intend to highlight these natural features, cultural patterns and inter-relationships. We also want to share the new perspective that we gain by looking down on this unique region from space. Satellite imaging, aerial and ground photography will graphically illustrate the stories told by some of the finest ecologists in New England and Canada. It will be an exceptionally rich book written for the lay public and will be distributed throughout the Northeast."—*The Island Institute*

Title: Coloring Books: Once Upon the Coast of Maine and Gulf of Maine Marine Coloring Book

Target Group: Grades K-8

Available from: Maine Department of Marine Resources Education Division, Station 21, Augusta, Maine 04333-0021; telephone (207) 624–6578; fax (207) 624-6024

Cost: Free

COMMENT

These simple but engaging coloring books are ideal for young children. Budding artists will become familiar with many of the Gulf water's coastal creatures depicted on these pages. *Once Upon the Coast of Maine* tells the story of a family's trip to Boothbay Harbor and is especially suited to very young children (K-4). *The Gulf of Maine Coloring Book* , for a slightly older crowd (5-8), contains more detailed drawings and more information about marine plants and animals.

EXCERPTS

"The children are having fun playing in the sand. They make sure that they do not step on the beach grass."—*Once Upon the Coast of Maine.*

"Hermit crabs are orange to reddish brown in color. The shell they inhabit is colored depending on what type of snail used to live in it."—*Gulf of Maine Marine Coloring Book.*

Marine Mammal Stranding Hot-Line

If you find a stranded marine mammal, call the National Marine Fisheries Service or the New England Aquarium at (617) 973-5247 Trained volunteers will rescue and care for the animal until it can be released.

82

Title: Ocean Adventure! Marine Information Programs and Tours

Target Group: General public (all ages)

Available from: Ocean Adventure! U.S. Rt. 1, Box 1151, Newcastle, ME 04556; telephone (207) 563–2318 or 1-800-696-0550

Cost: Offsite Outreach Program: Single program $65, half-day $160, full-day $250; Aquarium admission $4 adult, $2.50 child; group rates available

COMMENT

Located in a small but lively "ocean museum" and aquarium in mid-coast Maine, Ocean Adventure's programs about marine resources and life in the Gulf of Maine can be customized for a variety of audiences. Shows can be presented at the aquarium or off-site and can be arranged to fit into existing curriculums. Individual programs last 45-90 minutes, depending on the level of audience participation. All involve hands-on experiences, underwater videos, photos, fishing gear and more.

EXCERPT

Examples of topics available from *Ocean Adventure!*

- *Live Animal Touch Tank:* Marine animals to observe and hold to learn life histories as well as respect for other life forms.
- *Unhuggables:* How Fishermen catch Fish: Hands-on program on commercial fishing methods using actual fishing gear and videos.
- *Gulf of Maine: A Sea Within A Sea:* Why this distinct sea is unique and very productive, how tides work and why the ocean is salty. Uses underwater video, charts.

Title: Fins & Flippers: The Ultimate Hands-On Experience!

Target Group: Grades 2 – 8

Available from: The Chewonki Foundation, RR2, Box 1200, Wiscasset, ME 04578; telephone (207) 882-7323; fax (207) 882-4074

Cost: One presentation $85; two presentations $170; three presentations $240; four presentations $300; each additional presentation $75; plus transportation costs at $.25 per mile from Wiscasset

COMMENT

This is another of The Chewonki Foundation's popular outreach programs (see pages 37 and 119 for others). *Fins & Flippers* is a two-part presentation; each part is 45 minutes long. A slideshow examines the four major groups of marine mammals, describing their habitats and adaptations and discussing the threats they currently face. After the show, students are divided into groups. Each group works together to assemble a 16-foot pilot whale skeleton while it becomes the prop for a discussion of the intricacies of form and function. It's an engrossing, satisfying project. The resulting form brings home the size and grace of this cetacean and should make anybody want to see—and protect—the real live thing in its own natural habitat.

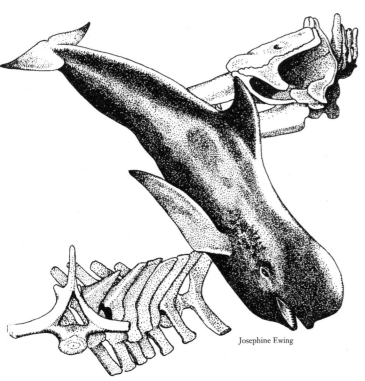

Josephine Ewing

Title: Space Available: Learning From Satellites

Target Group: Classroom teachers

Available from: The Gulf of Maine Aquarium, PO Box 7549, Portland, ME 04112; telephone (207) 772–2321; fax (207) 772–6855

Cost: Expenses underwritten by Gulf of Maine Aquarium sponsors, no cost to teachers

83

COMMENT

Space Available: Learning From Satellites is designed to instruct teachers in using and interpreting real-time satellite imagery in the classroom. The Gulf of Maine Aquarium plans to hold several teacher workshops using a satellite receiving van for demonstrations. Teachers participating in the workshops will have access to the receiving van for their classroom use. Teacher handbooks contain background information, reproducible classroom handouts and activity suggestions. Although the program covers a range of satellite-related topics and provides general training in "bringing remote sensing down to earth," programs related to marine habitats in the Gulf of Maine include *Tracking Sea Turtles, Charting the Gulf of Maine, Creating Plankton, Plumbing the Depths, The Invisible Line, How Animals Cope with the Cold,* and *Rescue at Sea.* (Other programs offered by the aquarium, All about Turtles and Keep it Clean, are described on pages 48 and 101.)

For the Tracking Sea Turtles Program, students will receive—via satellite transmission modem—primary data that identifies the current location of six adult female Kemp's Ridley turtles, the ratio of time spent above and below the surface and the water temperature. The challenge is to track the migration routes as revealed by the radio transmissions. This is a great way to put technology to work and learn about the planet along the way. Call the Aquarium for the teacher workshop schedule.

EXCERPTS

"In little over a third of a century, the launching of a satellite has gone from stopping the business of the nation to guaranteeing it runs like clockwork. Today, satellites are commonplace tools of technology, like clocks, telephones, and computers. Satellites serve us for navigation, communications, environmental monitoring and weather forecasting.

Appropriately, the word *satellite* means an *attendant.*"—*Gulf of Maine Aquarium*, Space Available: Learning from Satellites

"All eight species of sea turtles are threatened or endangered, primarily because of the destruction of their breeding grounds, poaching of their eggs for food, and marine pollution. Sea turtles spend almost all their lives at sea, but like all reptiles, the females must lay their eggs on land. When they come on shore, sea turtles have to contend with predators, poachers, and loss

of their breeding beaches to seaside hotels and resorts. In some places, coastal pollution has destroyed their food supply of shallow water grasses and seaweeds. In the ocean, adult sea turtles have only two enemies: sharks and people... Many islands and coastal areas now protect breeding sea turtles, but to sustain their populations we need to be able to protect them throughout their range. Yet little is known about their habits and migration routes. Radio tags on some sea turtles allow them to be tracked by satellites..."—*excerpted from* Space Available, *Tracking Sea Turtles Program*

**Gulf of Maine...
What Lives There?**

"Slip into the cool waters of the Gulf of Maine and meet the marine life that lives there. This slideshow and live sea animal presentation will open your eyes to a large variety of very special creatures that have learned to live in a harsh environment of cold water and pounding surf. We'll discuss and discover how they protect themselves and how they capture food, and students will have a 'hands on' opportunity to hold live periwinkles, sea urchins, and other marine life forms."
—*Gulf of Maine Aquarium, In-School Learning Opportunities*

84

Title: Status of Fishery Resources off the Northeastern United States

Target Group: High school, college students, teachers, fisheries professionals

Available from: Northeast Fisheries Science Center, 166 Water Street, Woods Hole, MA 02543; telephone (508) 548–5123; fax (508) 548–5124

Cost: Free

COMMENT

This annual publication is part of the National Oceanographic and Atmospheric Administration's Technical Publication Series. Far from being a dry compilation of statistics, this report offers a tremendous amount of information about marine environments and fish habitat in the Gulf of Maine. Following an introduction summarizing fisheries trends and the health of the ecosystem, the publication describes groundfish (*e.g.*, cod, haddock, hake, goosefish, cusk and tilefish), flounders (*e.g.*, yellowtail, plaice and sole), pelagics (*e.g.*, herring, mackerel, dogfish and skates), anadromous fish (*e.g.*, shad, bass, salmon and sturgeon), and invertebrates (*e.g.*, lobster, shrimp, sea scallop and ocean quahog). The text describes life cycles and includes black and white photographs, graphs of landings in recent years for recreational and commercial harvest, and additional information sources. This report puts a lot of fish information at your fingertips and is a great introduction to the research of the National Marine Fisheries Service.

Brenda Figuerido

EXCERPTS

"The fishery resources off the northeastern United States are harvested by a variety of fishing gear, including trawls, fill nets, traps, longlines and dredges. While each type of gear takes a different mixture of species, few fishermen target exclusively one species. The degree of mixture in the catches varies among the types of gear used in different areas. In addition, there are predatory and competitive relations among many of the fishery resources.— *Northeast Fisheries Science Center*, Status of Fishery Resources off the Northeastern United States for 1993

Atlantic Cod

"In U.S. waters, cod are assessed as two stocks; Gulf of Maine, and Georges Banks and Southward. Important commercial and recreational fisheries occur in both stocks. The commercial fisheries are conducted year-round with otter trawls and gill nets as primary gear. Recreational fishing also occurs year-round; peak activity occurs during the late summer in the lower Gulf of Maine, and during late autumn to early spring from Massachusetts southward... Total commercial cod landings from the Georges Bank and Gulf of Maine stocks in 1992 were 39,400 mt, down 29 percent from 55,400 mt in 1991. United States commercial landings in 1992 totaled 27,800 mt in 1991. United States commercial landings in 1992 totaled 27,800 mt, 34 percent less than in 1991 (42,000 mt), and the lowest since 1987...

At the current level of fishing mortality, commercial landings [in the Gulf of Maine] are expected to decline to 7,000 mt in 1993 and are likely to remain at or below that level in 1994. By 1994, the 1987 year class will no longer be a major component of the stock. To halt the declining trend in [fish stocks], fishing mortality needs to be markedly reduced. ...

The Georges Bank cod stock is at a very low biomass level and is over-exploited. Recovery of the stock will require a marked reduction in fishing mortality."
— *Northeast Fisheries Science Center*, Status of Fishery Resources off the Northeastern United States for 1993

Eastern Bering
Sea Ecosystem

Gulf of
Alaska
Ecosystem

California
Current
Ecosystem

Insular Pacific Ecosystem

Northeastern
Continental Shelf
Ecosystem

Southeastern
Continental Shelf
Ecosystem

Gulf of Mexico
Ecosystem

The seven large marine ecosystems of the United States, including the insular Pacific Hawaiian Islands. –from Northeast Fisheries Science Center, Status of Fishery Resources of the Northeastern United States

Title: Top Twelve Questions Asked about the Stellwagen Bank National Marine Sanctuary

Target Group: General audience

Available from: Stellwagen Bank National Marine Sanctuary Program, 14 Union Street, Plymouth, MA 02360; telephone (508) 747–1691; fax (508) 747–1949

Cost: Free

COMMENT

This simple, attractive brochure quickly answers basic questions about how Stellwagen Sanctuary came into being and what "sanctuary designation" means. Twelve questions and answers provide an overview of basic Sanctuary rules and describes appropriate activities in the Sanctuary. This handout would be useful in advanced classrooms studying marine resource protection.

A Meeting of Food and Light...

"The Stellwagen Bank National Marine Sanctuary encompasses 638 square nautical miles (842 square miles) of open ocean, stretching between Cape Ann and Cape Cod at the mouth of Massachusetts Bay. Here, the surface of the ocean may look no different than any other spot off the New England coast. But below the surface sits a geological feature that makes this part of the Gulf of Maine particularly productive and worthy of special protection.

Underneath the waves, the Bank reaches up from the depths, levelling off at an average of 100 feet below the water's surface and partially blocking the mouth of the bay. The shallow southwest corner has a depth of only 65 feet. Cold water containing nutrients from the depths creeps up along the Bank's flanks, reaching sunlight in the upper levels of the water column. This meeting of food and light supports a rich diversity of marine life ranging from small, single-celled plants to some of the largest animals alive today—the great whales. These majestic marine mammals...use parts of the Sanctuary for their spring and summer feeding grounds.

Visitors are welcome to the Stellwagen Bank National Marine Sanctuary—to traverse its waters, to fish its depths for a wide variety of species, to view its varied marine life and to study its secrets. This natural environment is one of nature's gifts all of us can share. But this gift, like others of value, requires care and attention in order to endure for the benefit and enjoyment of current users and future generations. To that end, the Sanctuary supports a wide range of research and educational efforts that contribute to better understanding and management of this area today and for years to come." —*excerpted from the National Marine Sanctuary Program's* Stellwagen Bank, An Investment in Our Nation's Environmental Future

Title: Guide to Some Trawl-Caught Marine Fishes From Maine to Cape Hatteras, North Carolina

Target Group: General audience

Available from: Northeast Fisheries Science Center, 166 Water Street, Woods Hole, MA 02543; telephone (508) 548–5123; fax (508) 548–5124

Cost: Free

COMMENT

Don't let the title fool you. This is a fun visual aid showing how fish are related to each other — a fish family tree of sorts. Described as "an identification guide to the commoner fishes caught during bottom trawl surveys" (conducted by National Marine Fisheries Service [NMFS] researchers to help keep track of fish stocks), the guide integrates line drawings with keys in a flowchart format that is easy to use, reproduce, and understand. People of all ages will be fascinated by the variety and intricacy of the underwater wildlife displayed here.

"**The Oceans Act of 1992 designated the Sanctuary in recognition of the national significance of the productive ecosystem at Stellwagen Bank that supports a wide diversity of marine life, including endangered northern right whales, humpback whales and fin whales...The high productivity of this area is due to upwelling of nutrient from the ocean bottom along the flanks of the Bank. When this cold, nutrient-rich water meets sunlight penetrating from above, blooms of plankton are the result—plankton that serves as the base of the food web for the region. Protecting this ecosystem is important for the environmental health of this section of the Gulf of Maine—for all of the creatures that reside here...**"
—*Stellwagen Bank National Marine Sanctuary Program*

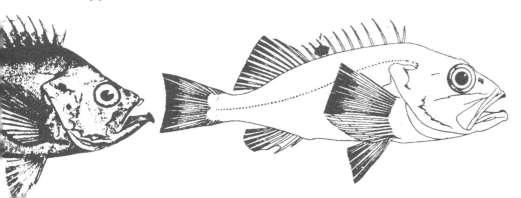

SUGGESTED HORSESHOE CRAB ACTIVITIES

Explorations

How does the horseshoe crab move?

—Observe all of their legs as it moves forward. Which pair of legs seems to provide the forward thrust? — Describe the shape of these legs in comparison with the others.

—Small horseshoe crabs are capable of swimming. How might they do this?

—Turn over the horseshoe crab. How does it right itself? The tail spine is not used as a weapon.

Horseshoe crab model

—Paint a 6" paper bowl brown inside and out. Cut out the two triangles as indicated below.

—Make some accordion style gills and a section of walking legs out of brown paper.

—Tape the gills and legs to the underside.

—Cut out a tail and attach it to the abdomen with a paper fastener.

Research

—Why is the horseshoe crab considered a "living fossil"?

—Why is the horseshoe crab not really a crab?

—Why is the horseshoe crab important to biomedical research?

—*excerpted from* A Teacher's Guide to Marine Life of the Gulf of Maine, *State of Maine Department of Marine Resources*

Title: ABC Fish of the Gulf of Maine

Target Group: General audience, high school and up

Available from: Maine Department of Marine Resources (DMR), Education Division, Station 21, Augusta, ME 04333-0021; telephone (207) 624-6578; fax (207) 624-6024

Cost: Free

COMMENT

This book is a quick, comprehensive summary of lots of information about familiar and unfamiliar fish in the Gulf of Maine, along with extra material about fish life and fish parts. Amazingly, there really are enough individual species (if you use both common and Latin names) to span the alphabet. You'll read about Jumping Mullet and Numbfish, Quadracus and Unicorn Fish. We'll let you find out what X, Y, and Z are.

EXCERPTS

"The most interesting thing regarding this fish [Numbfish] is its ability to give electric shocks when anyone touches it. The two large electric organs, each of which occupies one side of the front part of the disk, make up about one-sixth of its total weight. The shock from a large [numbfish] in rested condition may be strong enough to throw a full grown man to the ground...It is believed that it stuns its prey by its electric shocks. Otherwise, it is difficult to conceive how so sluggish a fish could capture active prey."—*Maine DMR*

"The Gulf of Maine is the boreal [northern] limit for the warm-water-loving bluefish. For this reason, they visit our area only periodically. When they do visit, bluefish are one of the most ferocious and bloodthirsty fish in the sea, leaving in their wake a trail of dead and mangled mackerel, menhaden, herring, alewives, and other species on which their prey."—*Maine DMR*

"A female cod may lay 1,000,000 eggs a year. These eggs float at the surface. The larvae are part of the plankton until they reach about 1.5 inches; then they go to the bottom to find food."
—*Maine DMR*

Title: A Teacher's Guide to Marine Life of the Gulf of Maine

Target Group: High school teachers

Available from: Maine Department of Marine Resources, Education Division, Station 21, Augusta, ME 04333-0021; (207) 624-6578; fax (207) 624-6024.

Cost: $5

COMMENT

This Department of Marine Resources publication provides substantial information on marine life in the Gulf of Maine. From sea anemones (*Metridum senile*) to short-finned squid (*Illex illecebrosus*), all kinds of species are represented here with classifications and itemized descriptions of habitats, movements, growth trends, nervous systems, and circulatory systems. Each detailed fact sheet is followed by accompanying diagrams of the organism, a list of the related species in the Gulf of Maine, and suggested activities for comparing, examining, and observing each marine animal. A glossary of terms is included for easy reference; teachers should have no trouble integrating these terms into their lessons. For more from Maine's Department of Marine Resources see entries for *Once Upon the Coast of Maine*, the *Gulf of Maine Coloring Book*, and the *ABC Fish of the Gulf of Maine*.

EXCERPT

The objective of the Department of Marine Resources, Education Division is to develop a citizenry that is marine literate and has a basic awareness of the marine environment and its resources. This project is dedicated to providing educators with training and materials in marine education. Training may be received at 'in-service' workshops, teacher recertification courses, or other scheduled sessions."
—*Maine DMR*.

Title: **Atlantic Coast Piping Plover Lesson Plans**

Target Group: Grades 5 – 7

Available from: U.S. Fish and Wildlife Service, New England Field Offices, 22 Bridge Street, Room 400, Concord, NH 03301; telephone (603) 225-1411; fax (603) 225-1467

Cost: Free

COMMENT

This week-long curriculum package explores the life and times of the piping plover, a threatened species currently protected by the Endangered Species Act. Individual lessons teach about piping plover habitat, survival needs, its behavior, and response to human activity. Lessons also examine why the plover is threatened and describe how we can work to help it survive. Lesson plans are presented in a lively format that includes group simulation games, a fully scripted slide program, and hands-on exercises in nest construction and habitat management. The package comes complete and ready-to-teach. Instructional materials for all activities, along with supplemental information brochures are included, but you'll need to gather a few props like a rope, a beach ball, some dried beans, and other fun stuff. Your students will find themselves learning a lot about this species, a lot about the importance of habitat protection, and they'll have a good time in the process.

EXCERPTS

"These lesson plans are designed to actively engage students in learning about the piping plover. The plans involve a simulation game in which students simulate the feeding behavior of the birds and explore factors that disturb both the feeding and nesting of the plover. The plans also include an area manage-ment activity in which the students construct a nest for a fictitious ground-nesting bird that might theoretically live on the school property. They then create models of this bird and its eggs and finally develop and carry out a manage-ment plan to protect the nest area."—*USFWS New England Field Office, Atlantic Coast Piping Plover Lessons Plans, Overview*

"Atlantic coast piping plovers winter along the southeastern coast of the U.S., the areas that surround the Gulf of Mexico, and even the Bahamas and West Indies. In spring, they migrate to where they'll breed: the eastern coast of North America from North Carolina to Newfoundland and southeastern Quebec. When they arrive in March or April at their east coast breeding sites, they settle on largely uninhabited beaches." —*USFWS New England Field Office, Atlantic Coast Piping Plover Lessons Plans, Slide Program*

> **"The Atlantic Coast piping plover is listed as 'threatened' under the Endangered Species Act, and it receives most of the same legal protection it would if it were listed as endangered. The difference is that threatened means extinction is less imminent. ...Recovery efforts are aimed primarily at protecting the plovers' breeding habitat to help prevent the plover population from dwindling further, which would necessitate reclassifying the species as endangered."** —*USFWS*

Julie Zickefoose

Title: **The Rocky Shore: A Complete Guide to Conducting Successful Field Trips for Grades K–12**

Target Group: Teachers, grades K–12

Available from: The Seacoast Science Center, Odiorne Point State Park, 570 Ocean Blvd., Rye, NH 03870; telephone (603) 436–8043; fax (603) 433–2235

Cost: $11.95

COMMENT

The first of a series of teacher guides developed by the Seacoast Science Center and the University of New Hampshire Cooperative Extension/Sea Grant Program, *The Rocky Shore* offers conveniently organized, step-by-step information about trip planning, classroom preparation, chaperone guidelines and safety, followed by a succinct and comprehensive illustrated summary about the rocky intertidal zone. More than forty classroom and field activities are suggested, classified by grade level. Also included are suggestions for field trips in the New Hampshire coastal area, a "marine vocabulary," and a "Bibliography of the Sea." (You'll find all this information in 32 pages.) A companion guide for field trips to salt marshes (*The Salt Marsh, Teacher Guide #2*) is also available (see p. 71).

> *"There are seven different habitats in the 330-acre park. Salt- and freshwater marshes, a freshwater pond, the rocky intertidal zone and a sandy beach, meadows and wooded uplands, and the Gulf of Maine can all be visited within an hour's walk on our trails. Most of these areas are handicapped accessible; all of them are accessible through our indoor habitat exhibits.*
>
> *We have a full complement of programming available from naturalist-led walks throughout the park to slideshows on marine and natural and cultural history. Most groups prefer to have a combination of organized and free time so that they can explore the exhibits and park at their own pace. We specialize in marine programs for families and senior citizens.*
>
> *Rates for programs are based on group size and format: minimum program fee is $60. To schedule a program, call the Program Director at (603) 436–8043."*
> —Seacoast Science Center

EXCERPTS

"In this guide you will find the necessary information to plan a successful field trip to the shore along with many ideas to ensure that it is educationally rewarding as well. Although some of the information enclosed is specific to the rocky shore at Odiorne Point State Park and the Seacoast Science Center, it represents the type of information field trip leaders should know (*e.g.*, trip logistics and emergency phone numbers) no matter where they go with their classes."—*Seacoast Science Center*, The Rocky Shore

"The field of environmental education has increasingly moved away from the identification approach to learning. Concept learning allows participants to think and explore for themselves and is adaptable to any environment from the rocky shore to your back yard. It connects a student to the natural world by making them a part of that world, not an outsider observing the life within. We hope this personalized approach to "scientific" learning makes students aware of the vital role they play in the health of our world."
—*Seacoast Science Center*, The Rocky Shore

A sample activity from The Rocky Shore:

Back to Back
(Classroom Activity 4–8)
Purpose: Help students become familiar with life on the rocky shore. Improve students' descriptive skills.
Materials: Drawing boards, paper, marine objects, pencils.
Method: Students sit down in groups of two, back to back. Give one a drawing board and paper, and the other a marine object. The student with the object describes it and the other student tries to draw it without seeing it or knowing what it is. When the object is guessed, switch roles and use a new marine object.

"Our mission is to provide high-quality programming and exhibits which interpret the natural and cultural history of coastal and marine environments. We limit our scope to the geographic area of the Gulf of Maine watershed."
—*Seacoast Science Center*

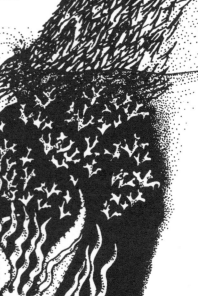

Patricia Miller

Title: Mr. and Mrs. Fish Outreach Programs

Target Group: Grades K–6

Available from: Mr. and Mrs. Fish Marine Education Program, Southern Maine Technical College, Fort Rd., South Portland, ME 04106; telephone (207) 799–6234; fax (207) 767-9645

Cost: Call to arrange program and fees (prices vary)

COMMENT

Mr. and Mrs. Fish will come to your school and present a 60-minute educational assembly on a variety of marine topics of your choice. This traveling show can be arranged for the entire school. Mr. and Mrs. Fish have a real knack for keeping a large audience of diverse ages (no class should miss this) spellbound for a solid hour. After the first hour, Mr. and Mrs. Fish split up and each "fish" meets with different grade levels for the rest of the day to teach about life in the sea. This fish program makes for a memorable, funny and fact-filled day. Call Mr. or Mrs. Fish to schedule a visit and discuss details.

EXCERPT

"There's something fishy about Deb Sandler. One day she's a starfish, the next, a whale. But it's all part of a day's work for Deb and her husband, Jeff, both marine biologists from Portland, Maine. They dress as sea creatures to teach elementary-school children about the ocean and the environment in a way they'll enjoy and remember.

The couple has over 60 hand-made costumes. In a nautical version of 'the tortoise and the hare,' … they dress as a sea turtle and a jellyfish. The story dramatizes how sea turtles lay their eggs, as well as how sick they get from eating plastic bags dumped into the ocean. Then the fish thank the children for throwing their garbage into a trash can. "What's important," says Deb, "is that they have a feeling for the ocean as an exciting place—one they want to keep healthy."— A Fishy Tale, *Woman's Day Magazine* November 27, 1990

Title: Treasure in the Eel's Cave, An Educational Video from Mr. and Mrs. Fish

Target Group: Grades K–4

Available from: Mr. and Mrs. Fish Marine Education Program, Southern Maine Technical College, Fort Rd., South Portland, ME 04106; telephone (207) 799–6234; fax (207) 767-9645

Cost: $15

COMMENT

If you've never seen them live, this is the next best thing. Often described as "a zany duo," Mr. and Mrs. Fish are real people, but it's possible to forget that in the course of their presentations, which have enthralled young children (and adults, too!) in the Gulf of Maine region for years. *Treasure in the Eel's Cave* is a humorous, 25-minute video introducing young children to a variety of concepts ranging from fish shapes to uses of seaweeds in everyday life. In the story, Mr. and Mrs. Fish assume several different fish roles (and costumes) in an effort to escape the predatory clutches of a big, hungry fish. The video also includes live footage of sea creatures, doing exactly the same things—for real. This is learning that's fun. Older children will enjoy it, too.

Title: Colonial Nesting Seabirds: An All-Inclusive Curriculum Unit

Target Group: Grades K–6

Available from: Petit Manan National Wildlife Refuge, U.S. Fish and Wildlife Service, Box 279, Milbridge, ME 04658; telephone (207) 546-2124; fax (207) 546-7805

Cost: Free on a first-come basis to teachers within driving distance of the Refuge. (The kit is too large to mail.)

COMMENT

This curriculum package is exactly what it says it is: all-inclusive. Developed by Amanda Reed, it provides a bounty of information about colonial nesting seabirds in the Gulf of Maine, all arranged to be accessible, intriguing, and fun for everyone from kindergarten through sixth grade (and grown-ups too!). The kit (complete with slides, feathers, nests, models, stuffed birds, and costume materials) is accompanied by a teacher's guide with lesson plans for a week-long session on the lives and habitat of colonial nesting seabirds. Lessons proceed from an "Introduction to Habitat" (Day 1) through "Morphology: Feet, Wings, Beaks, Sounds, Odors, etc." (Day 2), to "Bird Love: Courtship, Nesting, Eggs, and Fledging" (Day 3), "Predation and Migration" (Day 4), and finally "Human Impact: What You Can Do" (Day 5). Each lesson plan is tiered for grades K-1, 2-3 and 4-6. Along the way, students can learn the "Seabirds of Maine Song," make a bird mobile, and construct a tern mask. Then, after completing the program, students receive a U.S. Fish and Wildlife Service Seabird Diploma, which includes a pledge by the recipient "to use my new knowledge to help educate people on the ways of Colonial Nesting Seabirds...and to use what I know in a productive way, and carry the information and ideas over to other areas of life."

EXCERPTS

"To begin, show the students all the prepared specimens already put out in the classroom. Tell them that they are scientists from "Star Trek's" starship *Enterprise* who have been sent to figure out the likenesses and differences between the different birds, as well as their habitats. Let them touch the study skins and look closely at them. Encourage them to look at all the physical aspects of the birds, making careful observations (body shapes, feet, color, bills, etc.) Ask them if they know any of the names of the birds. Go around to each bird and tell the students the common names. Encourage them to use the correct names of the different birds so they get used to the different common names...puffin, petrel, eider, razorbill, etc. Remind them of 'habitat' [from Day 1]—ask them to explain it briefly. Ask them to think about where the different birds might live on the island (10 minutes). Ask for three Starship volunteers willing to wear seabird simulation costumes to help the group of scientists decipher differences/likenesses even more..."—*USFWS, Petit Manan National Wildlife Refuge*, Colonial Nesting Seabirds, "Morphology: Feet, Wings, Beaks, Sounds, Odors, Etc." *for K-1*

"Tell the students that they are going to become bird architects and carpenters/constructors. First, they must design the bird like an architect. Give the students the bird stamps. Using your discretion (5 minutes), give the students time to freely explore the stamps so that playing is mostly out of their system when the "task" begins. After exploring, tell the students that they are going to design a bird or birds that they think would be interesting. Tell them that they will have to explain their designs, why they chose which parts, how they would work together and in which habitat they would live (using adaptation as well), so that they might think of these points during the designing. If desired, have them color their birds (10-15 minutes)." —*USFWS*, Colonial Nesting Seabirds, "Morphology," *from Day 2, for grades 4-6*

Title: **Our Living Oceans**

Target Group: General audience, high school and college students, teachers, fisheries professionals

Available from: Northeast Fisheries Science Center, 166 Water Street, Woods Hole, MA 02543; telephone (508) 548–5123; fax (508) 548–5124

Cost: Free

COMMENT

This national summary of the status and trends in U.S. living marine resources includes sections on major commercial fish stocks, marine mammals and large pelagic fish. This 150-page softcover book contains a clear, easy-to-read overview section, a glossary of scientific principles and terms, and a general discussion of fishery issues and management strategies for the future. Unit synopses following the overview present information about hundreds of marine species. The Gulf of Maine is included in the information presented in the northeast Atlantic region. Appendices list common and scientific names of the species described in the book and provides a must-have list of acronyms and abbreviations. If you're interested in what's happening in the ocean, this attractive, well-written publication is worth your time.

EXCERPTS

"Our Living Oceans...provides a scientific overview of the health of the nation's marine fisheries as well as protected marine mammals and sea turtles. These national resources are under the stewardship of the National Marine Fisheries Service (NMFS)...this report synthesizes, for the public, results from extensive NMFS scientific programs aimed at evaluating and monitoring our living marine resources. The management of these resources is described, and important issues and recent progress are highlighted."—*National Marine Fisheries Service (NMFS), "Preface,"* Our Living Oceans.

"A population is a group of animals that are genetically related owing to interbreeding. Ideally, populations should be considered distinct groups for fishery management purposes. But it is difficult to determine which individuals of a species form a population, and it may not be practical to manage them as a population. Thus, this report uses the term "population" to identify interbreeding biological groups. The term 'stock' is used to identify groups of animals for management purposes."—*NMFS*

"Northeast demersal (groundfish) fisheries include about 35 species and/or stocks, primarily in New England waters, but also off the Mid-Atlantic states. In New England, the groundfish complex is dominated by members of the cod family (cod, haddock, hakes, pollock), flounders, dogfish sharks and skates."—*NMFS*

"Ocean pelagics are highly migratory species that include swordfish, bluefin tuna, yellowfin tuna, bigeye tuna, albacore, skipjack tuna, blue and white marlin, sailfish, longbill spearfish... In the Atlantic Ocean, swordfish and bluefin tuna have long provided important fisheries, while in recent years yellowfin tuna have increased in importance to U.S. fishermen... Since Atlantic oceanic pelagics migrate widely and are harvested over broad oceanic areas by U.S. and foreign fishermen, both national and international management are necessary."—*NMFS***

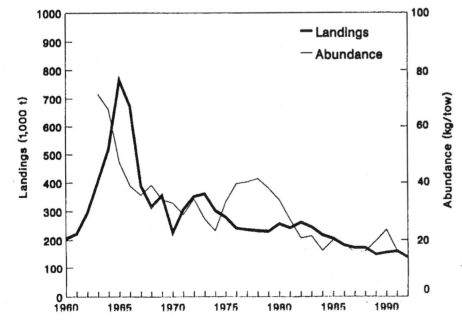

Total commercial landings and abundance indices for principal groundfish and flounders off the New England coast, 1960-92. From Northeast Fisheries Science Center, Our Living Oceans.

92

Title: All About Oceanography: A Fun-Filled Activity Book

Target Group: Grades K–12

Available from: Woods Hole Oceanographic Institution Sea Grant Program, CRL 209, Woods Hole, MA 02543; telephone (508) 289-2398; fax (508) 457–2172

Cost: $2 each (quantity and teacher discounts available)

COMMENT

"This is not just your average coloring book ," says Woods Hole Oceanographic Institution (WHOI) about their activity book. "*All About Oceanography* provides information and illustrations depicting various disciplines of oceanography. The book, highlighting research conducted at Woods Hole Oceanographic Institution also includes interesting oceanography trivia, crossword and word-search puzzles, and a comprehensive glossary. Examples of subject areas covered include: hydrothermal vent communities, the history of marine exploration, the use of satellites in oceanographic research, the Gulf Stream, the hydrologic cycle, erosion, marine mineral deposits, ocean floor topography, aquaculture, red tide, the importance of computers in oceanographic research, cetaceans, the chemistry of seawater, exploring historic shipwrecks, and much more. Useful for any age, the book can be used as a coloring book, a reference book, or both." This book offers a wonderful combination of activities and information, the kind of easy-to-color drawings that inspire you to stay inside the lines.

> *"Thanks to movies and television, sharks have received a reputation as dangerous killers of the oceans. In fact, most types of sharks are not only harmless, they are shy and avoid humans when possible."*—Woods Hole Oceanographic Institution, All About Oceanography

EXCERPTS

"Oceanography is a young science that is still growing and changing. When WHOI was first established in 1930, most ocean studies were done from the decks of sailing ships. To early oceanographers, the sea was mysterious, huge and sometimes dangerous. Since they couldn't see very far below the water's surface, scientists had to

lower instruments into it from their ships to learn about the ocean's depths, currents, plants and animals, and water chemistry. *Atlantis*, a 142-foot sailing ketch, was WHOI's first research vessel, and many important discoveries were made from its decks. Marine biologists collected plants and animals with nets, chemical oceanographers collected water in huge sampling bottles to learn about the chemistry of seawater, and marine geologists studied the bathymetry of the ocean bottom by measuring the time it took for sound to bounce off the seafloor and back up to the ship."—*Woods Hole Oceanographic Institution*, All About Oceanography

"We all know that the ocean is salty, but did you know that the ocean also contains elements, gases, chemical compounds, and minerals? Some people compare the ocean to a 'chemical soup' because it contains so many 'ingredients.' Chemical oceanographers and marine geochemists study seawater and ocean muds to learn more about the ocean's resources, like food (fish, shellfish, seaweed) and energy (underwater deposits of oil and minerals)."—*Woods Hole Oceanographic Institution*, All About Oceanography

> *"A glass of water with one teaspoon of salt has approximately the same salinity as the ocean."*
> —*Woods Hole Oceanographic Institution*, All About Oceanography

E. Paul Oberlander, All About Oceanography, *Woods Hole Oceanographic Institution*

Title: Marine Education: A Bibliography of Educational Materials Available from the Nation's Sea Grant College Programs

Target Group: Teachers

Available from: Woods Hole Oceanographic Institution Sea Grant Program, CRL 209, Woods Hole, MA 02543; telephone (508) 289-2398; fax (508) 457–2172

Cost: $2 per single copy; $1.50 per copy for bulk orders in lots of fifty

COMMENT

This attractive and readable bibliography (compiled by the Mississippi-Alabama Sea Grant Consortium and arranged geographically by Sea Grant College Program), "has proven useful to a wide range of educators as a tool to help students explore and understand our oceans and Great Lakes. It includes curricula and supplemental materials, including fact sheets, posters, booklets, field guides, how-to guides for classroom experiments, project and field trips, and other useful materials." This is the publication's fourth printing; demand in the past has far exceeded supply. Individual entries in the bibliography are available from the Sea Grant program or institution that developed them. Materials listed are usually available free or at nominal cost.

Titles available include:

A Field Guide to Economically Important Seaweeds of Northern New England. Susan White, editor; MaJo Keleshian, illustrator and designer. MSG-E-92-4 1992. 30 pp., $3.50 Includes illustrations and descriptions of selected seaweeds, suggestions of foraging and preparation, and recipes for some of the more commonly used species. Mail check payable to University of Maine to: Sea Grant Communications, University of Maine, 5715 Coburn Hall, Room 30, Orono, ME 04469–5715.

Citizen's Guide to Sources for Marine and Coastal Information in Massachusetts. Sixth revised edition. Compiled and edited by Madeleine Hall-Arber. MITSG 94-17. 170 pp. $5. This valuable reference book lists more than 170 Massachusetts agencies, information centers, and organizations concerned with coastal affairs. Each entry includes office hours, address and telephone number, as well as a brief description of the objectives, specialties and services of each organization. A subject index provides easy reference by area of interest. Address requests to: MIT Sea Grant College Program Publications, 292 Maine Street/Building E38-300, Cambridge, MA 02139.

Title: Field Guides for Eastern Shore Marine Environments

Target Group: General audience

Available from: Woods Hole Oceanographic Institution Sea Grant Program, CRL 209, Woods Hole, MA 02543; telephone (508) 289-2398; fax (508) 457–2172

Cost: $1 per set of five

COMMENT

This set of five placemat-like guides (written by Barbara Waters and illustrated by Carole Eldridge) is easy to read, extremely "user-friendly," and can be colored by young and willing, crayon- and-marker-wielding hands. The guides, "recently reprinted by popular demand include: Salt Ponds, Tidal Flats, Rocky Shores and Wooden Structures, Sandy Shore and Dunes, and Salt Marsh. The oversized guides (11" x 17") describe, on one side, the characteristics of each environment. The other side illustrates a cross section of each environment and the plants and animals that inhabit it, labeled with common and scientific names. We suggest laminating them for years of use in the classroom or in the field." Make them last; they're worth it.

EXCERPT

"The creator and guardian of our sandy beaches and dunes is the Beach Grass. This is a perennial, tough, native grass that can withstand some flooding, salt spray, drought, strong winds and building (*accreting*) sand. It is the first plant to be seen growing on a forming sand dune...When a healthy stand of grass develops, the stems break the force of winds and blowing sand. Grains of sand come to rest at the base of the stem and a good stand of grass can accumulate up to 4 feet of sand in a year's time... Whenever beach grass is destroyed, the dune begins to disintegrate and blow away."

—*WHOI*, Field Guide to Eastern Shore Marine Environments, *"The Sandy Shore and Dunes"*

"The many shallow pools of water left on a tidal flat by retreating water are good places to look for marine life. Fuzzy, pink shells move about, home for the hermit crabs, both the Long-Clawed Hermit Crab and Broad-Clawed Hermit Crab. The shells once contained live snails. When taken over by the hermit crabs they often become covered with a reddish 'fur,' which is a colony of hydroid animals, commonly called Snail Fur. With a 10x hand lens you can see that this 'fur' is a mat of single, flowerlike polyps."

—*WHOI*, Field Guide to Eastern Shore Marine Environments, *"Tidal Flats"*

Title: Schooling: New England Aquarium Education Department Newsletter

Target Group: Teachers, all grade levels

Available from: New England Aquarium Teacher Resource Center, Central Wharf, Boston, MA 02110-3399; telephone (617) 973-6590; fax (617) 973-0251

Cost: Free subscription to teachers; published twice a year.

COMMENT

Schooling, the New England Aquarium's education newsletter published twice a year, will keep teachers up to date on the Aquarium's multifaceted programs, teacher workshops, conferences, special events, publications, aquarium news, and more. Anyone who teaches marine or environmental studies should be on this mailing list. Special issues feature a wealth of information on topics such as the Aquarium's Whale Day program, Stellwagen Bank Sanctuary, and the recent Jellies exhibit. Whatever the subject, *Schooling* will provide teachers—and any other readers—with ideas about how to be involved in a wide range of conservation efforts and outreach projects, and it will direct readers how to best utilize the Aquarium's resources. Get this publication; it's informative and fun to pour over at any time, for any reason.

EXCERPTS

"We aim to increase people's understanding of acquatic life and environments, to enable people to conserve the world of water, and provide leadership for the preservation and sustainable use of aquatic resources.… This mission reflects the fact that it is no longer enough to simply teach about environments, or even about environmental problems. We must be active in solving these problems, and empower students to act with us on behalf of our lakes, rivers, and oceans. Environmental problems are complex. We cannot always provide a simple answer. We can provide information, skills for problem solving, and ideas for action. In the end, each of us, students, teachers, and even museum directors, must solve each problem for ourselves."
—*New England Aquarium Education Department, "Schooling," fall issue, 1993*

Title: New England Coastlines: New England Aquarium Education Department Curriculum Guide

Target Group: Teachers, all grade levels

Available from: New England Aquarium Teacher Resource Center, Central Wharf, Boston, MA 02110-3399; telephone (617) 973-6590; fax (617) 973-0251

Cost: $5

COMMENT

"*Coastlines—A curriculum package to help teachers, chaperones, and students prepare for a fun and rewarding field trip or outreach program.*"

Coastlines is the Aquarium's packaged guide providing background information and activity ideas on coastal and conservation issues for students of all ages. Filled with worksheets for a host of activities such as scavenger hunts, art exercises, writing exercises, suggestions for student designed simulations, chaperone ideas for field trips to the aquarium, exercises to learn about animal behavior and habitats, the possibilities seem endless in this neatly presented and exceptionally well organized program. What is in this guide can easily be woven into existing curriculums on marine science and should be used in conjunction with visits to the Aquarium (hopefully many of them) and with other Aquarium resources.

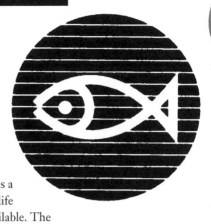

Title: New England Aquarium Teacher Resource Center

Target Group: K-12 teachers

Available from: New England Aquarium Teacher Resource Center, Central Wharf, Boston, MA 02110-3399; telephone (617) 973-6590; fax (617) 973-0251

Cost: Whale Kits, Coastal Kits, $15/week plus shipping (C.O.D.); other materials available free.

COMMENT

Made up of two collections of materials for K-12 teachers, a lending libary and a noncirculating curriculum collection, The New England Aquarium Teacher Resource Center is a gold mine for those seeking materials for marine and environmental studies programs. (Then again, the entire aquarium is a gold mine; see telephone numbers of additional Aquarium programs.) Shark's jaws, walrus tusks, sea-life puppets, books, costumes, turtle shells, "Whale Kits," and "Coast Kits" are some of the materials available. The large kits are available for rent; each comes with a two-week curriculum and supporting materials for each unit. Other materials and loan items are available free. A wealth of material designed for use in bilingual and special education classes is also available. Just about anything a teacher would want to "study the world of water" and "bring the ocean to your school," can be found here. Appointments are necessary to use the center and can be arranged for days, evenings or weekends.

EXCERPT

"Aquariums and zoos play a valuable role in the conservation of wildlife and environments. The New England Aquarium is much more than just a museum of aquatic life— it is a not-for-profit institution dedicated to education, conservation, and research. And through the exhibition of aquatic life, the New England Aquarium hopes to stimulate interest in and concern for animals and their habitats."—*excerpted from* "Take a Look Beneath the Surface," *New England Aquarium*

New England Aquarium titles for ages 7-11 available at the New England Aquarium Gift Shop (617) 973-5266:

Rescue of the Stranded Whales
Window on the Deep—Adventures of Underwater Explorer Sylvia Earle
Don't Blink Now—Capturing the Underwater World of Sea Creatures
Alligators to Zooplankton—A Dictionary of Water Babies
Do Fishes Get Thirsty? Questions Answered by the New England Aquarium
The Red Sea
Pomona— the Birth of a Penguin

Monster Myths—The Truth about Water Monsters
Night Reef—Dusk to Dawn on a Coral Reef
Fish Tales
What is a Fish?
Dive to the Coral Reef
Sea Jellies
Search for the Right Whale

DEPARTMENTS AND OTHER PROGRAMS AT THE NEW ENGLAND AQUARIUM

Group Reservations: (617) 973-5206
• Field trip information and reservations
• Auditorium reservations
• Behind-the-Scenes Tours
• Aquarium explorers classes

Education Department: (617) 973-5232
• Outreach information and reservations
• Teacher workshop reservations
• "Sleep-with-the-Fishes" Overnights reservations

Whale Watch:
• Information (617) 973-5277
• Reservations (617) 973 5281

"Science at Sea" Harbor Tour: (617) 973-5207

New England Aquarium Library: (617) 973-5237

Sponsor-a-Right-Whale: (617) 973-6582

New England Aquarium Information: (617) 973-5200

96

Title: The Whale Conservation Institute Research and Education Programs

Target Group: All ages

Available from: The Whale Conservation Institute, 191 Weston Road, Lincoln, MA 01773; telephone (617) 259-0423; fax (617) 259-0288

Cost: Costs for programs vary; contact for further information. Memberships available; rates range from $15-250.

COMMENTS

"Once upon a time, way back at the beginning of human time…we all had the right kind of admiration and awe for whales. It got lost. And in that moment, we not only lost something beautiful but something vital to our understanding of nature and our place in it.—*Dr. Roger Payne*

Founded in 1971 by Dr. Roger Payne, an international authority on whale behavior, the Whale Conservation Institute (WCI) is an established leader in whale conservation and cetacean research. Programs and educational opportunities with the Institute are extensive; what is mentioned here represents only a part of their work. The Institute's resources include the 94-foot research vessel *Odyssey*; over 25 years of data on more than 1,200 individually known right whales (making this the longest continuous study of any whale species based on identified individuals); widely distributed educational curricula; the world's largest collection of humpback whale song recordings; and a cross-referenced library of more than 3,500 technical papers, books, and publications. In addition, the Institute continues to develop award-winning media programs like *In the Company of Whales* (see page 97),works to establish marine sanctuaries and reserves around the world, influences important policy and legislation pertaining to commercial whaling practices and other major threats to marine mammals, and publishes several newsletters and reports to keep members and others updated on scientific and legislative developments. Their task is large, but WCI's commitment to the species and its preservation is obvious. The whales of the world should be happy to have people like these on their side.

EXCERPTS

Programs through the Whale Conservation Institute include:

The Education Today Program

The Education Today Programs work to improve the science literacy of K-12 students by linking the practice of science to the study of the environment. Our Interactive Video Curriculum, Elementary Whale Study Curriculum and formal assessment programs comprise this initiative.

The Right Whale Research Programs

Institute programs continue to redefine the state-of-the-art in whale research. More than 25 years of data on over 1,200 identified individuals create a context for discovery rarely encountered in field science and unmatched by any other cetacean research initiative. Dr. Payne and Institute scientists have developed many of the benign research techniques now used by cetacean researchers throughout the world.

The Odyssey Ocean Research Program

The Ocean Research Program creates a continuous platform for the Whale Conservation Institute at sea. The Odyssey Expeditions promote the Institute's global conservation efforts through research initiatives and through the introduction of scientists from developing countries.

The ECOTOX Program

Studying the link between toxin accumulation in the marine environment and the breakdown of immune systems in marine mammals, the Institute's toxicology studies currently focus on measuring baseline levels of ocean toxins and determining the basis of unusual skin lesions on the right whales.—*adapted from WCI program information brochure*

Title: "In the Company of Whales" Video

Target Group: General public

Available from: The Whale Conservation Institute, 191 Weston Road, Lincoln, MA 01773; telephone (617) 259-0423; fax (617) 259-0288

Cost: $28

COMMENTS

"You can't encounter a whale...and not remember it for the rest of your life."—*Dr. Roger Payne*
This Emmy-nominated, 90-minute documentary on whales was produced by the Discovery Channel and the Whale Conservation Institute. Hosted and narrated by the Institute's Dr. Roger Payne, the film examines whale behavior and explores the significant threats that face marine mammals. Produced over a period of eighteen months, from locations off five continents, it is the largest production ever done by The Discovery Network. A moving and compelling voyage into the "watery realm" of the whale; we should all dare to take this trip.

EXCERPTS

"We have to respond to the warning the whales are giving us about the oceans and we have to cease business as usual. By educating the public through programs like *In the Company of Whales*, I think people will wake up and realize the problems we are facing and start to take action and save our marine life. The truth is we are in the middle of a war. We just don't know it yet. It's a war with ourselves and where the weapons of our destruction are our own practices which destroy the environment. Once we recognize that, then we can do something about it, but not until we recognize it."—*Dr. Roger Payne, WCI*

"Don't despair....Do act. Time is running out, but I think that we can change our future. And once that change gets going it will be, I predict, exactly the same thing as when the Berlin Wall came down. There was no evidence or hope whatsoever that it was going to happen. And once it started, it happened so fast all you could do was watch. I think that's what will happen once people decide to take the health of our seas seriously and recognize the peril we and whales are in. It will happen very fast. Everyone will take up the call and recognize how we can all make a difference in the health of our seas and, ultimately, our own health."—*Dr. Roger Payne, WCI*

Title: New England Dolphin Outreach Project Educational Programs

Target Group: General public, grades K-12

Available from: New England Dolphin Outreach Project, 800 Mere Point Road, Brunswick, ME 04011; telephone (207) 729-1543; fax (207) 729-9915

Cost: Contact for more information on program costs

COMMENT

Thanks to the efforts of groups like this one, awareness of and commitment to this much loved species of whales is increasing, just as their very survival becomes more critical due to die-offs, driftnet catches and dolphin slaughters by foreign fishermen. Operated in affiliation with the Dolphin Research Center out of the Florida Keys (Flipper's original home as well as current home to 15 Atlantic bottlenose dolphins and one spotted dolphin), the New England Dolphin Outreach Center runs an increasing number of programs for school and community groups including slide shows, videos, lessons on dolphin anatomy and physiology, behavior, and research while focusing on conservation and the continued protection of dolphins and their environment. For anyone who has a soft spot for these remarkable animals and wants to know more, this is the group to contact. Even if you don't know anything about dolphins, the lessons learned here will surely win your affections—as well as your curiosities— for the Flippers of our oceans.

EXCERPT

"The New England Dolphin Outreach Project was created to raise human awareness of the species of whale known as dolphins. It is a program born of the love of dolphins and other marine animals and a deep concern for their immediate and future well-being. We humans are fascinated by these mystical creatures and saddened by their plight on Earth."—*New England Dolphin Outreach Center*

Twenty-four hour Marine Stranding Hot Line at the New England Aquarium: (617)973-5247

For additional information on Dolphins contact:

The Dolphin Research Center PO Box 522875 Marathon Shores Florida Keys, FLA 33052-2875

telephone (305)289-1121; fax (305) 743-7627

Other materials available from the Whale Conservation Institute:

Songs of the Humpback Whale
Cassette $10; CD $12

Whales Alive
Cassette $10; CD $12

Where the Whales Are
Book $12.95

Deep Voices (sounds of the right, blue, and humpback whale)
Cassette $10; CD $12

HUMAN SYSTEMS, ISSUES AND IMPACTS

Many people are surprised to learn that the Gulf of Maine watershed is the third most densely populated coastal region in the United States. By 2005, the human population in the coastal region between the seacoast of New Hampshire and southern Maine is expected to double from what it was in 1985. In all, more than five million of us live in the Gulf of Maine watershed.

We have many reasons for being here, many expectations for the region's resources, and many reasons to understand and protect the natural systems that are at the foundation of the Gulf of Maine ecosystem.

Similarly, we have a profound impact on the plant and animal communities that share the watershed with us. This chapter highlights materials and sources of information that concern human interaction with other living communities in the Gulf of Maine and its watershed.

Red Tide and More...

As coastal populations grow and ever greater amounts of nutrient-rich sewage are discharged to marine waters, the risk of water-quality problems grows, particularly in embayments where flushing and currents are restricted. Eutrophication may play a role in the incidence of toxic "tides," including red tide, which result in the closure of thousands of acres of clam flats each summer.

   In 1988, a bloom of a toxic marine alga, Gymnidinium nagasakiense, in the upper reaches of Casco Bay caused a major die-off of lobsters, clams, worms, and other benthic organisms. While nutrient runoff has been blamed for the bloom, few data exist to substantiate the claim.—*Gulf of Maine Council on the Marine Environment, 1989,* Sustaining Our Common Heritage

Economic Values

It is not difficult to think of economic ways in which people depend on the natural world. In the Gulf of Maine, direct benefits include commercial fishing, shellfishing, aquaculture, and the related processing and distribution systems that support these activities (marine construction and repair, retail fuel and supplies, fish processing, and marketing). Although currently in serious decline, the groundfish industry in the Gulf still provides a harvest valued at more than half a billion dollars annually, employing 20,000 fishermen on more than 1,600 boats in both the U.S. and Canada. In 1994, more lobsters were harvested in the Gulf than in any previous year—a catch of over 38 million pounds, generating $98 million in revenue for the State of Maine.

Tourism is a major contributor to both state and provincial economies in the region. Figures compiled within the last decade indicate that recreational fishing and hunting expenditures in Maine, Massachusetts, and New Hampshire exceeded $900 million annually. At the same time, "non-consumptive" recreational expenditures associated with wildlife (*e.g.*, photographing and observing wildlife) in the Gulf of Maine region (1988) are more than $486 million. Seventy-five percent of the economic activity on Cape Cod is directly attributed to the tourist industry, which generates over $1.5 billion each year. Revenue estimates from nature tourism (*e.g.*, whale-watching, camping and boating) average approximately $6 billion a year, supporting over 200,000 jobs in the Gulf watershed.

Environmental Costs

Habitats throughout the Gulf of Maine watershed have been seriously compromised by wetland loss, pollution, habitat fragmentation, over-harvesting, and other cumulative effects of human development. As development continues along the coast, natural process in the Gulf's estuaries are increasingly disrupted.

Approximately 90 percent of coastal wetland loss in the Gulf of Maine results from human actions, including industrial, residential, and harbor development, dam construction, and pollution from chemicals and debris. A major threat to the Gulf's marine ecosystems is the cumulative, long-term effect of persistent toxic chemicals in marine waters.

Habitat for Atlantic salmon is threatened by dams lacking effective upstream and downstream passage facilities, riverside land-use practices, and some forms of aquaculture. Habitat on islands critical for nesting seabirds, eagles, and osprey is threatened by development and growing pressure from recreational use. Increasingly intensive harvesting has strained the ability of commercial fish stocks in the Gulf to recover. For many species of groundfish, populations in the Gulf are at record low levels, prompting the New England Fisheries Management Council, in December, 1994, to close fishing grounds in Georges Bank and enact severe restrictions on groundfish harvest elsewhere in the Gulf.

Boothbay Harbor and Casco Bay have levels of contaminants that equal or surpass those found in Boston or New York Harbor.
—*The Wild Gulf Project*

Start Here...

People throughout the watershed are addressing the impact of human use on the Gulf's natural habitats and ecosystems. Federal, state, and provincial agencies are cooperating across jurisdictional lines, joining with nongovernmental environmental organizations, the academic community, and private individuals to develop management plans and solutions that minimize damage and protect the Gulf and its living resources. The following descriptions will begin to give you an idea of the level of commitment, enthusiasm, and determination these groups, organizations and individuals are contributing to the future of the watershed. Use these ideas, think of more, talk to students, talk to neighbors, become a sustainable part of your ecosystem.

Specific information for this introduction was drawn from recent publications of the Gulf of Maine Council on the Environment (Sustaining our Common Heritage), *the National Marine Fisheries Service, the U.S. Fish and Wildlife Gulf of Maine Project, and the Clean Annapolis River Project.*

Jon Iuoma

100

Title: Department of Marine Resources Fisherman's Library Video Collection

Target Group: General audience

Available from: The Library, Maine Department of Marine Resources Fisheries Laboratory, McKown Point, West Boothbay Harbor, ME 04575; tel. (207) 633-9551, (207) 633-9527; fax (207) 633-9641

Cost: Films can be borrowed for two weeks

COMMENTS

Maine's Department of Marine Resources (DMR) provides an exceptional resource at their library in West Boothbay Harbor. The library resources are bound to get anyone remotely interested in the fishing industry to think more about the fisheries issues affecting all the Gulf region and beyond. Gathered from a variety of places including state and federal agencies, commercial establishments, and interested individuals (many fishermen and women among them), a wealth of information is represented here: films on fishing methods and gear, aquaculture, research and biology, and historical and sociological views of the industry. Below is a sample list of titles; there are approximately 65 videos available in the library.

Legal Aspects of Clam Flats—University of Maine Sea Grant staff member interviews Alison Reiser of the Marine Law Institute on legal issues relating to clam flats.

The Gulf of Maine—Not Just Another Fish Story—A film for general audiences that describes the richness of the waters of the Gulf of Maine, and its diverse fishing industry.

Fisherman's Battle: Undersea Research in the North Atlantic—A study by the Massachusetts Division of Fisheries and the National Undersea Research Program of NOAA to determine the impact of fishing gear on the fish stocks in the North Atlantic.

Safety and Survival at Sea (4 tapes) (1987)—Safety equipment and survival procedures; medical emergencies at sea; fire prevention & control; fishing vessel stability.

Harvesters of the Sea—Shows the pride and independent spirit of a Maine fisherman.

The Blue Planet (1988)—One segment of the public television broadcast, "The Planet Earth." The film follows scientists employing new technologies to study the global ocean from underwater and from space. (60 minutes)

The Water Talks to Me—Provides a close look at a traditional fishing community caught in the midst of change. Shot in the port of Gloucester, MA, and on vessels in the North Atlantic, the impact of declining fish populations on the lives of two off-shore fishermen, a father and son, is examined. (30 minutes)

Merrymeeting Bay—12 towns, 6 rivers, 1 bay. Merrymeeting Bay talks to the viewer about what Man has done to it over the past 300 years. (General audience).

Sea of Green: The Maine Gold Rush—A well-produced video on the sea urchin industry in Maine, including information on diver safety issues. A must-see video for anyone considering going into the urchin business. (25 minutes)

Farmers of the Sea—Aquaculture techniques used in various countries around the world. (56 minutes)

The River Farmer—Reminiscences by Ed Myers about his aquaculture business on the Damariscotta River estuary in Maine.

Making New Waves: Aquaculture in Maine—Aquaculture industry members, environmental organizations, shorefront landowners and scientists express their views and concerns about the rapidly growing aquaculture industry in Maine. (30 minutes)

Lobster Special: the Catch of Tomorrow—Lobster research at the University of Maine is discussed.

The biggest source of plastic debris in Gulf of Maine waters is recreational boaters. Plastic trash can cost marine mammals and seabirds their lives; it can also be expensive to you! It is illegal to discard trash into ocean waters.
—National Marine Fisheries Service

Title: Keep it Clean Program

Target Group: Grades 2 -8

Available from: Gulf of Maine Aquarium, PO Box 7549, Portland, ME 04112; telephone (207) 772-2321; fax (207) 772-6855

Cost: $50 per program, plus mileage

COMMENT

The Gulf of Maine Aquarium has developed an innovative and participatory program to study water-quality issues and learn about safe water-use practices. *The Keep it Clean Program* is an outreach project committed to teaching about water—where it comes from, how it effects us, how we effect it. Students learn about the Sebago Lake watershed in detail and then locate their own schools in relation to the watershed. By studying a model of a watershed community, students learn about water pollution and the widespread effect of pollutants on every facet of the watershed. But learning doesn't stop there. Once students see the havoc wreaked on water supplies by pollution, they learn how to clean up the mess and gain an appreciation for how to avoid polluting water sources in the first place. Handouts for students include copies of the special water-quality issue of *Minnow*, (see page 21) and a leaflet entitled "Keep Out Phosphorous" which promotes the "Be a good KOP!" concept and describes the dangers of phosphorous in our water supplies. As with other materials from the Gulf of Maine Aquarium (See pages 21, 48, and 83) this is one more well-organized, artfully presented program for children—a timely testament to the Aquarium's commitment to environmental and marine education.

EXCERPTS

"Phosphorous makes plants grow faster. Phosphorous is a natural fertilizer that occurs in rocks and soil, as well as in phosphorous detergents, sewage leach-fields, and man-made fertilizers. When it enters a pond, it becomes the single most important ingredient in promoting algae blooms.

Phosphorus fertilizes the microscopic plants, called algae, making them grow rapidly. Nearly as rapidly, they die off. Their breakdown by small micro-organisms—bacteria and fungi—uses up much of the oxygen dissolved in the water, the same oxygen fish and animals need to survive. Algae blooms can kill fish, turn the water green and murky, make rocks slippery, and give drinking water an unpleasant taste and odor. If plants along the

shoreline intercept the phosphorus before it can reach the pond, they will use it for their own growth and keep the pond clear.
—*excerpted from "Keep Out Phosphorous," a phosphorous information sheet produced by the Gulf of Maine Aquarium and the Portland Water District*

Phosphorous Pollution Solutions
- Replace pine needles that have been raked up, put down mulch, or plant undergrowth that will absorb water.
- Replace a straight foot path with a curving one. This will re-direct water from the path into vegetation, where it will slow down and be absorbed.
- Plant a vegetable buffer strip—a variety of trees, shrubs, and ground cover. Grass alone is not enough.
—*Gulf of Maine Aquarium and the Portland Water District*, Keep Out Phosphorous

102

Title: Center for the Restoration of Waters "Living Machines" Information

Target: General audience

Available from: The Center for the Restoration of Waters, Ocean Arks International, 1 Locust Street, Falmouth, MA 02540; telephone (508) 540-6801; fax (508) 540-6811

Cost: General information materials free; membership rates are $15, students; $30, individuals; $35, Canadian members; $45, families; $100, supporters; $1000, patrons. (Membership includes subscription to *Annals of the Earth* and course announcements.)

COMMENT

"Restore the lands, protect the seas, and inform the Earth's stewards."
—*John and Nancy Jack Todd*

Ocean Arks International (OAI) has buckets of material available on their "Living Machine" technology, a timely and innovative approach to finding "sustainable alternatives to waste disposal, fuel production, heating and cooling, air purification, and food production."

Recipients of major support from the U.S. Environmental Protection Agency for "developing and demonstrating ecological concepts for water purification and for healing damaged aquatic ecosystems," OAI's Center for the Restoration of Water is now working in at least ten different sites where their Living Machines are either operational or are under construction. These projects include a water-purification system at Flax Pond in Harwich, Massachusetts, a zero discharge waste facility for the Audubon Society at Corkscrew Swamp in Naples, Florida; state-of-the-art-sewage-treatment facilities in Maryland and Rhode Island; and the development of household-scale Living Machines for "unplugged" houses in Canada. In Puerto Rico, OAI is developing a system to purify sewage water currently being discharged into a marine sanctuary so that it can be used for irrigation, reforestation, and ecological development; and in Providence, Rhode Island, OAI plans to convert a Living Machine sewage-treatment plant to a center demonstrating ecological technologies for urban food production. Additionally, the Center publishes *Annals of the Earth* three times year. The journal, printed on newsprint, features an impressive list of international contributors and readers and serves as an "intellectual forum for the presentation of leading edge environmental thought."(See box below.)

"The exchange of ideas feeds the roots of new thought. To this end, the Center for the Restoration of Waters publishes *Annals of the Earth* to disseminate the ideas and practice of ecological sustainability throughout the world. It seeks through written communication, to foster the emergence of a new global culture. Published three times yearly, *Annals* has an international roster of scholarly, philosophical, and ecological writers who deal with planetary issues from a wide range of perspectives. While *Annals* covers and chronicles the Center's activities, it also publishes articles that range in subject from the philosophy of ecology, basic biology, hands-on environmental projects, to the Gaia Hypothesis. Distributed worldwide, *Annals* is an intellectual forum for the presentation of leading-edge environmental thought."—*Ocean Arks International*

EXCERPTS

"Ocean Arks International is a non-profit research organization dedicated to the use of ecological knowledge to solve water pollution problems. Founded in 1981 by John and Nancy Jack Todd, Ocean Arks began a new phase in the research and implementation of the ideas that first took form at the New Alchemy Institute (also founded by the Todds)... Drawing on what we have learned of the ecology of aquatic ecosystems at New Alchemy, we have created a family of technologies called 'Living Machines' that are now able to restore waters currently polluted by human and industrial waste to EPA standards."

—*John Todd, President, Ocean Arks International*

"The Maryland AEES [Advanced Ecologically Engineered System for Sewage Treatment] Living Machine takes its sewage from the neighboring Ballenger Creek Sewage Treatment Facility after it has been screened and degritted. The first stage of treatment takes place in the anaerobic bio-reactor.

Cosmic Fish Swimming in Restored Waters

Fredrick Franck

There the organic constituents in the waste are subjected to the active bacterial breakdown that takes place there in the absence of oxygen. From the digester, sewage flows into a series of aerated tanks, where different communities of bacteria continue the breakdown process. The fluidized bed tanks, filled with buoyant pumice rock, provide more microbial surface area and exposure to ecological purification processes. These processes involve more and more diverse ecosystems of algae, protozoa, snails, fish, and plants as the waste moves downstream. Any accumulated sludges are settled out and removed at the clarifier tanks, located just before the marshes. The large engineered marshes, planted with a wide variety of plant species, are the last stage in the natural filtration and cleansing of the waste stream. The gravel media and plant roots perform the final polishing of an effluent that, after its journey through the biological cogs of the Living Machine, is of advanced quality. Effluent purity approaches that of drinking water, without the addition of harmful chemicals."—*Ocean Arks International, "Maryland Living Machine Process Description"*

103

Title: Adopt River Connections, A Handbook

Target Group: Grades K-12, general public

Available from: Penobscot River and Bay Institute, Box 214A, Brooksville ME 04617; telephone (207) 326-4822

Cost: Contact for information

COMMENT

This 10-page handbook explains the Adopt River Connections (ARC) program sponsored by the Penobscot River and Bay Institute, and provides various ways to initiate the program in the Penobscot River watershed. Suggestions are readily transferable to other watersheds. The handbook offers general guidelines and suggestions about how to "adopt" a river, but the beauty of this particular program is that it embraces anything that fosters involvement in—and awareness of—the complexities of watersheds like the Penobscot River and Bay region. Groups or individuals who participate in the program earn the title of River Keeper, along with a card to prove it!

ARC ABC's
A. **A**dopt a River Connection.
B. **B**ecome a keeper of that connection.
C. **C**onnect with others. (Learn from your connection and teach others.)

EXCERPTS
ARC=Adopt River Connections
"Mitakuye Oyasin"
This Native American message meaning *we are all related* suggests that there are many River Connections to adopt. Here are some Penobscot Institute Adoption Agency suggestions to get your ideas flowing:
- ADOPT NON-GAS DRIVEN BOATS— Improve or create public access to a local stream, lake or river for light, nonintrusive boats (canoes, kayaks, Windsurfers, rowboats, and the like.)
- ADOPT INJURED LAND NEAR WATER — Campaign for clean-up and removal of hazardous materials and structures from areas in or near wetlands and open water in your community.
- ADOPT WATER CONSERVATION — Make water bricks for toilets to reduce water consumption. Sell them to raise money for a water conservation publicity campaign.
- ADOPT A WILD PLACE— Improve a wildlife area in your community. Make, rescue, or improve a self-sustaining wildlife preserve that includes a variety of overlapping habitats. Make sure there is a clean and adequate water source. Put in a self-guided nature trail.

- ADOPT EACH OTHER— Start an environmental action club. Adopt a code of environmental ethics. For example, traditional Native Americans try to "live lightly on the earth" and leave the environment undamaged by their activities. They also try to envision how their actions will affect things seven generations from now. We like the "Seven Virtues" cited by a Penobscot leader, T. Sapier. They are — honesty, humility, courage, respect, responsibility, generosity, and acceptance and tolerance. The Penobscot Institute believes these or a similar set of ethics will provide a measuring stick for any proposed environmental activity the club might undertake. Use your code of ethics to guide your actions as you list and select important environmental issues to work on in your community.
- ADOPT RIVER HISTORY — Make a river history timeline. Select events from the timeline that affected the river. Write and produce a time lapse play or series of skits that show different ways humans have related to and used the river over time. Put one episode in the future.
—*The Penobscot River and Bay Institute*, Adopt River Connections, A Handbook

Title: Watershed Protection and You: It's Our Water

Target Group: General audience

Available from: New Brunswick Environment, PO Box 6000, Fredericton, NB, Canada E3B 5H1; telephone (506) 457-4846; fax (506) 457-7823

Cost: Free of charge for New Brunswick residents; available in English or French; for anyone ordering the series from outside New Brunswick, a shipping charge will be applied.

COMMENT
New Brunswick Environment's watershed protection program, "It's Our Water," includes an introductory brochure and four booklets focusing on the following issues: landscaping, safe on-site sewage disposal, agriculture and forestry, and responsible construction activities in designated watershed areas. All four booklets convey important information, outlining suggested steps for acting safely and responsibly. This water protection program was initiated to address the fact that "In New Brunswick, about 300,000 residents—about 40 percent of the population—obtain their water supplies from surface watersheds."

Four steps to a safe on-site sewage disposal system:
- Find out whether you live in a watercourse setback zone
- Obtain an On-site Sewage Disposal Permit
- Be careful of what goes into your sewage disposal system
- Practice good sewage disposal system maintenance

—*The Watershed Protection Program and You*, It's Our Water, *Safe on-Site Sewage Disposal Systems*

EXCERPT
"Clean water is essential to all living things—not just people, but also wildlife, trees, plants and the thousands of tiny organisms which are vital to a healthy environment. It supports our present quality of life, and enables us to enjoy many recreational activities... One contaminated watershed can mean undrinkable water for thousands of people. What's more, cleaning up the damage can take a great deal of time and money. It's far better to prevent contamination in the first place—which is why the New Brunswick Government has developed a Watershed Protection Program."—*New Brunswick Environment, the Watershed Protection Program*

Title: Citizen's Guides to Ocean and Coastal Law

Target: General audience, high-school and college students

Available from: University of Maine Sea Grant Communications, 22 Coburn Hall, University of Maine, Orono, ME 04469; telephone (207) 581-1440, fax (207) 581-1423

Cost: $1 per booklet

COMMENT
These Citizens' Guides, developed by the Marine Law Institute at the University of Maine, are a series of 14 pamphlets designed to help local officials, planning volunteers and the general public understand recent federal and state developments in ocean and coastal law. Intended for a wide spectrum of readers, the guides advise local governments and coastal citizens on how to effectively advocate for the wise use, conservation, and development of marine and coastal resources. The guides cover topics such as cumulative environmental impacts of coastal development, laws regulating coastal water pollution, submerged lands lease decisions, land use regulations to implement comprehensive plans, the Marine Mammal Protection Act, and planning for sea-level rise.

Other materials available from the Sea Grant Communications Office at the University of Maine:

- *The Cultured Clam: Raising Soft-shelled Clams Downeast* —A video focusing on the Beals Island Regional Shellfish Hatchery, demonstrating the steps involved in [establishing] the first shellfish management program in the country.

- *Making New Waves: Aquaculture in Maine* —A documentary video focusing on current issues and opportunities in Maine aquaculture, including interviews with industry members, environmental organization representatives, landowners, town and state personnel, scientists and others.

- *Field Guide to Economically Important Seaweeds of Northern New England*—A 30-page guide with illustrations and descriptions of selected seaweeds of the Maine/New Hampshire coast plus suggestions on foraging and preparation, and recipes for some of the more commonly used species.

Title: Cape Cod National Seashore National Environmental Education Development Program (NEED)

105

Target Group: Educational groups of all ages

Available from: Cape Cod National Seashore NEED Program, Salt Pond Visitors Center, Eastham, MA 02642; telephone (508) 255-3421; fax (508) 240-3291

Cost: $100 per 24 hour period; no more than 36 participants

COMMENT

The NEED Program (Cape Cod National Seashore's National Environmental Education Development Program) is a unique kind of environmental education experience located at an old Coast Guard facility in Eastham, Massachusetts, on Cape Cod. Designed to accommodate groups of no more than 36 participants, the program focuses on the historical and natural features of the Cape through several different curriculums developed by the National Park Service. Each participating group tailors its own program, schedules its own activities and discussions, and provides its own meals while staying at the program site in Eastham. Group leaders are advised to participate in one of the program's teacher/leader workshops to prepare them for facilitating discussions and activities and to teach them about the facility and the local region. The beauty of this program (other than the scenery) is that its content is limited only by its participants' imagination and depth of creativity. All kinds of instructional materials are available from the National Park Service (which suggests that at least three of their own topics be considered), but any group can use its own ideas that are in keeping with the environmental mission of the program. Descriptions of a few of the lesson plans are listed below.

EXCERPTS

Curriculum topics offered (as described by the National Park Service in the NEED Program brochure) include:

Archaeology...New Discoveries Answer Old Questions
Students focus on the "hows" and "whys" of archaeological excavation processes. Group activities include recognizing objects from varying time periods of human occupation. A 30-minute video tape is available highlighting the recent archaeological discovery at Coast Guard Beach in Eastham which dates back 8,000 years.

Recycle...We Have an Alternative
Students focus on landfill problems on Cape Cod and participate in recycling at the NEED building. A visit to the municipal recycling center may be arranged to coincide with your stay.

Biodiversity...Makes a World of Difference
Students focus on global, national, and local reasons for species and habitat protection. The lesson plan touches on extinction, the need for genetically diverse populations, and what is needed beyond preservation of endangered species.

More Than Just Cleaning the Shoreline...Seeking the Source
Students focus on the multiple impacts of marine debris on Cape Cod's shoreline and how scientific inventories help to identify sources.

Reminders from the National Park Service:
- Groups are reminded not to walk on, or over, any sand dunes
- Groups must stay clear of nesting shorebird areas (posted during spring and early summer) Also kite-flying is prohibited during nesting season.
- Archaeological features must not be disturbed or collected (leave items where they are found, and report them immediately).

Adopt the pace of nature:

her secret is patience.

—R. W. Emerson

Additional Educational Resources and Activities on Cape Cod:

Massachusetts Audubon Society, South Wellfleet (508)349-2615

Cape Cod Museum of Natural History, Brewster (508) 896-3867

Center for Coastal Studies, Provincetown (508) 487-3622

Salt Pond Visitor Center (508) 255-3421

106

MEMBERSHIP INFORMATION

Individual—$20

Family/Nonprofit group/Association—$30

Professional Group/Association—$100

Corporation:

1-25 employees—$75

26-75 employees—$125

76+—$200

Title: Moosehead Maritimes Beach Sweep and Litter Survey Kit

Target Group: General audience

Available from: The Clean Nova Scotia Foundation, PO Box 2528, Central, Halifax, NS Canada B3J 3N5; telephone (902) 420-3474; fax (902) 424-5334

Cost: See sidebar for membership fees. Kits are available to participating individuals and groups free of charge.

COMMENT

These kits offer great suggestions for involving communities, schools, and businesses in the worthwhile task of cleaning up our shorelines and promoting education about the devastating effects litter has on wildlife and our environment. A handy guide demonstrates how to organize a Beach Sweep and suggests ways for getting started—identifying a site, placing posters, contacting media, attracting volunteers, and arranging trash pick-ups. Safety precautions, a general checklist, and suggestions for post-clean-up activities are included along with tips for writing news releases for radio, television, and newspapers. Complete kits include, the guide, posters, data cards for participants to record their findings, and labeled garbage bags—recyclable, of course. This project is organized by three environmentally dedicated Canadian agencies—the Clean Nova Scotia Foundation, the Environmental Coalition of Prince Edward Island, and Huntsman Marine Science Centre—and is sponsored by Moosehead Breweries, Ltd. For additional information on the *Beach Sweep Activities Guide* adapted specifically for school use, see the following entry.

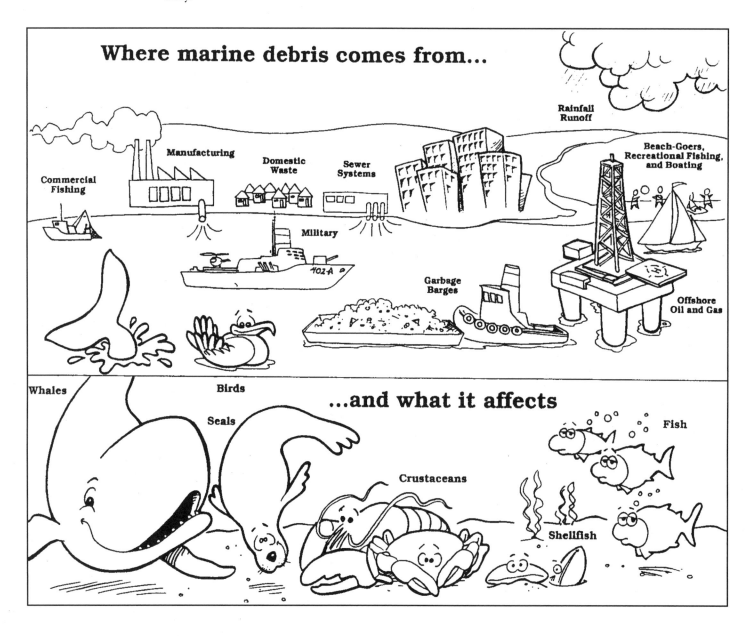

Where marine debris comes from...

Rainfall Runoff

Manufacturing

Domestic Waste

Sewer Systems

Commercial Fishing

Military

Beach-Goers, Recreational Fishing, and Boating

Garbage Barges

Offshore Oil and Gas

...and what it affects

Whales

Birds

Seals

Crustaceans

Fish

Shellfish

EXCERPTS

"By becoming involved in Beach Sweep, individuals can play an active role in protecting the coastal and marine environment for which the Maritimes are famous. A Beach Sweep can also serve as an excellent 'focus activity' for participating organizations to educate children and the general public about avoiding and preventing beach litter. This guide is designed to help coordinate a safe, educational and fun event."

"Most of the litter left on beaches consists of plastics… As well, glass pieces, wood, and metal cans are found in abundance on the shoreline. Plastic poses a particular problem since the same qualities that make it useful—lightness, strength, and durability—also enable it to persist a long time when disposed of in sensitive environments. One researcher of marine debris has stated that the global seas already contain so much plastic trash that even if dumping were to cease immediately, plastic litter would continue to wash ashore for one hundred years."—*Moosehead Maritimes Beach Sweep Kit organizational guide.*

Safety and Environmental Tips

(—from Beach Sweep Data Card)
1. Be careful with medical waste.
2. Do not go near any large drums.
3. Be careful with sharp objects.
4. Stay out of dune areas.
5. Wear gloves.
6. Don't lift anything too heavy.
7. Be careful of natural habitats— avoid Piping plover nesting areas.

Title: Moosehead Maritimes Beach Sweep and Litter Survey School Activities Guide

Target Group: Grades K-8

Available from: The Clean Nova Scotia Foundation, PO Box 2528, Central, Halifax, NS Canada B3J 3N5; telephone (902) 420-3474; fax (902) 424-5334

Cost: Free to schools

MOOSEHEAD
Canada's Oldest Independent Brewery

COMMENT

This activity guide expands on the topic of marine debris education by providing a series of hands-on activities and projects in which students can participate. In addition to the "Beach Sweep and Litter Survey Kit" detailed on page 106, activities include units on the meaning of adaptation and habitat, the effects of plastics on marine wildlife, the effects of oil spills on marine birds, poisons in our food chain, a role-play exercise based on the issue of ocean dumping by corporations, a "recycling relay" in which students race to distinguish recyclables from nonrecyclables, and some fun worksheets with word games and identification exercises. Clearly, the investigative and research-oriented methods in these lessons—and their manageable size and scope for this age group—make these learning opportunities important ones for students and teachers together.

EXCERPTS

"The strong ties of the ocean to the Maritime way of life connect us in many ways. Our heritage, our livelihoods, our homes are part of the waters that surround us. Each year, the Moosehead Maritimes Beach Sweep and Litter Survey draws thousands of volunteers to our shorelines to take part in coastal clean-up projects. However, a beach clean-up is only a small part of the learning that can occur on our shores. With this in mind, we have developed this series of educational activities to take your Beach Sweep studies to a new level.

   Your special day at the beach can have many remarkable and unforgettable moments. The development of these educational materials seeks to further explore the adventures that can result from studying our coastal environment."
—"*Moosehead Maritimes Beach Sweep and Litter Survey School Activities Guide*"

Some suggested Beach Sweep follow-up exercises:

• Write a Letter to the Editor, informing the public of your beach clean-up results.

• Design posters on the marine debris problem. These can be posted in boating stores, fishing supply stores, marinas, yacht clubs, etc.

Analyze the information you've gathered on marine debris. Make bar graphs and pie charts after determining the percentages of different items found.

• Create a mural of the shore you have cleaned by placing on it a variety of the marine debris that was collected during Beach Sweep.

• Construct a garbage monster out of some trash collected on the beach.

• Erect a notice board on environmental issues. Encourage students to bring in articles and discuss the issues raised by each before posting the articles on the board.

• Adopt a beach. Commit your class to regular beach clean-ups
—*adapted from* "*The Moosehead Maritimes Beach Sweep and Litter Survey School Activities Guide*"

For Example:
Dilemma:
Crud Co., a major international sewage-treatment company, was contracted by the province to take over the municipal treatment facilities. In 1992, Crud Co., was caught dumping large amounts of lead-contaminated sewage directly into the Bay of Fundy on a regular basis. The corporation is being charged with a violation of the Environmental Protection Act. Crud Co., is pleading not guilty to the charge on the basis that the amounts of sewage sludge released into the bay were negligible.

Characters:
Prosecutor
Ecologist
Environmentalist
Defense Lawyer
Corporate official
Politician
Journalist
—*from* "*Ocean Dumping*" *role-playing activity*, The Moosehead Maritimes Beach Sweep and Litter Survey School Activities Guide

108

Title: Field Testing Manual for Water Quality, Department of Marine Resources, Fisheries Education Unit #18

Target Group: General public; high-school and college teachers

Available from: Education Division, Maine Department of Marine Resources, Station 21, Augusta, ME 04333-0021; telephone (207) 624-6550; fax (207) 624-6024

Cost: Free

COMMENT

Presuming you have an interest in learning more about water quality testing techniques, this manual will instruct you how to take part in Department of Marine Resources's (DMR) rigorous water-quality testing program in your own area. The manual describes the criteria for testing, standard testing procedures, the proper method for reporting data to DMR, and where to get testing materials. The information is very readable (even for the non-scientifically inclined), well-organized, and clearly instructional. The program represents a terrific opportunity for teachers to develop an exciting and productive water-quality unit for high school or college students, but homeowners and interested individuals can also get involved. The more that take part, the better.

EXCERPTS

"The Department of Marine Resources is interested in the quality of the water that enters the Gulf of Maine. One of DMR's programs involves the restoration of anadromous fish to their historical waters. To accomplish this task, DMR needs to know the quality of the water in each of these rivers, streams, and lakes and as many other environmental factors as possible.

With this in mind, DMR is establishing a database of information on as many water bodies as possible. This information will be used in long-range planning, restoration and eventual management of the anadromous fisheries resources once re-established in that water body or system.

Your data could play a very important role in the development of this database and the eventual restoration of anadromous fish to the area. This is a real work-type activity where participants encounter the actual problems of field testing under a wide range of conditions. You will develop skills in scientific testing, recording of data, the interpretation of that data and report writing, all scientific skills that developed in a meaningful situation, besides learning a great deal about the natural environment, *i.e.* what factors influence that environment positively and adversely."—*Department of Marine Resources, Education Division*

"The site selections for your testing and sampling activities are very important. First of all, they must be accessible at all seasons of the year and under all weather conditions. You must return to those sites every time you test. The sites must be meaningful sites preferably in the open stream, river, or lake. …Select your sites with an eye to the water body as a whole."—*Department of Marine Resources*

"The volume of water that flows through a site per day is known as the flow rate. This is a critical factor in fisheries management as it determines how fast pollutants move, how much replenishment of water occurs, thus bringing in more nutrients, gases and much more."—*Department of Marine Resources*

> *"If you walk out into the water to obtain the sample, always let the water settle for a minute and take the sample from the upstream side."*
>
> —*Department of Marine Resources*

If you would like to obtain training in the use of equipment, DMR's Education Division has workshops dealing with the topic. These workshops are free to the teachers in any school that would like to participate in the testing program. DMR also offers summer courses that deal with the theory and practice of water quality and fisheries management.
—*Department of Marine Resources*

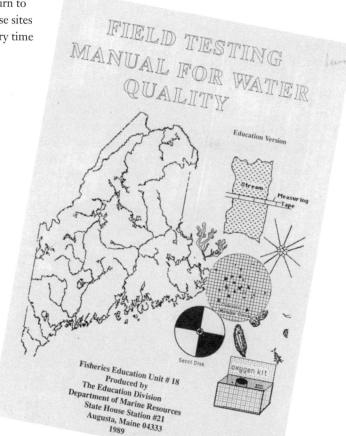

FIELD TESTING MANUAL FOR WATER QUALITY

Education Version

Fisheries Education Unit # 18
Produced by
The Education Division
Department of Marine Resources
State House Station #21
Augusta, Maine 04333
1989

Title: **Fish Banks Game, Ltd.**

Target Group: Grades 9-adult

Available from: Fish Banks, Ltd., Institute for Policy and Social Science Research (IPSSR)-Hood House, University of New Hampshire, Durham, NH 03824; telephone (603) 862-2186; fax (603) 862-1488

Cost: $100 per game kit, ($5 for each additional game disk), plus shipping and handling. For further information, an "Awareness" video is available for $5.

COMMENT

Fish Banks, Ltd. is a highly engaging interactive simulation about the fishing industry. Touted as "the game that changes the way your students think about management of natural resources, economics, and group problem-solving," and identified as an "exemplary educational program of the National Diffusion Network," Fish Banks is designed to teach students, in teams, about fisheries depletion, management strategies, negotiation, natural resource management, and group communication skills. Designed for either a Mac- or IBM-compatible computer, the entire program can be played over a 3-hour time frame or it can be played in individual segments. Six-hour training sessions are available (and advised in order to get the most out of this unique teaching tool) for high school and college teachers and can be arranged for your school site; or you can attend one of the scheduled trainings offered all across the country. Training information and an introductory "Awareness" video are available when you order your "game kit." Materials include the program, a game board, wooden ships, fish money, and administrator's and materials manuals which help explain and initiate the game. Fish Banks is a fun—and meaningful—computer game for our vid-kid generation.

EXCERPTS

"No review can convey the involvement (should I say excitement?) of actually taking part in the ongoing and unfolding experience generated by this well-designed simulation."—*David Crookall, Editor of* Simulation and Games, *June, 1990*

"This computer-assisted simulation can be used with diverse groups of 6 to 40 students. Sessions have been conducted in 26 countries, with 15-year-old students in [the former] Soviet Georgia, environmental studies majors in many U.S. universities, and high school students across the country. All these groups find the game engrossing, though they naturally take different lessons away from their sessions.

Fish Banks is used by high school and college teachers of science (environmental, biological, marine, life, earth), social studies, mathematics, economics, organizational management, ethics and business. Interdisciplinary teams find Fish Banks to be extremely valuable."—*Fish Banks, Ltd.*

Fish Banks, Ltd. Improves:
- Academic achievement, especially in understanding sustainable management of natural resources
- Communication, negotiation, and group problem-solving skills
- Reasoning and higher-order thinking skills
- Motivation to use environmental resources sustainably
—*Fish Banks, Ltd.*

"The National Diffusion Network is a program of the U.S. Department of Education. It supports nationwide dissemination of locally developed rigorously evaluated, exemplary educational programs."

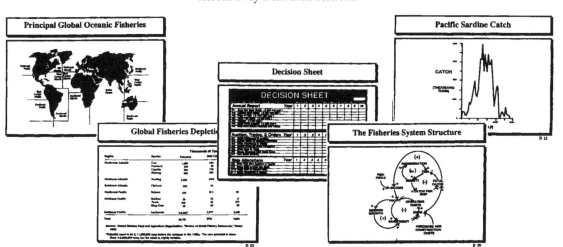

A comprehensive set of transparency masters is provided for introducing and debriefing the game

110

Title: Exploring Limits: Making Decisions About the Use and Development of Maine's Islands

Target: General audience

Available from: The Island Institute, 60 Ocean Street, Rockland, ME 04841; telephone (207) 594-9209; fax (207) 594-9314. Maine Coastal Program, Maine State Planning Office, Station 38, Augusta, ME 04333-0038; telephone (207) 287-3261; fax (207) 287-6489

Cost: Free

COMMENT

If you have heard of the Island Institute, you probably appreciate the extensiveness of their work with Maine island communities. Written in collaboration with the Maine Coastal Program at the Maine State Planning Office as part of the larger Islands Project, *Exploring Limits* illuminates their shared commitment to the people and the environments of island communities. In three chapters and five appendices, *Exploring Limits* introduces the premise that islands have limits simply because they are islands, and goes on to discuss six limiting factors of island living in detail: groundwater, social experience, vegetation and soil resiliency, nesting habitat, and scenic quality. The last chapter proposes a "comprehensive island management strategy" to be used by island planners in an effort to identify the issues that impact individual islands and their natural resources. Though *Exploring Limits* is intended to be a handbook, it is much more than a how-to manual. This well-researched document points to the universal need to create economic and environmental balance in our communities—islands or no islands—in order to sustain them.

EXCERPTS

"*Exploring Limits: Making Decisions About the Use and Development of Maine Islands* is intended to be both a primer on understanding the limits on use and development of islands and a how-to guide for assessing certain elements that make up an island's carrying capacity. We hope the publication will be interesting for people who haven't thought much about the limits of an island's natural resources, and useful for those who are working to assure that critical island resources are adequately protected as islands are used and developed."—*The Island Institute and Maine State Planning Office*, Exploring Limits: Making Decisions About the Use and Development of Maine Islands

"From a planning standpoint, islands accentuate limits because the amount of land is finite, and other natural resources can be depleted. Uses can conflict quickly, more so than on the mainland. Runoff from a poorly placed septic system can pollute the clamflats on which islanders are economically dependent. A leaking landfill can contaminate the drinking water for the entire island. Skyrocketing real-estate prices can drive working islanders off the island. Intensive recreational use of an uninhabited island can destroy vegetation or disrupt nesting seabirds. On islands, once a limit is exceeded, the damage is often irreversible." —*Maine State Planning Office and The Island Institute*, Exploring Limits

Island Institute

"The approach suggested in this handbook is quantitative, to the extent that "rules of thumb" are available to help establish limits for growth....Islanders, island owners, and policy makers for the offshore islands need to understand the implications of policy choices they make and decide on a case-by-case situation how much change is ultimately acceptable.

Empowerment of islanders, island owners, and others with jurisdiction over islands comes from having the courage to suggest that an island has quantifiable limits to growth, and the patience to engage in the process of determining what these limits may be. The consequences of failing to recognize these limits will irrevocably and unnecessarily change the islands as we now know them."
—*Maine State Planning Office and The Island Institute*, Exploring Limits

It's Time to Act!

Those qualities that typify island life often work against planning for their protection. The continuing accommodation to weather, the reliance on boat travel, the enduring nature of their island's rockbound shore tempt year-round island residents to believe that human impacts are insignificant in comparison to the forces of nature. The sense of isolation, proximity to wildlife, and the relative quaintness of island communities lull summer visitors into a false sense of security that their island will never change. However, to be complacent about the future of the islands will put them at risk; island wildlife, water supplies, environmental quality and community character are subject to limits rarely experienced on the mainland.

Christopher Ayres

It is the responsibility of all—residents, visitors, municipal, state and federal officials—to exercise stewardship of Maine's islands. With this book as a guide, those concerned about the future of the islands can begin to lay the foundation for protecting the qualities that make Maine's islands special places to live, work, or visit."—*Maine State Planning Office and The Island Institute*, Exploring Limits

Available from the Maine Coastal Program:

Waterways
Charting our Course
The Estuary Book
Coastlinks
Gulf of Maine Watershed Map
"A Guide to Local Planning and Regulation of Offshore Islands, Including Model Ordinances"

Available from the Island Institute:

The Gulf of Maine Environmental Atlas
The Island Journal
The Inter-Island News
The Working Waterfront
"Island Institute Publications: A comprehensive list of articles and reports published by the Island Institute"
Island conferences and workshops
Educational projects for island schools

"Both the charm and the challenge of island living are imposed by the island's distinct geographical boundaries."
—*The Island Institute*

Crouched hard on granite, facing a weathered sea, I breathe as slow as rock.

Harbor is one way to look; but voyages wash my eye, and old tides rock my butt.

Gulls root on the ledge, taught by every wind how spruces tug; snails

hug the tideline, hulls on their own horizon: bound as I am to the very edge.
—*Philip Booth*, Relations: Selected Poems 1950-1985

112

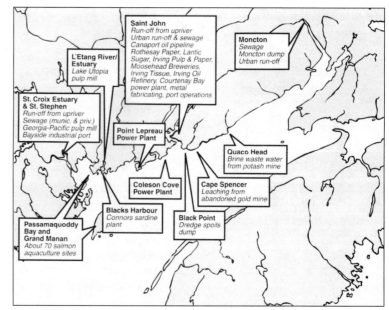

K. Matthews

Title: **Turning the Tide: A Citizens' Guide to the Bay of Fundy**

Target: General audience

Available from: The Conservation Council of New Brunswick, 180 St. John Street, Fredericton, NB, Canada E3B 4A9; telephone (506) 458-8747; fax (506) 458-1047

Cost: Free

COMMENT

"The Conservation Council, founded in 1969, is one of New Brunswick's leading environmental education and action organizations....CCNB is an independent voice for the environment. The Conservation Council promotes ecological awareness and promotes responsible solutions to our environmental problems."

Turning the Tide is a fascinating, comprehensive, and eminently readable source of information on the Bay of Fundy and the need for environmental action to protect its unique natural environment. Besides providing background materials on the status of resources around the Bay, the guide presents anecdotes—sometimes disturbing—from knowing individuals steeped in the Bay's history and lore. The last two chapters of the book describe an action plan for saving the region's resources (complete with information on what is already being done and who is doing it, and a list of potential protection sites), plus a section on the laws and mandates affecting the Bay of Fundy environment. This guide is thorough and specific in describing the resource qualities the Bay of Fundy possesses, and it also clearly illustrates the potential for destruction in light of the Bay's magnificent resources. *Turning the Tide* makes a strong case indeed for community action—a loud and poignant cry for anyone with a heart and mind for protecting this region.

"Levels of mercury contamination in striped bass in the St. John River are almost five times higher than what is considered acceptable for human consumption. According to recent studies, harbour porpoises in Passamaquoddy Bay and around Grand Manan carry five times more DDT and three times more PCBs than the beluga whales in the St. Lawrence River....

This persistent pollution destroys livelihoods, damages and kills marine life and puts people's health at risk. The greatest barrier to solving the problem is the old attitude, still common today, that the Bay of Fundy's giant tides will take care of whatever we dump into it. Based on even the limited information we have on the effects of pollution, we know this is not true."
—*Janice Harvey*, Turning the Tide: A Citizens' Guide to the Bay of Fundy, *The Conservation Council of New Brunswick*

EXCERPTS

"If the bay can't support fish, it won't be able to support other life and activity dependent on it. Whales, dolphins, sea and shore birds, aquaculture operations, tourism, recreational fishing—all of these will disappear along with the fishing industry. If we allow this to happen, then ultimately we have given up on ourselves.

There is a way out. It's common sense. If we take care of the fish, of where they live and what they eat, they will recover and our coastal communities will recover.

We all want to ensure that the Bay of Fundy continues to provide for the critical needs of marine mammals, sea and shorebirds and fish. Our future is bound up in theirs. Sadly, we often dismiss the small impacts human activity may have on the bay's ability to do this.

What we often do not see is the combined effect, over so many years, of all these minor actions. It is time to take stock and determine the limits we must put on our activities in order to allow the Bay of Fundy to function as a healthy marine ecosystem.

The problems created when humans and marine species interact are complex and may have serious economic implications. Solutions must be found that allow coastal communities to continue to draw their wealth from the bay while not endangering its nonhuman residents. This will require patience, goodwill, commitment and an understanding that all the parts must be in place if the system is to function well.

Major sources of pollution affecting the Bay of Fundy.

The first step in this journey is to develop a better understanding of the Bay of Fundy as a marine ecosystem, the interdependence of plant and animal life in the bay and the impact of human activity on that natural relationship."
—*Janice Harvey,* Turning the Tide: A Citizens' Guide to the Bay of Fundy, *The Conservation Council of New Brunswick*

"The general decline in environmental quality in the Bay of Fundy is having even more subtle effects on our communities and economies. An exact cause and effect relationship is rarely possible. However, the gradual yet dramatic decline in fisheries from the head of the bay to the mouth must be seen in the context of 150 years of treating the Fundy tides as a flush toilet, among other abuses.

To rehabilitate the fisheries of Bay of Fundy, and to maintain our economy based on the bay, we must stop treating the bay as an aquatic dumping ground for human and industrial wastes. We must also understand that a decision to continue polluting is a decision to place in further jeopardy the livelihoods of those who harvest marine resources. It reduces our choices for future development. It pushes already vulnerable marine species and ecological functions closer to the edge of collapse. In sum, it sentences Bay of Fundy communities to a future of cultural, social, recreational, and economic decline."
—*Janice Harvey,* Turning the Tide: A Citizens' Guide to the Bay of Fundy, *The Conservation Council of New Brunswick*

Title: FishNET: Fisheries Conservation Education Network

Target: Elementary and secondary school teachers, students; fisheries organizations; coastal community residents

Available from: QLF Atlantic Center for the Environment, 55 South Main Street, Ipswich, MA 01938; telephone (508) 356-0038; fax (508) 356-7322

Cost: Contact Julie Early for information on FishNET programs or for information on how to become involved.

COMMENT

"QLF is a nonprofit organization incorporated in both Canada and the United States. It was founded in 1963 to promote the natural and cultural heritage of eastern Canada and northern New England. QLF's environmental division, the Atlantic Center for the Environment, advances science literacy through environmental education, wildlife research, technical assistance, leadership development and international programs."

FishNET is a community-based marine science and education program in the Gulf of Maine region, produced by the QLF/Atlantic Center for the Environment (based in Ipswich, MA). Activities include development of interdisciplinary marine science programs for elementary and secondary schools; science literacy outreach and mentoring programs; technical assistance for community development organizations; and creation of a binational network of professionals working on fisheries-related issues. Founded in 1993, FishNET was developed in order "to address the environmental, social and economic impacts of declining groundfish stocks on fishing communities of coastal New England and eastern Canada." In just two years, this innovative project has made major strides in identifying the concerns of fishing communities and their inhabitants, and has created a forum for important discussions, education, and research to take place, making significant positive impacts on the quality of life for all who live and work in the Gulf region.

EXCERPTS

The goals of FishNET are:
- To improve communication and understanding among scientists, fishers, and conservationists;
- To foster a bioregional outlook on fisheries resources; and
- To support families affected by the fisheries crisis.

FishNET achieves these goals by providing:
- Professional skills development and training;
- Marine trades and marine science education; and
- Local, regional,and international exchanges.

Some of the projects implemeted by FishNET include:
- Career-oriented marine trades course at Shead High School in Eastport, ME
- Storytelling and drama program for students of West Parish Elementary School, Gloucester, MA
- Marine Science field course at Chatham Junior-Senior High School
- Summer experimental oceanography program for secondary school students in Cartwright, Rigolet, and Makkovik, Labrador
- Development of a computer-based and field-oriented tidal pool unit for 7th and 8th grade students at Beatrice Rafferty Middle School in Pleasant Point, Maine —*adapted from FishNET information brochure*

Since use of the pesticide DDT was banned in the 1970s, the osprey population of the Gulf has increased. Bald eagles are also re-establishing themselves, especially in the Passamaquoddy Bay area.—*Gulf of Maine Council on the Marine Environment*

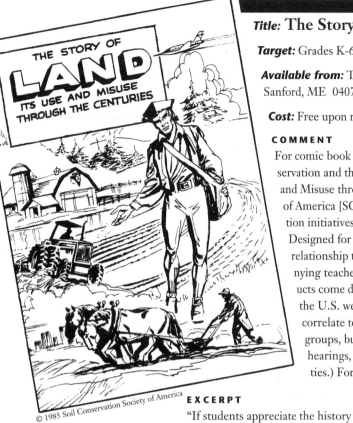

© 1985 Soil Conservation Society of America

Title: **The Story of Land Book and Teacher's Guide**

Target: Grades K-6

Available from: The York County Soil and Water Conservation District, 160 Cottage Street, Sanford, ME 04073; telephone (207) 324-7015; fax (207) 324-4359

Cost: Free upon request, plus postage

COMMENT

For comic book afficionados, young and old, this inventive approach to teaching about land conservation and the preservation of natural resources will have appeal. "The Story of Land, its Use and Misuse through the Centuries," published with a grant from the Soil Conservation Society of America [SCSA] in Iowa, deals with the history of land use, farming, and current conservation initiatives and issues in North America.

Designed for grades K-6, this packet of material addresses children's understanding of their relationship to the land and its future. Objectives for students are listed in the short accompanying teacher's guide. Students will learn what's important in making fertile soil; what products come directly and indirectly from farmed crops; who the key early conservationists in the U.S. were; and what actions affect land use in local communities. Most of the objectives correlate to activities described in the teacher's guide; some seem appropriate for younger groups, but most are geared for older students (vocabulary games, mock conservation hearings, research projects, and identifying local land-use issues in their own communities.) For a short unit on a huge topic, there is a lot to work with here.

EXCERPT

"If students appreciate the history of resource conservation and those who shaped it, they will better understand what is now going on in their own communities and how human action, or the lack of it, will affect the future of that community. [These activities are] designed to help students realize that each new event has a cause and exercises a future effect— that events have three dimensions—THEN (cause), NOW (action or lack of), and TOMORROW (effect).—*SCSA*

...The care of the earth is our most ancient and most worthy and, after all, our most pleasing responsibility. To cherish what remains of it, and to foster its renewal, is our only legitimate hope.—Wendell Berry, The Unsettling of America: Culture and Agriculture

Title: **The Casco Bay Estuary Project Water Quality Fact Sheets**

Target Group: General public, homeowners

Available from: The Casco Bay Estuary Project, 312 Canco Road, Portland, ME 04103; telephone (207) 828-1043; fax (207) 828-4001

Cost: Free

COMMENT

A series of fact sheets available from the Casco Bay Estuary Project cover water-quality issues within the watershed. "Nonpoint Source Pollution," geared for high-school-age and general readers, addresses the causes and effects of nonpoint source pollution and recommends strategies to reduce it. A second sheet, "A Clean Bay Begins at Home," discusses many ways that homeowners can reduce pollution by changing simple day-to-day habits: install low-flow toilets and shower heads to reduce your use of water; use a mixture of liquid castille soap and baking soda or Borax for an all-purpose cleaner; use compost and mulch in your garden instead of chemical fertilizers. Several other practical and easy alternatives to the dangerous flow of household chemicals into our water supplies are listed. Both sheets are worth reading and considering carefully: post them on the refrigerator door or somewhere where you can refer to them often. (See page 22 for information on the project's poster of the Casco Bay watershed region.)

C. Michael Lewis

EXCERPTS

Cars: Moving Oil Spills

"Just driving in your car produces hazardous wastes that can end up in the Bay. Burning gasoline and other fossil fuels produces toxic chemicals known as petroleum aromatic hydrocarbons (PAHs) which are released into the air with automobile exhaust, and deposited onto Bay waters. PAHs are also carried by runoff from roads and parking lots into the marine environment by nearby streams and rivers or through storm drains.

Products you use to maintain and clean your car can also produce hazardous waste. For example, every year Americans who change their own motor oil improperly dispose of an estimated 175 million gallons—roughly the amount contained in ten *Valdez* oil tanker spills. It takes just one quart of used oil to foul the taste of 250,000 gallons of water."—*The Casco Bay Estuary Project*

"You may not realize how your daily activities add to coastal pollution. How you maintain your septic system, clean your bathroom and kitchen, and fertilize your lawn can pollute Casco Bay or the lakes, rivers, and streams that eventually flow into it. Coastal pollution means lost jobs, inedible shellfish, closed beaches, and less wildlife. The good news is that you can do a lot to reduce pollution by changing your household habits today."—*The Casco Bay Estuary Project*

"The mission of the Casco Bay Estuary Project is to preserve the ecological integrity of Casco Bay and ensure the compatible human uses of the Bay's resources through public stewardship and effective management."—*The Casco Bay Estuary Project*

We need to develop an ethic of place. It is premised on a sense of place, the recognition that our species thrives on the subtle, intangible, but soul-deep mix of landscape, smells, sounds, history, schools, storefronts, neighbors, and friends that constitute a place, a homeland. An ethic of place respects equally the people of a region and the land, animals, vegetation, water, and air....An ethic of place ought to be a shared community value and ought to manifest itself in a dogged determination to treat the environment and its people as equals, to recognize both as sacred, and to insure that all members of the community not just search for, but insist upon solutions that fulfill the ethic. —*Charles Wilkinson*, Eagle Bird. *New York: Vintage Press, 1993, pp. 137-138*

116

Title: Waterways: Links to the Sea—An Activity Guide for Grades 3-5 Teachers on Cleaning Up Coastal Waters

Target Group: Grades 3-5, teachers

Available from: Shore Stewards Partnership, Maine Coastal Program, Station 38, 184 State Street, Augusta ME, 04333-0038; telephone (207) 287-3261; fax (207) 287-6489

Cost: Free. "An Introduction to Waterways: Links to the Sea," a fifteen-minute companion video for students, is available on loan from the Shore Stewards Partnership.

COMMENT

This succinct and attractive 36 page book accomplishes a lot in a little space. Divided into two major sections—"Water On the Move" and "Cleaning Up Coastal Waters"—each activity includes a list of materials needed in class, a sequence of steps to follow (with tips for keeping things going smoothly), and "extension" ideas for taking the lessons farther afield. Activities in "Water on the Move" address the concept of a watershed, the water cycle, and the Gulf of Maine. "Cleaning Up Coastal Waters" teaches about sources of pollution threatening the Gulf and actions students can undertake to reduce water pollution.

Activities in *Waterways* have been designed for use either in sequence or individually as self-contained units. The book is illustrated with black and white drawings, and individual pages (like the "Home Water Use Inventory Sheet") are easily reproducible for hand-outs. Appendices list additional reading; a compilation of other water quality-related resources such as videos, annual coastal/marine events, field programs, and teacher workshops; and a glossary of words related to water ecology that we should all add to our vocabulary.

> "Point sources of pollution, visible discharge pipes that are usually regulated, include sewage treatment plants, paper mills, industrial waste pipes and oil terminals.
>
> Nonpoint source pollution is runoff that does not come from a discharge pipe or visible 'point' source. It may include soot, dust, oil, animal waste, litter, sand, salt and chemicals from everyday sources that are difficult to identify and locate. Activities like fertilizing lawns, walking pets, changing motor oil and driving all contribute to nonpoint source pollution: with each rainfall, pollutants are washed from lawns and streets into stormwater drains and groundwater, eventually reaching the ocean."
> —*Shore Stewards Partnership*, Waterways: Links to the Sea

Jon Luoma

EXCERPTS

"This guide is a resource for those who teach Maine's youngest 'Shore Stewards.' While there are many excellent marine science curricula for grade school students...there are few activities that discuss the effects of human actions on coastal ecosystems...The guide is intended primarily for teachers of grades 3-5, but can be used (with some adaptations) by instructors of younger age groups. (A similar guide for grades 6-12, *Charting Our Course*, is available through the Maine Coastal Program).—*Shore Stewards Partnership*, "*Introduction,*" Waterways: Links to the Sea

"For centuries, people saw the sea as a 'bottomless pit,' an ideal dumping ground. Since the ocean covers nearly three-fourths of our world, people assumed that materials dumped into coastal waters would be diluted or dispersed. This belief that the 'solution to pollution is dilution' has been shattered in recent years. We have seen declines in fish and shellfish populations, mysterious die-offs among marine mammals, and growing concerns about water pollution threatening human health."—*Shore Stewards Partnership*, Waterways: Links to the Sea

A sample activity from "Part One: Water on the Move..."
Watersheds—Links to the Gulf

Summary: In this activity, a model will be used to demonstrate the watershed concept....

Materials: Aluminum foil (or newspaper covered by plastic); large rectangular pan or basin (or a child's swimming pool for a larger model); wooden blocks or bricks; water and watering can with "shower spout" or several small paper cups with holes punched in the bottom (note: test prepared cups to be certain that surface tension of water does not prevent flow through holes); and a map (a laminated map will last longer).

Procedure:
- Introduce the class to the idea of a watershed... Stress the fact that by living in the Gulf of Maine watershed, we are all connected to the Gulf—even if we seem to live far away from the coast. All of the water bodies students described in "At Home With Water" [earlier activity] are ultimately linked to the Gulf.
- Using a map of your county...locate your community and the major bodies of water in your area. Discuss the idea of **tributaries** [explained in the Glossary], and find which smaller streams and rivers flow into a major river in your area...

Highlight all these streams and wetlands and draw a line around what you and your students think are the boundaries of that river's watershed. Ask students: what is the body of water nearest to your school? Where is its water source and how does it reach the Gulf?

- To illustrate the watershed concept, work with students to create a model. Tear off a piece of aluminum foil that is slightly larger than the pan. Crumple the foil to make dips and gullies to represent stream and river beds (you can also use crumpled newspaper with plastic covering it). At one end of the foil, form a larger basin or pocket—this will be the "Gulf" and will collect water that runs from the tributaries. Place blocks in the corners at the other end of the pan to make hills by shaping the foil over the blocks. Make a valley between the hills, and raise this end of the pan a bit higher than the end with the "Gulf." Explain to the class what the model represents, noting that higher elevation or bumps in the foil are land areas, while cracks and dips are bodies of water.
- Students can then make it "rain" with the cups filled with water, or you can produce "rain" using the watering can. Observe how the water runs off of the land, into the tributaries, and eventually into the bay.

Keep this model: it will be used to complement other activities in this guide. If desired, a permanent display can be made using plaster of Paris.

—adapted from Shore Stewards Partnership, Waterways: Links to the Sea

Jon Luoma

The Shore Stewards Partnership at the Maine State Planning Office brings together citizen volunteers, educators, policy makers and scientists in an effort to help Maine's coastal communities reduce marine pollution and protect coastal waters. The Shore Stewards Partnership uses a unique combination of financial, technical and organizational contributions from state government, the university system, and private philanthropy to offer assistance to local groups. The Partnership supports local water quality initiatives through an information clearinghouse, a quarterly newsletter, regional workshops, educational materials, technical support for local water-quality monitoring groups and two local grant programs. **For more information contact the Shore Stewards Partnership at (207) 287–3261.**

118

Title: Aquaculture in Maine Booklet

Target: General audience, high school, and college

Available from: University of Maine Sea Grant Communications, 22 Coburn Hall, University of Maine, Orono, ME 04469; telephone, (207) 581-1440; fax (207) 581-1423. Maine Aquaculture Innovation Center, 141 North Main Street, Suite 203, Brewer, ME 04412; telephone (207) 989-5310. Maine Aquaculture Association, PO Box 535, Damariscotta, ME 04543; telephone (207) 563-1456

Cost: Free

COMMENT

Developed jointly by the University of Maine Sea Grant Program and the Maine Aquaculture Innovation Center, this 34 page booklet provides information on aquatic species cultured in Maine. It describes steps for getting started in aquaculture, including site selection and leasing regulations, and shipping and marketing strategies. It also includes a directory of Maine producers, suppliers, government agencies, aquaculture associations and consultants, business development and funding agencies, and educational and professional development programs. Useful information for the entrepreneur with a yen for exploring sustainable resources.

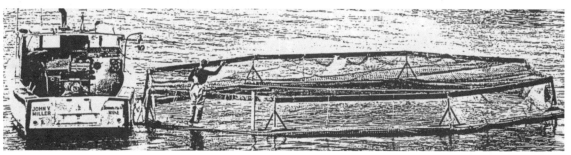

EXCERPTS
What is Aquaculture?

Aquaculture is the controlled cultivation and harvest of aquatic plants and animals and offers the possibility of expanding domestic supplies, thereby reducing fishery product imports in the United States, which now total over two and half billion dollars.

Is the Maine Coast Suitable for Aquaculture?

According to University of Maine marine economist James Wilson, the physical circumstances of the Maine coast (high tides, a heavy nutrient load, and protected embayments) are nearly ideal for culturing seafood, and with the exception of Alaska, the most extensive resource of this kind in the United States.

What Are Some of the Specific Problems Facing Maine's Aquaculture Industry?

Current constraints on the industry include seed availability; hatchery technology; mechanization of cleaning, growing, and fouling control; site selection for hatchery, nursery, and grow-out operations; overwintering methods and storage; automation in harvest and processing equipment; storage facilities; disease and pollution control; red tide monitoring, prevention, and controls; and improved growth rate and winter-hardy stock development.
—*University of Maine Sea Grant College Program*, Aquaculture in Maine, *1989*

"How will Maine's seafood industry differ by the year 2000? Perhaps the most startling changes will occur within the aquaculture sector. By the end of the century, farmed fish and shellfish will represent over 50 percent of the value of all seafood products...

While farm-raised products will never replace wild harvests, by the year 2000 the culture of aquatic species will transform a hunting/gathering approach to fisheries into an investment/management approach using husbandry of marine animals as the basis for predictable landings.

Presently over 15 percent of total fish and shellfish landings in the United States are farm-raised. However, since seafood consumption has risen more than 25 percent in the last five years, supply has continued to lag behind demand. Over half the seafood now eaten in this country is imported. Excluding petroleum products, seafood imports account for 28 percent of our annual trade deficit. As demand for seafood continues to increase and wild stocks level off or decline, aquaculture offers the only alternative to imports."
—*University of Maine Sea Grant College Program*, "Introduction," Aquaculture in Maine

Title: **The Chewonki Foundation Natural History Outreach Programs: "Too Much Trash?" and "Rhythms of Farm Life"**

Target Group: Grades 4-5 (Too Much Trash!); K-5 (Rhythms of Farm Life)

Available from: The Chewonki Foundation, RR2, Box 1200, Wiscasset, ME 04578; telephone (207) 882-7323; fax (207) 882-4074

Cost: One presentation $85; two presentations $170; three presentations $240; four presentations $300; each additional presentation $75; plus transportation costs at $.25 per mile from Wiscasset.

COMMENT

Like Chewonki's other outreach programs these natural history lessons provide children of all ages with dynamic hands-on learning experiences both in and out of the classroom. These two programs emphasize human use of resources and examine how we can do more to conserve. Each program is distinct, presented by trained staff in small groups fostering lots of participation, problem-solving discussions, and valuable time for reflection. While the recycling program ("Too Much Trash!") can be offered at any suitable location, the "Farm Life" program is presented at Chewonki's own small farm and provides a unique experience in observing and participating in the daily rhythms of life on a working farm. Both experiences are important lessons in taking and sharing responsibility for the conservation of our resources. For descriptions of other Chewonki outreach programs, see pages 37 and 82.

Josephine Ewing

EXCERPTS

Too Much Trash!

Choices that we make in our everyday lives effect the amount and types of trash we produce. We explore the concepts related to recycling, composting and the reuse of durable products.
Through several activities, students develop personal, meaningful strategies to reduce their contribution to the waste stream and they are encouraged to implement their own personal action plan.—*The Chewonki Foundation, Natural History Lessons program description*

The Rhythms of Farm Life: A field trip to the farm

The site for this introduction to farming principles is Chewonki's small, diversified, saltwater farm. The visit includes a tour of the woodlot, the vegetable garden, composting center, and animal barn to demonstrate the cyclical patterns of our farm. Seasonal tasks, such as sheep shearing, may be demonstrated. All students have an opportunity to make butter from the farm's cream.—*The Chewonki Foundation, Natural History Lessons program description*

"Environmental issues and natural history are a part of all our lives. When the world gathered in June 1992 in Brazil to address the plight of endangered species, a forecast of dwindling resources, and the effect of human society on the global climate, it was the single largest conference in the history of humankind. We believe that environmental ethics are learned, and that group problem-solving is central to the lesson. The programs presented here may help you as a parent, teacher, camp director, librarian, or business manager to enhance the environmental literacy of your children, students, or peers.—*The Chewonki Foundation*

"The naturalist, ornithologist and painter, Roger Tory Peterson, directed the nature study program at Chewonki in the late 1920s and early 1930s, and he wrote the first edition of A Field Guide to the Birds while at Chewonki. That legacy of nature and conservation study remains at the heart of all that we do at Chewonki."—*The Chewonki Foundation*

120

Title: The Penobscot: A Moving Experience

Target Group: Grades K-12

Available from: Penobscot River and Bay Institute, Box 214A, Brooksville ME 04617; telephone (207) 326-4822

Cost: Contact for further information

COMMENT

Developed in conjunction with the Penobscot Riverkeepers 2000 1994 Expedition, "Teachers on the River" Program, *The Penobscot: A Moving Experience* curriculum focuses on the theme of river transportation in past, present and future. As a result, students are encouraged to think about a host of issues related to the watershed. As part of the multidisciplinary curriculum, several different handouts are provided in an activity packet sent out to participating classrooms for use before, during and after the teacher's experience on the river. Pre- and post-trip activities are suggested and lessons for the class to take part in with their substitute teacher (provided by the program while their own teacher is out on the river) are included. Curriculum materials also include a follow-up unit on the several ways that transportation affects the river, allowing for more long-term involvement with sustainability, stewardship, and community issues. Particular emphasis is placed on the Adopt-River-Connections (ARC) projects as described in the ARC Handbook (see p. 103). This group has developed an innovative and creative way to teach stewardship and responsibility by directly involving and inspiring teachers.

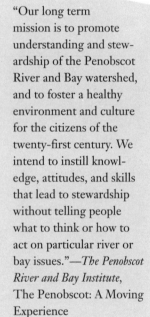

"Our long term mission is to promote understanding and stewardship of the Penobscot River and Bay watershed, and to foster a healthy environment and culture for the citizens of the twenty-first century. We intend to instill knowledge, attitudes, and skills that lead to stewardship without telling people what to think or how to act on particular river or bay issues."—*The Penobscot River and Bay Institute*, The Penobscot: A Moving Experience

EXCERPTS
To Build a Boat Launch?

• After presenting information on the river's past and present, have students participate in the simulation entitled "To Build a Boat Launch?" In this simulation, students represent various interests before a public hearing for a proposed boat launch. Every class member is assigned a specific role, such as fisherman, dam owner, farmer, powerboater, canoeist, etc. Each is expected to act out his or her role and try to sway a local planning board vote.

• With the whole class, write a news article on the "new" way their river is going to be used (a new wildlife refuge, a power plant/dam, an industrial plant, etc.) Have students write individual letters to the editor in response to the article.

• Follow a log from stump to plank. Students could research the process from growing the tree, to felling it, getting it to the mill, milling it, marketing it, and finally, using it. Or go at it mathematically, either finding out how long the total process takes, or how much money is generated in the process.

• For younger children, role play. When they enter the classroom for the "Teacher on the River" day, have them step back in time. They can spend the day as Native Americans, lumberjacks, early settlers, etc.

—*Penobscot River and Bay Institute*, The Penobscot: A Moving Experience

Some Stewardship Advice
—*from The Penobscot River and Bay Institute:*

• Before undertaking stewardship action, assess the situation to determine if the action is wise, appropriate and worth doing. Use various methods of citizen action such as persuasion, consumer action, political action, legal action, and eco-management. Finally, evaluate the effectiveness of the actions you take.

• Avoid superficiality. Be honest, responsible, and thorough in your gathering and assessment of information. Explore alternative actions. Consider legal, social, and economic consequences. Do you have the time, skills resources, and courage to take the action you are considering?

• Respect, listen to, and tolerate other people's points of view. Humility and generosity towards others will help communications and can lead to interactive problem solving.

• Avoid propagandizing and the inappropriate use of children to that end.

121

Title: For Your Lake's Sake Information Pamphlet

Target: General audience, waterfront homeowners

Available from: The York County Soil and Water Conservation District, 160 Cottage Street, Sanford, ME 04073; telephone (207) 324-7015; fax (207) 324-4539

Cost: Free upon request, plus postage

COMMENT

This pamphlet folds out to a small poster and is packed with information on steps to conserve the quality of water in the lakes of our Gulf of Maine region. One side describes phosphorous—where it comes from, and how badly it can harm our waters. The other side includes a respectable list of do's and don'ts for anyone—homeowner or not— interested in preserving the pristine quality of lake waters. Anyone who owns lakefront property, however, may want to take particular heed of this pamphlet; it's practical, informative, and serves as an effective reminder of where the responsibility for protecting our resources lies. Post this pamphlet on a kitchen wall, the refrigerator door, in the laundry room, garage, or the tool shed. You may even want to keep a few extras around to share with friends.

EXCERPTS

"Residential homes introduce new substances into a watershed, many of which degrade water quality. In a developed watershed, water picks up salt, oil, gas, and lead from roads; pesticides and fertilizers from home gardens and landscaping; effluent from septic systems; and substances disposed of on the ground by homeowners."—*The York County Soil and Water Conservation District*

"Pristine lake waters add beauty and diversity to the landscape… These waters are one of Maine's prime resources, and it is in our best interest to protect them. We must all assume responsibility for maintaining water quality by breaking old habits and taking positive actions which will limit the amount of phosphorous and other contaminants which reach the lakes. This pamphlet explains how lakes are affected by land use and explains how homeowners can protect water quality for their own future and for generations to come."—*The York County Soil and Water Conservation District*

Lakeshore activities requiring a DEP permit

- Dredging or filling below the normal high-water line or on adjacent land such that material might be washed into Great Ponds.
- Construction or repairing permanent structures below the normal high-water line (including piers, docks, retaining walls, etc.)

Shoreland Zoning

- All nonwater dependent uses must meet shoreland setback requirements.
- Decks and additions must meet shoreland setback requirements
- A buffer strip of vegetation must be retained between a new use and the normal high-water mark, except for a maximum opening 30 feet wide for every 100 feet of shoreline.

See your local shoreland ordinance for other land use standards in the Shoreland Zone.
—*The York County Soil and Water Conservation District, "For Your Lake's Sake"*

Once polluted, recovery of a lake is extremely slow. Unlike rivers and streams, lakes are slow to exchange their water, and the amount of phosphorous entering a lake from its watershed remains relatively constant."—The York County Soil and Water Conservation District

122

Manomet Observatory is an independent, nonprofit institution. Conservation Sciences Quarterly is published by Manomet four times a year and is available to members. For membership information, contact the Manomet development office at (508) 224-6521.

Title: Taking Stock of Our Fisheries: The Groundfish Crisis in the Gulf of Maine

Target: High school teachers

Available from: Manomet Observatory for Conservation Sciences, PO Box 1770, Manomet, MA 02345; telephone (508) 224-6521; fax (508) 224-9220

Cost: Free, plus $3 shipping and handling, as long as materials last

COMMENT

Developed in response to the growing concern about the status of natural resources in the Gulf of Maine, *Taking Stock of Our Fisheries* brings the issue of fisheries depletion and "mismanagement," to the classroom to inspire "input to this important natural resource rebate." Six chapters of readings, activity sheets, fact sheets, field trip and discussion suggestions cover topics such as historical and cultural perspectives of New England, the natural history and ecology of fisheries, fishing technology, natural resource management, suggestions for becoming involved in environmental issues, and a comprehensive list of additional resources (books, government documents, other teacher guides, magazine articles, videos and sea-going educational programs.) On the whole, this curriculum is a remarkable combination of teaching tools that will educate high-school students about the issues, providing opportunities for scientific and technical exploration as well as introducing students to the rigors of policy- and decision-making. Tackling these critical issues is both timely and urgent; by creating this important teacher guide, Manomet Observatory demonstrates its commitment to environmental education and to the "conservation of natural resources for the benefit of wildlife and human populations throughout the Americas"—reason enough for any teacher with an orientation towards our Gulf region to have a look at what this curriculum offers.

"New England communities need to work together to develop regional solutions to fishery issues. The solutions incorporate programs to protect the stocks on a long-term basis and to address the economic and social needs of communities. The challenge requires innovative ideas and a willingness to explore different ways of thinking."
—*Manomet Observatory for Conservation Sciences*, Taking Stock of our Fisheries: The Groundfish Crisis in the Gulf of Maine, 1994

EXCERPTS

"Manomet Observatory (MO) is a center for long-term environmental research and education. MO's studies improve understandings of wildlife populations and natural systems, and foster conservation action throughout the Americas.

MO's environmental education program focuses on improving science education in the schools. Special emphasis is placed on developing a citizenry that is concerned about the environment and that has the skills and commitment to work toward solutions to natural resource challenges."
—*Manomet Observatory for Conservation Sciences*, Taking Stock of our Fisheries: The Groundfish Crisis in the Gulf of Maine, 1994

"During the early to mid-1800s, New England's cod, herring, and mackerel fisheries accounted for 80 percent of the nation's $5 million catch of those species, with Massachusetts dominating the scene. It is estimated that 12,000 people earned their living as fishermen, with many more involved in support industries...

Today New England groundfish stocks are in crisis. What has happened to this renewable resource? In 1963, 55 percent of marine life in the Gulf of Maine were cod-like fish and 24 percent were skate and dogfish. In 1993, 11 percent are cod-like fish and 74 percent are skate and dogfish showing a cataclysmic change in species composition. The groundfish biomass of cod-like fish is so low, that it is not able to replenish itself to keep at a sustainable level; and yet our economy is built on it...

We all, whether we are fishermen or fish consumers, have an interest in maintaining healthy stocks of fish, as with all our natural resources. How do we as a society better manage our resources? We need to see that common resources are collectively owned by all of us, so that we become responsible stewards. We must be prepared to consider the consequences of poor management activities. Specifically, this means we need to better compute environmental costs (such as depletion or habitat destruction), take into account the benefits of resources and come up with better ways to measure the intrinsic values (such as aesthetic). Finally, we need to see that people are part of the natural system; therefore long-term management plans should include humans in the formula."—*Manomet Observatory for Conservation Sciences*, Taking Stock of our Fisheries: The Groundfish Crisis in the Gulf of Maine, 1994

Title: U.S. Coast Guard Marine Pollution Information Kit

Target Group: General audience, boatowners, oceanfront homeowners

Available from: U.S. Coast Guard Headquarters, Marine Environmental Protection Division, 2100 2nd St., Washington DC 20593; telephone (202) 267-0518

Cost: Free

COMMENT

Along with the U.S. Coast Guard's pamphlet stating their "commitment to environmental excellence," this information contains a placard to post on your boat citing dumping restrictions, posters with summaries of garbage, sewage, fuel and oil discharge laws, and suggestions for keeping the seas clean. A "Clean Water Notebook" lists pertinent questions and answers about the ecological impact of boat sewage discharge, and an enclosed coloring book for the younger set features the pollution-fighting fish, Officer Snook. A "How's the Water?" pamphlet folds out as a colorful promotional poster urging public involvement while listing agency numbers and addresses at the bottom. For boatowners, and anyone living or working close to the sea, this information kit is a must; for educators and anyone else concerned about the water quality of our oceans, this kit will inform you of our Coast Guard's tough stance on pollution control. You should know what they are up to and how it affects you.

EXCERPTS

"The Coast Guard is working aggressively in partnership with federal, state, and local agencies, environmental interest groups and private industry to provide for long-term environmental quality. Central to our environmental quality effort are the preservation of maritime biodiversity and the prevention of

degradation to the maritime ecosystem from land-based and sea-based activities...Our environmental program is multifaceted, focusing on marine emergency preparedness, transportation management, environmental law enforcement, and pollution response."—*U.S. Coast Guard,* A Commitment to Environmental Excellence

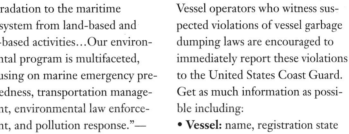

Vessel operators who witness suspected violations of vessel garbage dumping laws are encouraged to immediately report these violations to the United States Coast Guard. Get as much information as possible including:

- **Vessel:** name, registration state and number, country flag, characteristics, course and speed, approximate distance from land.
- **Location** of incident (GPS or Loran coordinates if possible), time, and date.
- **What was discharged?**
- **Witnesses** on your vessel and any other in the area.

Report illegal dumping directly to the National Response Center at 1-800-424 8802. If this is not possible, contact your local USCG station or Marine Safety Office via VHF channel 16. Talk with the duty officer.

Citizen report forms and information about the federal garbage dumping restrictions are available from: the **Center for Marine Conservation—pla., 1725 DeSales NW, Washington DC 20036; (202) 429-5609.**
—*excerpted from "MARPOL Garbage Dumping Restrictions" placards*

"What scientific proof exists that links boat sewage and health hazards?"

From a scientific point of view, the link between boat-waste discharge and harm to the general public's health is not absolutely proven. Circumstantial evidence, however, is very convincing and has led many state regulatory agencies to believe that boats directly contribute to the degradation of shellfish beds and swimming beaches. Furthermore, studies of our Great Bays...have identified numerous sources of 'nonpoint' pollution such as urban stormwater runoff, failing septic tank systems, and agriculturally applied toxins. Boat wastewater is just one of these, but together, nonpoint sources represent approximately half of the pollution entering our waterways."
—*excerpted from* Clean Water Notebook, *vol. 1, "Ecological Impact of Boat Sewage Discharge," Sealand Technology, Inc., Big Prairie, Ohio*

Title: **NOAA Marine Debris Information General Public Information Packet**

Target: General audience

Available from: NOAA Marine Debris Information Office, Center for Marine Conservation, 1725 DeSales St. NW., Washington DC 20036; telephone (202) 429-5609; fax (202) 872-0619

Cost: Free

DON'T TEACH YOUR TRASH TO SWIM!

COMMENT

NOAA's Marine Debris Information Office distributes information packets that include several brochures on the dangers of plastic pollutants (showing some photographs likely to stir and enrage your passions.) Packets also include a report on the Marine Plastic Pollution Research and Control Act of 1987 that prohibits dumping of plastics into the sea and restricts garbage dumping. A list of educational materials, publications, videos, and a newsletter entitled "Coastal Connection" is also included. Published by the Center for Marine Conservation, "Coastal Connection" advocates "beach cleanup events, Citizen Pollution Patrols, and other efforts to eliminate marine debris that injures wildlife, fouls our beaches, and threatens boater safety." Agency offices for the Center are located on both coasts (in Washington, DC and in San Francisco, CA)—a telling indication of the problem's scope. Addresses and numbers are provided in the kit for further information on this collaborative national and international effort.

EXCERPTS

"We hope these materials will help you better understand the marine debris issue while encouraging you to join us in an effort to combat pollution of the sea."
—*NOAA's Marine Debris Information Office*

"As we all work hard to guard our coastal environments against the damage caused by ocean-and land-based debris, we must keep in mind that we humans also benefit from cleanups, beyond the aesthetic value of clean beaches. By insuring the safety of our wildlife, we are taking a step to guarantee the preservation of nature's web, the network of interdependency upon which all beings depend for survival."—*The Center for Marine Conservation, "Coastal Connection," Fall, 1993*

George Antonelis

Marine scientists now consider plastic to be the most widespread human threat to marine species. The National Wildlife Federation estimates that, worldwide, over one million birds and 100,000 marine mammals die each year as a result of ingesting plastic, or becoming entangled in it. Birds can die after consuming various small plastic particles, mistaking them for crustaceans or fish eggs, their normal prey. The indigestible plastic then blocks their intestines, causing ulcers and—ultimately starvation. More than 50 of the 280 bird species known consume plastic. Turtles such as the endangered Loggerhead ingest plastic bags, mistaking them for jellyfish—one of their favorite foods. Marine mammals and fish also become entangled in plastics such as discarded fishing gear and six-pack yokes. Unable to move normally or feed, the entangled animals often die from exhaustion, exposure, or starvation.
—*Maine Coastal Program,* Charting our Course: An Activity Guide for Grades 6-12 on Water Quality in the Gulf of Maine

THE WILDGULF DIRECTORY OF RESOURCES

The *Wild Gulf Almanac* "Directory of Resources" on the following pages is included to further assist you in exploring the endless supply of educational resources pertaining to the Gulf of Maine. Because inevitable obstacles like time, peoplepower, and deadlines did not allow us to include all of the materials which we know to be available region-wide, we have tried to list as many of those names as possible in an attempt to include important individuals, agencies, programs and the like—all of whom make significant contributions to the preservation of our fragile Gulf environment.

The Directory started out as a simple appendix, the purpose of which was to supplement the resources written up in preceding chapters. What follows is the result of our recognizing that there is nothing simple at all about the volume of existing materials, programs, and groups of people dedicated to protecting this unique region. Compiled from a variety of sources including the Gulf of Maine Council on the Marine Environment's 1991 *Gulf-Links*, this section serves as a vital supplement to the *Almanac,* making it an even more thorough and informative document.

To find your way to specific listings, please note that the directory is organized first by category or type of listing (Databases and Computer Networks; Educational Organizations and Programs; Governmental Agencies; Media Resources; Museums and Aquariums; Nonprofit Organizations; Parks and Sanctuaries; Research Programs and Organizations; and Annual Events). Then, it is arranged by state or province (Maine, Massachusetts, New Hampshire, New Brunswick, Nova Scotia). Each entry lists the organization name, address, a contact person, phone and fax numbers, e-mail numbers where available and a short description or mission statement. At the end of the directory there is a page designated for your responses to and comments on the *Wild Gulf Almanac*.

In this inaugural issue, we see the *Wild Gulf Almanac* itself in fledgling form. The Directory must be seen as an indication of the possibilities for this publication in subsequent issues as we strive to make the *Almanac* more comprehensive and useful to all of you and always more beneficial to this beautiful place called the Gulf of Maine.

DATABASES AND COMPUTER NETWORKS

EcoNet

18 DeBoom Street
San Francisco, CA 94107
ph: 415-292-6717

An on-line global computer network that can be used to find information about environmental education programs and activities as well as information about specific environmental issues and events. An excellent avenue for communication with other people interested in environmental issues around the world. Basic charges plus user fees.

EE-Link

National Consortium for Environmental Education and Training
School of Natural Resources
University of Michigan
430 E. University Avenue
Ann Arbor, MI 48109-1115
ph: 313-998-6726
fax: 313-936-2195
e-mail: eelink@nceet.snre.umich.edu

An on-line source of environmental education information providing access to teaching resources and materials, articles, conference listings, literature, other databases, and grant information.

ERIC Clearinghouse for Science, Mathematics, and Environmental Education

1200 Chambers Road, Room 310
Columbus, OH 43212-1792
ph: 614-292-6717

The ERIC database contains information about environmental education materials available from a variety of sources. Many of the resources are available on microfiche. Contact ERIC for a free list of database locations for your state, a state-by-state list of environmental education coordinators, a list of environmental education publications available through ERIC, and basic information about how to use the system.

Global Rivers Environmental Education Network (GREEN)

GREEN Project
721 East Huron Street
Ann Arbor, MI 48104
ph: 313- 761-8142

A program designed to get kids in grades K-12 actively involved in helping to protect their local rivers. Participants monitor water quality and develop action plans to help cleanup local problems. In addition, kids are provided with opportunities to network with other students working on similar issues around the world.

Technical Education Research Center (TERC)

2067 Massachusetts Avenue
Cambridge, MA 02140
ph: 617-547-0430

TERC develops innovative programs in science, mathematics, and technology for schools and other learning environments. Recognized as the developers of the National Geographic Kids' Network for elementary-age students, TERC offers a Global Laboratory in which high school students can monitor local environmental quality and share data (in such areas as air pollution, global warming, and ozone depletion) with other schools and groups over telecommunications networks.

GAIN (Global Action and Information Network)

GAIN-Online
740 Front Street 355
Santa Cruz, CA 95060
ph: 408-457-0130
fax: 408-457-0133

National Geographic Kids Network

PO Box 98018
Washington, DC 20090-8018

Through software and communications, students help conduct original scientific research on real-world issues. Subscription fee of $115 includes eight weeks of access to the network, 120 minutes of telecommunications time; assistance to a research team; data analysis by a unit scientist; and announcements. Kit cost for each unit an additional $375. Units include "What's in Our Water" and "Weather in Action."

(Compiled with assistance from the *Teacher's Guide to World Resources*, The World Resources Institute, Washington, D.C.)

EDUCATIONAL ORGANIZATIONS AND PROGRAMS

Note: Many important educational opportunities and programs are offered by organizations and agencies listed under other headings.

Maine

Audubon Expedition Institute
PO Box 365
Belfast, ME 04915
contact: Anna McKim
ph: 207-338-5859
fax: 207-338-1037

Offers traveling college and graduate degree programs with study throughout North America (credit awarded through Lesley College). Degrees focus on Environmental Education with a deep ecological perspective.

Bates College
Department of Education
111 Bardwell St. #22
Lewiston, ME 04240
contact: Peter B. Corcoran, Ed.D.
ph: 207-786-6064
fax: 207-786-6123

The Department of Education at Bates College offers undergraduate courses in environmental education.

Bowdoin College Environmental Studies Program
Bowdoin College
Brunswick, ME 04011
contact: Becky Koulouris, Coordinator
ph: 207-725-3629

Offers a major B.A. program in Environmental Studies, a resource room containing environmental periodicals, an environmental lecture series and a marine research station.

Center for Marine Studies
5715 Coburn Hall #14
University of Maine
Orono, ME 04469-5715
contact: Robert Wall, Director
ph: 207-581-1435
fax: 207-581-1426
e-mail: robert_wall@voyager.umeres.maine.edu

Provides leadership in developing research programs, emphasizing the Gulf of Maine, its coastal zone and related cold-water regions.

The Chewonki Foundation
RR2, Box 1200
Wiscasset, ME 04578
contact: Don Hudson, Executive Director; Sarah Bright, *Wild Gulf Almanac* Editor
ph: 207-882-7323
fax: 207-882-4074
e-mail: chewonki@igc.apc.org

Provides educational experiences that foster understanding and appreciation of the natural world and emphasize collective effort. The 400-acre coastal campus offers residential environmental education programs for students in grades 5-12, Camp Chewonki, and Maine Coast Semester (for college-bound 11th graders). Natural history outreach programs are held in Maine schools and communities, and wilderness expeditions are run throughout the Northeast region. Publications include *Pathways to a Sustainable Future* (a waste management curriculum), the *Wild Gulf Almanac*, and a quarterly newsletter.

College of the Atlantic
105 Eden Street
Bar Harbor, ME 04609
contact: Carl Little, Director of Public Affairs
ph: 207-288-5015
fax: 207-288-4126
e-mail: ckl@ecology.coa.edu

COA offers a B.A. and M. Phil. in Human Ecology, which includes programs in marine and coastal studies, environmental policy, environmental design and environmental education. Other programs include a summer field studies program for K-12 students; summer field studies for teachers; an island research center on Petit Manan island; and a weekly summer lecture series on ecological topics. Faculty and staff are available to give talks on coastal ecology.

Eagle Hill Field Research Station
PO Box 9
Steuben, ME 04680
contact: Joerg-Henner Lotze, Director
ph: 207-546-2821
fax: 207-546-3042
e-mail: eagl@maine.maine.edu

Provides intensive, week-long seminars and workshops in natural history for scientists, teachers and naturalists. Publishes the Maine Naturalist, a quarterly journal with scientific research reports, general interest articles, and field notes (subscriptions $30/yr.).

Earthminders, Partners in Environmental Education
Department of Environmental Protection
Station 17
Augusta, ME 04333-0017
contact: Barbara Welch
ph: 207-287-7682

A coalition of organizations promoting environmental education in Maine, Earthminders produces resources for schools and community groups (such as the *Maine Environmental Education Matrix 1995: A Directory for Teachers*).

Environmental Studies Center
University of Maine
11 Coburn Hall
Orono, ME 04469
contact: Nick Houtman, Natural Resource Communicator
ph: 207-581-1490

Helps develop and apply research dealing with terrestrial and freshwater resources. Offers informational digests on land and water resources, a directory of Maine's natural resource organizations ($3), and a slide program on Maine's natural resources ($15 rental).

128

RESOURCES

Gulf of Maine Marine Education Association (GOMMEA)
PO Box 2652
South Portland, ME 04106
contact: Mary Cerullo, President
ph: 207-799-6406

Fosters educational initiatives on the Gulf of Maine watershed that develop scientific knowledge and sound stewardship among educators, students and citizens. Offers an annual conference each fall and a newsletter for members.

KIDS Consortium
Southern Maine Technical College
2 Fort Road
South Portland, ME 04106
contact: Caroline Allam, Managing Director
ph/fax: 207-774-4530
e-mail: Carolkids@aol.com

Helps schools create learning opportunities that challenge students to solve real-life problems (*e.g.*, working on water quality, environmental stewardship and wildlife protection). KIDS provides free workshops for educators, and a 90-minute video and information on student-led projects.

Lobster Institute
5715 Coburn Hall #22
University of Maine
Orono, ME 04469-5715
contact: Jean Day
ph: 207-581-1448
fax: 207-581-1423
e-mail: jean_day@voyager.umeres.maine.edu

A cooperative venture of the lobster industry and the University of Maine, the Institute generates information about the American lobster to help conserve and enhance the resource. Provides a library with journal articles, reports and pamphlets on lobsters; a periodic *Lobster Bulletin*; and seminars and conferences.

Maine Energy Education Program
219 Capitol Street
Station 130
Augusta, ME 04333-0130
contact: Tom Boothby, Project Coordinator
ph: 207-624-6820

Offers energy education workshops, resource materials and in-class presentations for teachers and students statewide.

Maine Environmental Education Association
PO Box 9
Wiscasset, ME 04578
contact: Don Hudson, Treasurer
ph: 207-882-7323
fax: 207-882-4074
e-mail: chewonki@igc.apc.org

Promotes environmental education in Maine through sharing of ideas, resources, information and programs among educators, organizations and individuals. Annual conference each spring; "Connections" newsletter for members.

Maine Maritime Academy
Castine, ME 04420
contact: John Staples, Public Relations Director
ph: 207-326-4311

Specializes in marine-oriented programs at the undergraduate and graduate levels, with emphasis on engineering, transportation, management and ocean science. Resources include laboratory support, an 80-foot oceanographic research vessel and a conference center.

Maine Mathematics & Science Alliance
PO Box 5359
Augusta, ME 04332-5359
contacts: Thomas Clark, Executive Director; Francis Eberle, Science Specialist
ph: 207-287-5881
fax: 207-287-5885
e-mail: feberle@agate.net

Promotes systematic reform in math and science curriculum, instruction and assessment in Maine schools and communities. "Beacon Centers" are run in Brunswick, Union, York and Scarborough. Maintains a resource library of materials and math/science standards, and organizes regional groups of math/science teachers. "Navigator" newsletter for participating communities.

Maine Science Teachers Association
RR 1, Box 934
Coopers Mills, ME 04341
contact: Don Berthiaume
ph: 207-967-0032

A statewide organization of K-6 science educators, MSTA promotes the teaching and learning of science in Maine.

Maine/New Hampshire Sea Grant Program
5715 Coburn Hall #21
University of Maine
Orono, ME 04469-5715
contacts: Kathleen Lignell, Susan White
ph: 207-581-1440
fax: 207-581-1423
e-mail: kathleen_lignell@voyager.umeres.maine.edu
susan_white@voyager.umeres.maine.edu

Supports statewide cooperation in marine research, education and advisory services focused on the Gulf of Maine. Research topics include fisheries management and development, coastal development, and coastal erosion.
Communications office has publications catalogue with educational booklets, brochures, posters, reports, videos and speaker's list.

MEDUSA — Undergraduate Science Consortium

University of New England
Department of Life Sciences
11 Hills Beach Road
Biddeford, ME 04005
ph: 207-283-0171, ext. 410

Promotes science and research at undergraduate institutions through collaboration on interdisciplinary projects. Resources include a laboratory manual for use along Maine's coast, a computer network, and a database of students and faculty.

Mr./Mrs. Fish Marine Education Program

Southern Maine Technical College
South Portland, ME 04106
contact: Deb and Jeff Sandler
ph: 207-799-6234
fax: 207-767-9645

Perform participatory dramatic presentations that teach about the marine world (available for all age ranges).

Ocean Adventure!

Route One
Edgecomb, ME 04556
contact: Phil Averill
ph: 207-563-2318, 1-800-696-0550

Offers interactive displays and exhibits of commercial fishing gear, and a children's play area.

Science Teachers Resource Center

University of Maine
206 Shibles Hall
Orono, ME 04469
contact: Mary Bird
ph: 207-581-2434
fax: 207-581-2423
e-mail: birdm@voyager.umeres.maine.edu

Offers a small library of K-12 curriculum resource materials on science, environmental and marine education for teachers, available for use on premises. Monthly colloquia during academic year.

Unity College Environmental Education Program

Unity College
Unity, ME 04988
contact: Marty O'Keefe
ph: 207-948-3131

Leading to a B.S. in Social Sciences, the Environmental Education Program combines coursework in natural sciences, with group process, teaching, outdoor skills, planning and administration.

University of Maine Cooperative Extension (UMCE)

5741 Libby Hall
University of Maine
Orono, ME 04469-5741
contact: Conrad Griffin, Community Development/Marine Specialist; Esperanza Stancioff, Water Quality Biologist (ph: 594-2104)
ph: 207-581-3168
fax: 207-581-1387
e-mail: cgriffin@umce.umext.maine.edu

UMCE provides educational support and organizational assistance to citizens, community leaders and organizations in developing programs in coastal resource management, fish health, water-quality education, 4-H youth education, aquaculture and harbor management. County offices offer a wide variety of audio-visual materials, leaflets, and pamphlets on marine-related subjects.

Androscoggin/Sagadahoc Counties
Nancy Coverstone
133 Western Avenue
Auburn, ME 04210
phone: 207-786-0376
fax: 1-800-924-7508

Cumberland County
Richard Brzozowski
96 Falmouth Street
Portland, ME 04103
phone: 207-780-4205
fax: 207-780-4382

Hancock County
Ron Beard
Boggy Brook Rd., RR5
Ellsworth, ME 04605
phone: 207-667-8212
fax: 207-667-2003

Kennebec County
Richard Verville
125 State Street
Augusta, ME 04330
phone: 207-622-7546
fax: 207-621-4919

Knox/Lincoln Counties
Leslie Hyde
375 Main Street
Rockland, ME 04841
phone: 207-594-2104
fax: 207-594-0801

Penobscot County
Gleason Gray
307 Maine Ave.
Bangor, ME 04401
phone: 207-942-7396
fax: 207-942-7537

Waldo County
Rick Kersbergen
RR2, Box 641
Belfast, ME 04915
phone: 207-342-5971
fax: 1-800-924-4909

Washington County
Louis Bassano
11 Water Street
Machias, ME 04654
phone: 207-255-3345
fax: 207-255-6118

York County
Frank Wertheim
RFD 2, Box 1678
Sanford, ME 04073
phone: 207-324-2814
fax: 207-324-0817

130

University of Maine Cooperative Extension

Tanglewood 4-H Camp and
Learning Center
375 Main Street
Rockland, ME 04841
contact: Leslie Hyde, Extension
Educator (environmental education); Jim Dunham, Tanglewood
Camp Director
ph: 207-594-2104
fax: 207-594-0801
e-mail: lhyde@umce.umext.maine.
edu

Organizational and technical support provided for land trusts and
community groups interested in
volunteer water-quality monitoring. Tanglewood summer camp
and school programs, along the
Ducktrap River in Lincolnville,
focus on marine ecology. Curricula
include *4-H Connections to the Sea*
and *4-H Earth Connections* (a
leader's guide to hands-on environmental education activities).

University of Maine

Department of Chemical
Engineering
105 Jenness Hall
Orono, ME 04469-5737
contact: Marquita Hill
ph: 207-581-2277

Provides information on environmental pollution issues and pollution prevention in the home.

University of Maine at Machias (UMM)

9 O'Brien Avenue
Machias, ME 04654
contact: Brian Beal, M. Gayle
Kraus
ph: 207-255-3313, ext. 289

UMM offers a marine ecosystem
concentration in the Environmental Studies B.S. degree, and a
marine biology concentration in
the Biology B.A. degree. UMM
also serves as technical advisor for
two outreach programs: the Cutler
Marine Lobster Hatchery and the
Beals Island Regional Shellfish
Hatchery.

University of New England

Department of Life Sciences
11 Hills Beach Road
Biddeford, ME 04005
contact: Stephen I. Zeeman
ph: 207-283-0171

Programs offered leading to a B.A.
in Marine Biology, Environmental
Science and Environmental
Studies. Courses, seminars, audio-
visual materials and a library available.

Wells National Estuarine Research Reserve

RR 2 Box 806
Wells, ME 04090
contact: Henrietta List
ph: 207-646-1555
fax: 207-646-2930

Wells Reserve presents educational
programs to school groups through
its DEPTHS curriculum. Visitor's
Center includes interpretive
exhibits, 7 miles of trail, classroom
and research space.

Massachusetts

Boston Partners in Education

145 South Street
Boston, MA 02111
contact: Mary Jane Curran
ph: 617-451-6145

Offers the program Aqua-
SMAARTS.

Boston University Marine Program

5 Cummington Street
Boston, MA 02215
contact: Jelle Atema, Director
ph: 617-353-2429
fax: 617-353-6340
e-mail: atema@bio.bu.edu

Trains undergraduate and graduate
students in marine biology and
geology, including a month-long
marine mammals course at Woods
Hole.

Boston Voyages in Learning

Charlestown Navy Yard
100 First Avenue
Charlestown, MA 02129
contact: Sara Benet
ph: 617-261-9180

Provides marine curriculum units,
audio-visual materials, books and
periodicals.

Cape Cod Cooperative Extension

Deeds & Probates Building
Barnstable, MA 02630
contact: Karl Rask, Marine
Specialist
ph: 508-362-2511, ext. 585

Educates the public about marine
resource issues and conducts
regional study on disease-resistant
oysters, coastal erosion and freshwater aquaculture. Mobile saltwater aquarium, slide shows, lecture
series, publications and technical
assistance available.

Cape Cod Environmental Education Resources Center

Cape Cod Community College
Route 132
West Barnstable, MA 02668
contact: Brenda J. Boleyn
ph: 508-362-2131, ext. 363

Offers a *Groundwater Resource
Guide* and annual meeting.

Cape Outdoor Discovery

47 Old County Road
East Sandwich, MA 02537
contact: David DeKing
ph: 508-224-3040

Residential programs (from 2-5
days) available for school groups
and organizations (including men-
tally/physically challenged).

Center for the Restoration of Waters

Ocean Arks International
One Locust Street
Falmouth, MA 02540
ph: 508-540-6801

Offers tours of the center (which
includes a Solar Aquatics boat-
waste treatment plant and pond
remediation project) and materials
for teachers.

E. F. Schumacher Society
Box 76-A, RD 3
Great Barrington, MA 01230
contact: Susan Witt
ph: 412-528-1737
fax: 413-528-4472

Works to realize the vision of British economist E. F. Schumacher for a sustainable economy and environment through education and implementation of model programs. Member of SHARE and maintains several local currency program. Provides lecture series and hosts visiting scholars.

Environmental Careers Organization
286 Congress Street, Third Floor
Boston, MA 02210-1009
ph: 617-426-4375

Offers paid, short-term environmental positions for senior undergraduate and graduate students, recent graduates and others seeking entry-level environmental jobs. Offers books on environmental careers and a Minority Opportunities Program.

Marine Education Center of Cape Ann (MECCA)
PO Box 3015
Gloucester, MA 01930
ph: 508-281-2687

Provides in-school and outdoor programs, an environmental resource library and a newsletter.

Massachusetts Bays Education Alliance
PO Box 185
Hingham, MA 02043
contact: Faith Burbank
ph: 617-740-4913

Provides grants, speakers, information about events and meetings, and a *Summary of Massachusetts Environmental Organizations*.

Massachusetts Bay Marine Studies Consortium
PO Box 255660
Boston, MA 02125
contact: Roger Stern
ph: 617-287-6540

Offers undergraduate courses in coastal science and policy; community education programs and lectures (Mass Bay Classrooms); and hosts the biannual Massachusetts Marine Environment Symposium (in April 1996 and 1998).

Massachusetts Marine Educators
c/o Institute for Learning and Teaching
Graduate College of Education
University of Massachusetts - Boston
Boston, MA 02125
contact: Michael Borek
ph: 617-287-7666

Promotes marine literacy through the provision of curricula, workshops, a speakers' bureau and a newsletter "Flotsam and Jetsam."

Massachusetts Maritime Academy
Marine Fisheries Education and Training Program
101 Academy Drive
Buzzards Bay, MA 02532
contact: John Callahan, Director
ph: 508-830-5000, ext. 2103

Supports development of the fishing and boating industries through vessel safety education, oil spill contingency planning, courses, curricula, workshops, tours and a library.

New England Environmental Education Alliance
PO Box 105
Glendale, MA 01229
contact: Jeff Schwartz, President
ph: 207-622-2209
e-mail: econet:jschwartz

Supports regional educators and statewide environmental education organizations through regional activities, an annual conference held each fall, a yearly newsletter and occasional special projects.

New England Environmental Network
Lincoln Filene Center
Tufts University
Medford, MA 02155
contact: Nancy W. Anderson, Director
ph: 617-381-3451

Promotes environmental citizenship through programs and courses. Hosts the annual New England Environmental Conference, a summer Environmental Leadership Training Institute and a fall Growth Management Forum. Publications include conference proceedings and a newsletter.

New England Science Center
222 Harrington Way
Worcester, MA 01604
contact: Lois Brynes, Program Director
ph: 508-791-9211
fax: 508-752-6879
e-mail: lois@nesc.org

On-site marine programs for groups; summer camp and workshops; field trips to study coastal ecosystems; and exhibits and programs on regional and global environmental dynamics. Offers a curriculum entitled *Tides of Change*.

Northeast Fisheries Science Center
166 Water Street
Woods Hole, MA 02543
contact: Teri Frady, Chief, Research Communications; Don Flescher, Education Coordinator
ph: 508-548-5123
fax: 508-548-5124
e-mail: tfrady@whsun1.wh.whoi.edu
dflesch@whsun1.wh.whoi.edu

Conducts research and analysis in support of the region's living marine resources. Public aquarium at the Center offers tours for the public.

132

Northeastern University

Marine Science Center
East Point
Nahant, MA 01908
contact: Morgan Hardwick-Witman
ph: 617-581-7370

Provides university courses, marine biology education for adults, exhibits, tours, lectures, seminars, publications and a library.

OceanQuest, Inc.

PO Box 1450
East Dennis, MA 02641
contact: Kathy Mullin, Executive Director
ph: 508-385-7656
fax: 508-896-4057

Offers oceanography cruises, classroom presentations, teachers workshops and other interactive programs (several of which focus on how global changes are affecting marine issues).

The Sacred Earth Network

267 East Street
Petersham, MA 01366
ph: 508-724-3443
fax: 508-724-3436

Provides training and support in the use of inexpensive computer technologies and leadership skills for local groups doing environmental work.

Sea Education Association, Inc. (SEA)

PO Box 6
Woods Hole, MA 02543
contact: Lucy Helfrich, Communications Manager
ph: 508-540-3954
fax: 508-457-4673

Fosters knowledge and appreciation of the oceans by providing academic programs in which students live, work and study at sea. Programs include SEA Semester for undergraduates, SEA Experience for teachers, and Science at SEA (two summer programs for high school students).

Thornton W. Burgess Society/Green Briar Nature Center

6 Discovery Hill Road
East Sandwich, MA 02537
contact: Mary Beers, Education Director
ph: 508-888-6870
fax: 508-888-1919

Offers curricula (*Bay Buddies* for grades 1-3); classroom field lessons (*Coastal Ecology by Rail* for grades 3-9, *Lessons in Field Ecology* for middle school); and salt marsh/tidal pool teachers' workshops.

Tufts University

Certificate Programs in Community Sustainability Professional and Continuing Studies
112 Packard Ave.
Medford, MA -2155
contact: Thea Sahr, Program Coordinator
ph: 617-627-3562
fax: 617-627-3017

Offers intensive professional training in nonprofit management and environmental studies on a flexible schedule designed for working adults.

University of Massachusetts Cooperative Extension/ Nutrition

202 Chenoweth Laboratory
Amherst, MA 01003
contact: Nancy Cohen
ph: 413-545-0552
fax: 413-545-1074

Provides practical, research-based information to the public. Conducts the "Seafood: New England's Healthful Harvest" program whose goals are to increase consumer knowledge of seafood selection, storage, preparation and nutritional content. An 11-minute slide presentation and factsheets ($1.50/set of 10) are available.

University of Massachusetts Cooperative Extension System

Water Resources Program
University of Massachusetts
Amherst, MA 01003-0099
ph: 413-545-4800
fax: 413-545-6555

Offers *Watershed to Bay: A Raindrop Journey*, a curriculum and teaching kit for grades 4-8 that provides hands-on experience with coastal watershed systems.

University of Massachusetts

Marine Station
PO Box 7128, Lanesville Station
Gloucester, MA 01930
contact: Ronald P. Athanas
ph: 508-281-1930

Provides educational and research opportunities for the Massachusetts public, technical advisory services, and a library.

Woods Hole Oceanographic Institution

Woods Hole, MA 02543
contact: Education or Information offices
ph: 508-457-2000
fax: 508-457-2188 (Education Office)

Woods Hole Oceanographic Institution Sea Grant Program

CRL 209
193 Oyster Pond Road
Woods Hole, MA 02543-1525
contact: Tracey Crago; Sheri DeRosa
ph: 508-289-2665; 508-289-2398
fax: 508-457-2172
e-mail: seagrant@whoi.edu

As part of the national Sea Grant network, it supports research, education and advisory projects to promote responsible use and understanding of ocean and coastal resources. Conducts research on

red tide; economic impacts of harmful algae blooms; coastal water-quality management and monitoring programs; contamination of edible marine resources; ; and on Boston Harbor and Massachusetts bays. Provides information and referral services, workshops, annual public lecture series and computerized publication and bibliographic databases. Oceanography reading lists, activity book ($2), field guides ($1/set), groundwater resource guide, and biannual *Nor'easter Magazine* (free) available.

Vernal Pool Association
62 Oakland Road
Reading, MA 01867
contact: Leo P. Kenney, Advisor
ph: 617-944-8200, ext. 33
fax: 617-942-9133
e-mail: vernalpool@whale.simmons.edu

Encourages the identification, study, appreciation and protection of vernal pools. Interested in involving other high school students in vernal pool studies. *Wicked Big Puddles*, a guide to the study and certification of vernal pools ($10.00 plus $3.00 postage) and a slide set of vernal pools and their organisms are available. Workshops at various conferences in eastern Massachusetts and/or by arrangement are conducted by Vernal Pool Association high school students.

New Brunswick

New Brunswick Community College
Fisheries/Marine Training
PO Box 427
St. Andrews, NB E0G 2X0

University of New Brunswick
Biology Department
PO Bag Service 45111
Fredericton, NB E3B 5A3
contact: Chair
ph: 506-453-4582

Offers undergraduate and graduate education in basic and applied life science, using research facilities and library holdings.

New Hampshire

Environmental Hazards Management Institute
PO Box 932
Durham, NH 03824
contact: Amy Dyer Cabaniss, Educational Programs Director
ph: 603-868-1496

Brings together stakeholders in environmental issues through innovative educational programs and products, conferences, publications, and consultation.

Great Bay National Estuarine Research Reserve
NH Fish & Game Department, Region 3
225 Main Street
Durham, NH 03824
contact: Peter Wellenberger
ph: 603-868-1095
Sandy Point Discovery Center
contact: Betsy Franz,
ph: 603-778-0015
Conducts research and education on the Great Bay estuary and operates an interpretive facility (Sandy Point Discovery Center). Tours, exhibits, curricula, maps, posters, brochures, workshops and internships are available.

Institute for Policy and Social Science Research
Hood House
University of New Hampshire
Durham, NH 03824
contact: Karen Burnett-Kurie, Extension Specialist
ph: 603-862-2186
fax: 603-862-1488
e-mail: klbk@christa.unh.edu

Supports the use of computer games and simulations for education concerning sustainable development. Game kits include Fish Banks, Ltd. (on fisheries management) and Stratagem (on sustainable development). Offers teacher trainings, simulation sessions, kits on disk, a resource library and videos/transparencies to accompany the book *Beyond the Limits: Confronting Global Collapse, Envisioning a Sustainable Future.*

Maritime Heritage Commission
c/o Greater Portsmouth Chamber of Commerce
Portsmouth, NH 03801
contact: Carrie Keating, Executive Director
ph: 603-436-1118

Coordinates waterfront events that heighten awareness of Portsmouth's marine and naval heritage and current maritime industries.

New Hampshire/Maine Sea Grant Program
Kingman Farm
University of New Hampshire
Durham, NH 03824-3512
contact: Sharon Meeker
ph: 603-749-1565
fax: 603-743-3997

See Maine/NH Sea Grant Program listing on page 128.

Student Conservation Association

PO Box 550
Charlestown, NH 03603
ph: 603-543-1700
fax: 603-543-1828

Offers opportunities for education, leadership and personal development in conjunction with public service in conservation. Provides programs around the country for high school and college students and young adults.

Nova Scotia

Canadian Network for Environmental Education and Communication

PO Box 1514
Antigonish, NS B2G 2L8
ph: 902-863-5984
fax: 902-863-9481

Encourages the exchange of information among Canadians involved in environmental education and facilitates discussion of the field in local and national contexts. Provides a database, newsletter and *Guide to E-Mail for Environmental Educators.*

EcoLogic Associates Environmental Education Consulting

PO Box 1514
Antigonish, NS B2G 2L8
contact: Anne Camozzi, Owner
ph: 902-863-3306
fax: 902-863-9481
e-mail: acamozzi@fox.nstn.ca

Supports adult environmental education through production of materials and programs (e.g., *4-H Environment Resource Guide*; *Adult Environment Education: Workbook to Move from Words to Action*; and *Aquatic Stewardship: An Inventory of Educational Resources*).

Marine and Environmental Law Program (MELP)

Dalhousie Law School, Weldon Building
Halifax, NS B3H 4H9
contact: David VanderZwaag
ph: 902-494-1045
fax: 902-494-1316
e-mail: dvanderzwaag@kilcom1.ucis.dal.ca

Offers curricular specialization in marine law and policy within undergraduate and graduate programs; holds workshops on ocean law and policy; and maintains library holdings on marine law and resource management.

Oceans Institute of Canada

1236 Henry Street, 5th Floor
Halifax, NS B3H 3Z5
contact: Peter Mushkat
phone: 902-494-3879

Pursues national and international research, education and training. Publications include *InfoOcean* (monthly information bulletin), *Coastal Nova Scotia* (education guide to natural and cultural resources) and *Planning Handbook for Nova Scotia Municipalities.*

School for Resource & Environmental Studies

Dalhousie University
1312 Robie Street
Halifax, NS B3H 3C3
contact: Ray Cote
ph: 902-494-3632

Offers interdisciplinary education and research in natural resource management (*e.g.*, harbor management, marine ecosystem modelling and climate impact assessment). Publications and resource collection available.

GOVERNMENTAL AGENCIES

Note: See also Parks and Sanctuaries & Research Programs and Organizations

Maine

Casco Bay Estuary Project

312 Canco Road
Portland, ME 04103
contact: Anne M. Payson, Public Outreach Director
ph: 207-828-1043
fax: 207-828-4001

Developing a conservation management plan to protect Casco Bay and its watershed. Offers educational talks and materials (watershed poster, fact sheets, homeowner tips to prevent pollution; 15-minute educational video, quarterly newsletter); and GIS database for the watershed (being developed).

Craig Brook/Green Lake National Fish Hatcheries

U.S. Fish & Wildlife Service
Hatchery Road
East Orland, ME 04431
contact: Peter Steenstra
ph: 207-469-2803

Conserves wild anadromous Atlantic Salmon populations in Maine rivers (through fry and smolt propagation).

Gulf of Maine Council on the Marine Environment

c/o Maine State Planning Office
Station 38
Augusta, ME 04333-0038
contact: Jim Doyle, Secretariat
phone: 207-287-1492
fax: 207-287-6489

A cooperative effort begun in 1989 by the states and provinces bordering the Gulf to prevent degradation of the regional environment. Committees support collaborative work on habitat protection, research, and environmental monitoring, reducing marine debris, data and information management, public education and environmental quality monitoring. Resources include a Gulf of Maine watershed map/poster, fact sheets, newsletters an annual report and the *Gulf of Maine Action Plan*. The Council Secretariat rotates each year to a different state/province: the Maine State Planning Office can provide current contact information.

Gulf of Maine Project
U.S. Fish & Wildlife Service
4R Fundy Road
Falmouth, ME 04105
contact: Lois Winter, Outreach Specialist
ph: 207-781-8364
fax: 207-781-8369
e-mail: R5ES__GOMP@mail.fws.gov
www: http://www.fws.gov/~cep/mainecep.html

Works in partnership with federal, state and non-governmental partners to identify coastal wildlife habitat and minimize or eliminate threats facing fish and wildlife. Offers presentations to land-use decision-makers, a display, wildlife fact sheets, an "Island Ethics" brochure and the *Wild Gulf Almanac*, and fact sheets about specific habitat protection efforts.

Maine Anadromous Fish Program
U.S. Fish & Wildlife Service
Craig Brook National Fish Hatchery
East Orland, ME 04431
contact: Gerry Marancik
ph: 207-469-6701

Coordinates federal, state and private efforts focused on anadromous fish restoration in Maine. Presents educational programs.

Maine Clean Water Program/Partners in Monitoring
Station 38
Augusta, ME 04333
contact: Kathleen Leyden, Shore Stewards Coordinator, 207-287-3261; Esperanza Stancioff, Water Quality Biologist, 1-800-244-2104
e-mail: spkleyd@state.me.us
ceskl@umce.umext.maine.edu

Provides start-up support, training and on-going technical assistance to community groups and schools interest in monitoring Maine's marine and estuarine waters. Provides training manuals and programs; data management software; "GulfTalk Listserv" (an electronic discussion group water quality available on internet); and a grants program for establishing water-quality labs. Ongoing opportunities for volunteers to work with existing groups or begin new ones. Sponsors a water-quality monitoring fair each spring.

Maine Coastal Program
State Planning Office
Station 38
Augusta, ME 04333-0038
contact: Aline LaChance
ph: 207-287-3261
fax: 207-287-6489
e-mail: spalach@state.me.us
www: http://www.state.me.us/spo/spohome.htm

Encourages cooperative federal/state/municipal management of coastal resources; ensures continuation of working waterfronts and public shore access points; provides technical assistance and land-use planning to coastal towns; supports the Gulf of Maine Program; and coordinates Coastweek, the Gulf of Maine Coastal Cleanup, the Shore Stewards Partnership and the Penobscot Bay Marine Volunteers. Resources include publications (including handbooks on island management issues, estuaries, sea-level rise, and coastal issues curriculum for grades K-12); five traveling displays; slide shows and videos on marine issues (see listing for *Sightings* under media resources).

Maine Department of Conservation (DOC)
Harlow Building, AMHI Complex
Station 22
Augusta, ME 04333-0022
contact: Marshall Wiebe, Public Information
ph: 207-287-4900
fax: 207-287-2400
e-mail: http://www.state.me.us

Manages coastal state parks and historic sites; provides coastal access for boats; manages a coastal educational program at Wolfe's Neck Woods, Freeport; manages state-owned submerged lands; does planning/zoning for certain coastal islands; investigates and maps marine geology; administers a coastal island registry; and assists with forest fire and insect protection. Departmental divisions include the Bureau of Parks and Recreation, Bureau of Public Lands, Land Use Regulation Commission, Maine Geological Survey, and the Maine Forest Service (see following listings). Publications include *Maine's Public Facilities for Boats Program* (free); *Rules and Regulations for State Parks and Historic Sites* (free); *Your Islands on the Coast* (free); and coastal marine environmental maps.

Bureau of Parks and Recreation
Station 22
Augusta, ME 04333-0022
contact: Patricia Bailey
ph: 207-287-3821

Maintains and interprets 14 state parks and 10 state historic sites and manages 52 public boat facilities (see chart, page 157). Free publications include *Outdoors in Maine*, *Self-directed Activities for Groups* and *Explore the Shore*.

135

Bureau of Public Lands

Station 22
Augusta, ME 04333-0022
contact: Steve Oliveri
ph: 207-287-3061
fax: 207-287-8111

Provides multiple-use management for all the state's public lands, including submerged lands. Grants leases for dredging, filling, erection of structures, and installation of cables and pipelines on submerged lands owned by the state. Maintains maps and records identifying all islands and manages a program to provide public with low-impact recreational opportunities on state-owned islands.

Land Use Regulation Commission

Station 22
Augusta, ME 04333-0022
contact: Fred Todd, Planning Supervisor
ph: 207-287-2631

Provide land-use planning, zoning, permitting and enforcement (growth management) in unorganized territories. Publications include *Comprehensive Land-use Plan for the Unorganized Areas of Maine; Land Use Districts and Standards*; and *A Preliminary Study of the Coastal Islands in the Land Use Regulation Commission's Jurisdiction.*

Maine Forest Service

Station 22
Augusta, ME 04333-0022
contact: Jeannie Knobil
ph: 207-287-1061

Offers grant programs for tree planting and community forestry education; furnishes technical assistance on forest management issues; and administers Project Learning Tree, a K-12 environmental education program that uses the forest as a window to the natural world.

Maine Geological Survey

Station 22
Augusta, ME 04333-0022
contact: Steve Dickson
ph: 207-287-2801
fax: 207-287-2353
University of Maine Geological Department
Boardman Hall
Orono, ME 04469
contact: Joe Kelly
ph: 207-581-2162
fax: 207-581-2202

Conducts research and resource inventories of Maine's offshore, nearshore and estuarine areas; maps offshore and gravel resources; studies geologic history and evaluates geologic stability of coastal areas. Resources include geologic and topographic maps, aerial photographs of coastal regions, marine geology publications and *Living with the Coast of Maine.*

Maine Department of Environmental Protection (DEP)

Ray Building, AMHI Complex
Station 17
Augusta, ME 04333-0017
contact: Deb Garrett
ph: 207-287-7688
e-mail: http://www.state.me.us/dep/mdephome.htm

DEP administers laws affecting coastal wetlands, sand dunes, discharge licenses, water-quality certification for net pen aquaculture, oil pollution, and site-location approval for major developments. Conducts research on toxic pollution and biological effects in coastal waters. Publications include *Watershed* (a citizen's guide to non-point source pollution); *Preserving and Protecting Marine Water Quality through Comprehensive Planning; Nuisance Blooms and Nutrients in Maine's Marine Waters; Toxic Pollutants in Maine's Marine Waters;* and *Maine's Marine Environment — A Plan for Protection.*

Maine Department of Human Services/Division of Health Engineering

Station 10
Augusta, ME 04333-0010
contact: W. Clough Toppan, Director
ph: 207-287-5697

Supports public health by regulating on-site sub-surface waste disposal systems and water quality supplied by public water companies; licensing restaurants, motels and camping areas; and licensing scuba tank-filling operations.

Maine Department of Inland Fisheries and Wildlife (DIF&W)

284 State Street
Station 41
Augusta, ME 04333-0041
contact: Lisa Kane
(Project WILD)
ph: 207-287-2871

Works to ensure that all species of wildlife and aquatic resources in Maine are maintained for their intrinsic and ecological values, their economic contribution, and their recreational, scientific and educational use by Maine people. Promotes Project WILD and Project WILD AQUATIC, K-12 conservation education programs, through training workshops and provision of curriculum guides (cost: $5 per person/workshop). Video programs, quarterly magazine ($9) and booklets available, including a guide for Maine wildlife watchers ($4.95).

Maine Department of Marine Resources (DMR)

Stevens Complex, Hallowell
Station 21
Augusta, ME 04333-0021
contact: Robin Alden, Commissioner
ph: 207-624-6550

Conducts scientific research, management, public information and education about Maine's marine resources; enforces marine regulations; and promotes Maine seafood. In-service and teachers'

workshops; marine curriculum enhancement programs; marine recreational fisheries education; consumer education materials and programs; speakers, slide shows; videos and publications.

Also located at: 624-6550:
Administration: Samantha Jones
Anadromous Fish: Lewis Flagg
Marine Development: Harold C. Winters
Marine Education: Elaine Jones
Marine Patrol: Joseph Fessenden
Market Development: Robert Beaudoin

Maine Field Office

U.S. Fish & Wildlife Service
1033 S. Main St.
Old Town, ME 04468
contact: Gordon Russell, Project Leader
ph: 207-827-5938
fax: 207-827-6099

Works to protect and enhance fish and wildlife and their habitats by assisting in coastal wetlands protection, working cooperatively with landowners, evaluating development, providing scientific data, and protecting endangered species.

Marine Water Quality Laboratory (DMR)

Lamoine State Park
Ellsworth, ME 04605
contact: Paul Anderson
ph: 207-667-5654

Marine Resources Laboratory (DMR)

(see listing under Aquaria and Museums)

Maine Department of Transportation (DOT)

Ports and Marine Transportation
Station 16
Augusta, ME 04333-0016
contact: Robert D. Elder, Director
ph: 207-287-2841
fax: 207-287-8300

Plan, develop and maintain marine infrastructure projects in the coastal zone; operate ferry services and market Maine's ports. Publications include *Planning Study of Maine Coastal Port & Harbor Needs* and *Port Traffic Statistics*.

Maine Historic Preservation Commission

55 Capitol Street, Station 65
Augusta, ME 04333-0065
contact: Earle G. Shettleworth, Jr.
ph: 207-287-2132
fax: 207-287-2335

Conducts coastal surveys of prehistoric and historic archaeological sites (*e.g.*, Native American shell heaps, early colonial settlements, and shipwrecks) and works to protect these resources. Has historic archaeological and architectural inventories, slide collections, bibliographies and published scientific studies.

Maine Natural Areas Program

Department of Conservation
Augusta, ME 04333-0093
contact: Sarah Holbrook, Information Manager
ph/fax: 207-287-2211
e-mail: sdsholb@state.me.us

MNAP conducts ongoing inventories and monitoring to document the location, condition and status of Maine's rare and endangered plants and animals, as well as exemplary natural features and communities. The program has a comprehensive data management system, technical publications, a listing of endangered and threatened plants, and a register of critical areas voluntarily protected by landowners.

Maine State Library

Cultural Building, Station 64
Augusta, ME 04333-0064
contact: reference staff
ph: 207-287-5600

Collects all state published documents and many federal ones; provides search services in national, on-line databases. Open weekdays 9-5 (and Saturdays during school year).

National Marine Fisheries Service

National Oceanic and Atmospheric Administration
Marine Trade Center, Suite 212
Two Portland Fish Pier
Portland, ME 04101-4633
contact: Robert Morrill
ph: 207-780-3322
fax: 207-789-3340

Provide fisheries statistics (*e.g.*, landings and harvest data) for Maine. See NMFS listing in Massachusetts for further information.

National Weather Service

National Oceanic and Atmospheric Administration
PO Box 1208
Gray, ME 04039-1208
contact: Albert W. Wheeler, Meteorologist
ph: 207-688-3216
fax: 207-688-3230
e-mail: awheeler@smtpgate.ssmc.noaa.gov

Issues weather warnings and forecasts to help protect life and property. Office tours can be scheduled for individuals or groups, with advance notice.

Penobscot Bay Marine Volunteer Program

Station 38
Augusta, ME 04333-0038
contact: Laura Taylor, Coastal Planner
ph: 207-287-3261
fax: 207-287-6489
e-mail: spltayl@state.me.us

Provides a professional training program for adult volunteers, enabling them to present coastal resource information to students, tourists and community groups. Five-week training follow-up support and resource library provided, in return for 30 hours of community service work.

137

138

Maine Shore Stewards Partnership

Station 38
Augusta, ME 04333-0038
contact: Kathleen Leyden, Shore Stewards Coordinator
ph: 207-287-3261
fax: 207-287-6489
e-mail: spkleyd@state.me.us

Encourages Maine citizens to protect coastal waters through stewardship activities and community education, and fosters cooperation among local groups working on water-quality issues. Provides information clearinghouse, mini-grants program for public education projects related to water quality and for volunteer monitoring projects. Offers two curricula on coastal issues, *Waterways* (for grades 3-5, with accompanying video) and *Charting Our Course* (for grades 6-12), and a newsletter, "The Ripple Effect."

U.S. Army Corps of Engineers

RR 2, Box 1855
Manchester, ME 04351
contact: Jay Clement, Project Manager
ph: 207-623-8367
fax: 207-623-8206

Administers the Federal Regulatory program for work performed in navigable waters in Maine and for discharges of dredged or fill material into all waters and wetlands.

Massachusetts

Aquatic Resource Education Program (AREP)

Massachusetts Department of Fisheries, Wildlife & Environmental Law Enforcement
Field Headquarters
Westboro, MA 01581
contact: Gary Zima
ph: 508-366-4470

Provides environmental education concerning fishing, including lectures, courses and temporary exhibits.

Cape Cod Commission

3225 Main Street
Barnstable, MA 02630
contact: Dan Hamilton, Public Information
ph: 508-362-3828
fax: 508-362-3136
e-mail: 74260.3152@compuserve.com

Provides planning, regulatory and technical assistance to the 15 towns that constitute Barnstable County, and coordinates a Coastal Resource Committee. Offers a library, GIS mapping and several newsletters.

Massachusetts Bays Program

100 Cambridge Street, Room 2006
Boston, MA 02202
contact: Susan Schneider, Public Information Specialist
ph: 617-727-9530, ext. 408
fax: 617-727-2754

A joint local, state and federal effort to restore and enhance the natural resources of Massachusetts and Cape Cod bays through development of a management plan and work with 49 coastal and 164 watershed communities. MBP provides speakers, regional workshops, volunteer opportunities, special events, research and demonstration projects, publications and a grants program.

Massachusetts Coastal Zone Management

Massachusetts Executive Office of Environmental Affairs
100 Cambridge Street, 20th Floor
Boston, MA 02202
contact: Anne Donovan, Public Outreach Coordinator
phone: 617-727-9530, ext. 420
fax: 617-727-2754

Protects and promotes responsible use of coastal resources through technical assistance on coastal issues and federal consistency review. Educational resources include publications, limited curricula, maps, posters, workshops and a "Shorewatch Series" of coastal videos.

Massachusetts Department of Environmental Management

Massachusetts Executive Office of Environmental Affairs
100 Cambridge Street, 19th Floor
Boston, MA 02202
contact: Susan Fairbanks, Director of Communications
ph: 617-727-3180
fax: 617-727-9402

Operates state forest and park system, including coastal parks and beaches. Administers coastal acquisition program and coastal engineering bureau; manages state piers; administers the flood hazard management program, ocean sanctuaries program and coastal access program. Resources include a coastal recreation brochure; flood hazard management handbook; coastal land inventory; speakers; and technical assistance to communities and agencies.

Massachusetts Department of Environmental Protection

Massachusetts Executive Office of
Environmental Affairs
One Winter Street
Boston, MA 02108
contact: Thomas Higgins
ph: 617-292-5500

Works to enforce environmental
laws, waste prevention, hazardous-
waste site cleanup and solid waste
management regulations. Offers
technical assistance bulletins,
audio-visual materials, workshops
and a speakers' bureau.

Massachusetts Department of Fisheries, Wildlife and Environmental Law Enforcement — Division of Marine Fisheries

Massachusetts Executive Office of
Environmental Affairs
100 Cambridge Street
Boston, MA 02202
contact: Noreen Whitaker,
Administrative Assistant to
Director
ph: 617-727-3193, ext. 371
fax: 617-727-7988

Works to manage and conserve the
living marine resources of
Massachusetts and promote the
commercial and recreational industries they support. Programs
include licensing of fishers and
dealers; applied marine research;
fishways; red-tide monitoring and
shellfish classification. Quarterly
newsletter and saltwater fishing
guide available.

Massachusetts Department of Public Health

Division of Food and Drugs
305 South Street
Jamaica Plain, MA 02130
contact: Richard Waskiewicz,
Director Food Protection Program
ph: 617-522-3700, ext. 6759
fax: 617-524-8062

Administers seafood inspection
program and studies offshore
marine biotoxins. Issues advisories
on food and seafood safety issues;
investigates food-born illnesses;
and provides information on food
safety issues.

Massachusetts Division of Conservation Services

Massachusetts Executive Office of
Environmental Affairs
100 Cambridge Street
Boston, MA 02202
contact: Joel Lerner
ph: 617-727-1552

Offers a speakers' bureau and
cosponsors the annual
"Envirothon," a competition to test
the natural resource knowledge of
high school students.

Massachusetts Executive Office of Transportation and Construction

10 Park Plaza, Room 3510
Boston, MA 02116-3969
contact: Joy Hearn, Manager
ph: 617-973-7000

Assesses new opportunities in
water transportation for public
transit. Provides advice on travel
opportunities by boat, route maps
and schedules, referrals and a
transportation library.

Massachusetts Natural Heritage and Endangered Species Program

Massachusetts Department of
Fisheries, Wildlife and
Environmental Law Enforcement
Route 135
Westboro, MA 01581
ph: 508-792-7270, ext. 200

Offers posters, a newsletter, and
fact sheets on rare species in
Massachusetts.

Massachusetts Water Resources Authority

Charlestown Navy Yard
100 First Avenue
Boston, MA 02129
contact: Neil Clark
ph: 617-241-4643

Provides videos, materials, pamphlets, tours and information on
water conservation and supply,
wastewater treatment and the
Boston Harbor project. Field trip
suggestions and visiting educator
available.

National Marine Fisheries Service

National Oceanic & Atmospheric
Administration
One Blackburn Drive
Gloucester, MA 01930-2298
contact: Thomas E. Bigford
ph: 508-281-9300

Prepares fishery management plans
for offshore stocks (in cooperation
with states and the regional fishery
management council); supports
research on interstate and commercial species; reviews impacts of
human activities; and manages protected species. Offers coastal slides,
brochures, posters, and speakers.

National Oceanographic Data Center

Regional Office
Woods Hole Oceanographic
Institute
Woods Hole, MA 02543
contact: George Heimerdinger
ph: 508-548-1400, ext. 2497
e-mail: gheimerdinger@whoi.edu

Stores and disseminates marine
environmental data derived from
research conducted in coastal and
open ocean waters.

National Park Service

15 State Street
Boston, MA 02109
ph: 617-223-5200

Manages national parks, monu-
ments, seashores and recreational
and historic areas; provides technical and informational services. See
Parks and Sanctuaries entries for
specific information.

New England Fishery Management Council

Suntaug Office Park
5 Broadway, Route 1
Saugus, MA 01906
contact: Douglas Marshall
ph: 617-231-0422

Prepares, monitors and amends (as
necessary) fishery management
plans for resources in the New
England region. Newsletter, public
service announcements and press
releases produced.

North Attleboro National Fish Hatchery

U.S. Fish & Wildlife Service
144 Bungay Rd.
North Attleboro, MA 02760
Contact: Larry Lofton
ph: 508-695-5002
fax: 508-695-5098

Conserves wild anadromous Atlantic salmon populations by rearing fry from 4,000,000 eggs for the Merrimack and Pawcatuk Rivers. Conduct large numbers of tours for school groups and other organized groups by appointment throughout the year. Also offer a wheelchair-accessible fishing pond stocked with rainbow trout.

PALMS Project

Massachusetts Department of Education
350 Main Street
Malden, MA 02148
contact: Susan Zellman
ph: 617-388-3300

Provides math and science curriculum through a partnership with pilot schools and cooperating museums and colleges.

Stellwagen Bank National Marine Sanctuary

14 Union Street
Plymouth, MA 02360
contact: Anne Smrcina, Education Coordinator
ph: 508-747-1691
fax: 508-747-1949
e-mail: asmrcina@ocean.nos.noaa.gov

Provides conservation and management that complements existing regulatory authorities; supports, promotes and coordinates scientific research on, and monitoring of, the sanctuary's marine resources; works to enhance public understanding and appreciation of the marine environment; and facilitates multiple uses of the sanctuary where compatible with resource protection. Brochures, newsletter, and videos available. Sponsors the annual MIMI Teacher's Conference.

U.S. Army Corps of Engineers

New England Division
424 Trapelo Road
Waltham, MA 02254-9149
contact: Larry Rosenberg, Chief of Public Affairs
ph: 617-647-8237
fax: 617-647-8850

Designs, constructs, and maintains projects for navigation, beach erosion control, hurricane protection, flood control, streambank erosion, and emergency response measures. Coastal projects include permitting, regulatory enforcement, dredging, and flood damage reduction. Offers technical and advisory services, legal and regulatory information, and health and environmental information.

U.S. Coast Guard Public Affairs Office

First Coast Guard District
408 Atlantic Avenue
Boston, MA 02110-3350
contact: James B. McPherson, Lieutenant Commander
ph: 617-223-8515

Works to prevent pollution incidents, enforce marine regulations, maintain waterways for navigation, promote vessel safety, and respond to marine emergencies. Coordinates joint U.S. and Canadian oil-spill response program with other agencies. Speakers available.

U.S. Department of Energy

One Congress Street, Room 1101
Boston, MA 02114
contact: Duane D. Day, Public Affairs
ph: 617-565-9705
fax: 617-565-9723

Promotes efficient energy use, reduced petroleum dependence and increased reliance on renewable energy. Legal, technical and energy data; curricula; and a speakers' bureau available.

U.S. Environmental Protection Agency

Northeast Region Office
J.F.K. Federal Building
Boston, MA 02203
contact: Public Affairs Office
ph: 617-565-9447

Administers programs in water pollution, waste treatment and disposal, and coastal planning (*e.g.*, the National Estuary Programs in Massachusetts and Casco bays, the Near-coastal Waters Program; and the Marine Protection Research and Sanctuaries Act). Resources include curricula on marine debris (*Turning the Tide on Trash*) and wetlands, videos on stormwater runoff, and speakers on marine debris, water quality, recycling and other topics.

U.S. Fish & Wildlife Service

Region 5
300 Westgate Center Drive
Hadley, MA 01035
contact: Tammy Hogan, Public Affairs Office
ph: 413-253-8328
fax: 413-253-8482

Coordinates activities on approximately 80 refuges and field stations throughout a 13-state region. Information available on curriculum and outreach materials south to Virginia) Calls for local materials should be directed to the nearest USFWS office. See other Governmental Agencis and Parks and Sanctuaries listings for specific information.

U.S. Geological Survey

Branch of Atlantic Marine Geology
384 Woods Hole Road
Woods Hole, MA 02543-1589
contact: Rich Signell
ph: 508-548-8700
e-mail: rsignell@nobska.er.usgs.gov
www: http://bramble.er.usgs.gov/

Conducts multidisciplinary investigations of such areas as mineral resources; metal and sewage contamination and transport processes; sediment studies; and quaternary stratigraphy of nearshore areas. Electronic and paper publications, maps, atlases, and databases available.

New Brunswick

Atlantic Coastal Action Program (Environment Canada)

45 Alderney Drive
Dartmouth, NS B24 2N6
contact: Karen Swan, Project
Officer
ph: 902-426-3766
fax: 902-426-4457
e-mail: swank@cpdar.dots.doe.ca

Assists communities to acquire the skills, information and partnerships necessary to develop and implement comprehensive environmental management plans. Publications include *ACAP: Communities in Action; Sharing the Challenge: A Guide for Community-based Environmental Planning; A Workbook for Use in ACAP Project Areas*; and a quarterly newsletter. Additional materials available from the community contacts.

Community Contacts in Coastal New Brunswick

Letang Estuary:
Eastern Charlotte Waterways Inc.
No. 4 Main Street
St. George's, NB E0G 2Y0
ph: 506-755-6001
fax: 506-755-6688
e-mail: ecwinc@nbnet.nb.ca

St. Croix:
Rob Ranier
St. Croix Estuary Project
(see listing in section on nonprofit organizations)

Pat Desmond & Allison Lowe
ACAP St. John Inc.
(see listing in section on nonprofit organizations)

Canadian Coast Guard

PO Box 7730, Station A
Saint John, NB E2L 4X6
contact: Wilfred G. Tucker, Senior
Representative, Fundy Zone
ph: 506-636-4701
fax: 506-636-4024
e-mail: tuckerw@tc.gc.ca

Maintains a safe, effective marine transportation system through vessel traffic services; aids to navigation; emergency response and joint response efforts with the U.S. Coast Guard.

Canadian Heritage, Parks Canada

Historic Sites
1045 Main Street, Third Floor,
Unit 106
Moncton, NB E1C 1H1
contact: Claude DeGrace
ph: 506-851-3083

Protects and administers national historic parks and sites.

Canadian Wildlife Service

Atlantic Regional Office
PO Box 1590
Sackville, NB E0A 3C0
contact: William Prescott,
Manager of Wildlife Conservation
ph: 506-364-5044

Manages migratory birds and the marine ecosystems that support them. Conducts seabird research and inventories; offers technical advice, publications, and speakers; and manages Machias Seal Island Bird Sanctuary.

New Brunswick Department of Fisheries and Oceans

PO Box 210
St. Andrews, NB E0G 2X0
contact: Hank Scarth, Area
Manager
ph: 506-529-5850
fax: 506-529-5858

Works to manage and protect the fisheries and fish habitats of southern and western New Brunswick through enforcement, licensing; maintenance of statistics; development and management of recreational fisheries, native fisheries and fish habitat; and fishing vessel insurance. Posters, videos and displays available.

Environment Canada

Environmental Protection
PO Box 400
Fredericton, NB E3B 4Z9
contact: George Lindsay, Manager
ph: 506-529-5050

Promotes environmental conservation and implements environmental policy for the Canadian government. Offers technical advice, program information and publications.

New Brunswick Department of Economic Development and Tourism

PO Box 6000
Fredericton, NB E3B 5H1
contact: Maurice Lavigne
ph: 506-453-2965

Works to attract investment and enhance the business community. Videos and brochures available.

New Brunswick Department of the Environment

Planning & Sciences Branch
PO Box 6000
Fredericton, NB E3B 5H1
contact: William Ayer
ph: 506-457-4846
fax: 506-457-7823

Preserves and enhances the environment of New Brunswick.

New Brunswick Department of Fisheries & Aquaculture

PO Box 6000, King's Place, York
Tower
Fredericton, NB E3B 5H1
contact: Barry Jones
ph: 506-444-5749

Develops and manages marine fisheries and aquaculture; conducts environmental impact evaluations for aquaculture; and works toward sustainable development.

New Brunswick Department of Health & Community Services
Community & Environmental Health
PO Box 5100
Fredericton, NB E3B 5H1
ph: 506-453-2360

Protects public health through water-quality monitoring, sanitary surveys and a shellfish working group.

New Brunswick Department of Municipalities, Culture & Housing
PO Box 6000
Fredericton, NB E3B 5H1
contact: Girard Belleveau
ph: 506-453-2171

Responsible for municipal government and land use planning in New Brunswick.

New Brunswick Department of Natural Resources and Energy
Fish & Wildlife Branch
PO Box 6000
Fredericton, NB E3B 5H1
contact: Pat Kehoe
ph: 506-453-2440

Conserves and manages wetlands and coastal habitats. Offers a coastal ethics brochure, landowner's wetland package, program brochures and information on the Daly Point Reserve.

New Brunswick Emergency Measures Organization
PO Box 6000
Fredericton, NB E3B 5H1
contact: Arthur Skaling
ph: 506-453-2133
fax: 506-453-5513

Works to mitigate the effect of natural and human-made disasters upon persons, property and the environment by participating in a regional response team and international emergency management group. Operates an automated emergency information system and a library with technical papers, audio-visual materials and public information on emergency planning, response and recovery.

New Brunswick Land and Water Advisory Committee
Department of the Environment
PO Box 6000
Fredericton, NB E3B 5H1
contact: David Besner
ph: 506-453-3703

Advises the provincial government with respect to major land and water issues; recommends a comprehensive land and water-use policy to the government.

St. Croix International Waterway Commission
435 Milltown Boulevard
St. Stephen, NB E3L 1J9
contact: Lee Sochasky
ph: 506-466-6550

Facilitates cooperative, integrated management of the St. Croix International Waterway's resources, and provides resource maps, research and historical documents, and slides of the estuary.

New Hamphire

Central New England Anadromous Fish Program
U.S. Fish & Wildlife Service
151 Broad St.
Nashua, NH 03063
contact: Matt Poole, Outdoor Recreation Planner
ph: 603-598-4392
fax: 603-595-3478

Coordinates federal, state and private efforts forum on anadromous fish restoration in the Merrimack and Pawcatuk Rivers. Presents programs on interdisciplinary watershed education and anadromous fish restoration.

Nashua National Fish Hatchery
U.S. Fish & Wildlife Service
151 Broad Street
Nashua, NH 03063
contact: Vic Segarich, Project Leader
ph: 603-886-7719
fax: 603-886-7720

Conserves wild anadromous Atlantic salmon populations by maintaining a broodstock population to produce eggs that are transferred to other hatcheries for fry, parr, and smolt production.

New Hampshire Coastal Program
New Hampshire Office of State Planning
2 1/2 Beacon Street
Concord, NH 03301-2361
contact: Kristine Cheetham
ph: 603-271-2155

New Hampshire Department of Environmental Services
Water Supply and Pollution Control Division
6 Hazen Drive
Concord, NH 03301
contact: Richard A. Flanders
ph: 603-271-3505

Controls and prevents pollution sources and protects or restores threatened surface and groundwaters through projects such as stormwater management, water-quality monitoring and shellfish sanitary surveys. Publications include *Good Neighbor Guide for HorseKeeping: Manure Management;* and *Guidelines for the Preparation of Site-specific Applications.*

New Hampshire Division of Parks and Recreation
Bureau of Marine Services
PO Box 856
105 Loudon Road
Concord, NH 03301
contact: Rich McLeod
ph: 603-271-3254

Operates fish piers, boat-launch facilities, state parks and historic sites along New Hampshire's coast. Coastal and park brochures and educational videos available.

New Hampshire Fish & Game, Region 3
Marine Fisheries Division
37 Concord Road
Durham, NH 03824
contact: John Nelson
ph: 603-868-1095

Regulates and promotes recreational and commercial marine fishing, and offers publications and newsletters.

New Hampshire Natural Heritage Inventory Program

New Hampshire Department of Resources and Economic Development
PO Box 856
Concord, NH 03302-0856
contact: Frankie Brackley Tolman
ph: 603-271-3623

Monitors threatened and endangered plant and animal species through field work, mapping efforts and database compilation.

New Hampshire State Port Authority

555 Market Street
Portsmouth, NH 03801
contact: Michelle Hart, Administrative Assistant
ph: 603-436-8500
fax: 603-436-2780

Oversees harbor management, including 1,400 moorings in the state's tidal waters. Offers a handbook, newsletter, video, and tours of facilities by appointment.

Rockingham Planning Commission

121 Water Street
Exeter, NH 03833
contact: Cliff Sinnott, Executive Director
ph: 603-778-0885
fax: 603-778-9183

Furthers sound land use and resource planning through resource inventories and mapping, open-space planning, promotion of land use regulations and mapping of critical areas.

U.S. Fish & Wildlife Service: New England Field Office

22 Bridge Street, Unit 1
Concord, NH 03301-4901
contact: Linda Morse, Communications Specialist
ph: 603-225-1411
fax: 603-225-1467
e-mail: r5es_nefo

Works to protect and enhance fish and wildlife and their habitats by assisting in coastal wetlands protection, evaluating development, providing scientific data and protecting endangered species. Resources include publications, technical reports, curricula, fact sheets, exhibits, maps, and atlases.

USDA Natural Resources Conservation Service

Federal Building
Durham, NH 03824-1499
contact: Dawn W. Genes
ph: 603-868-7581
fax: 603-868-5301

Works to reduce soil erosion and prevent nonpoint source pollution, providing financial and technical assistance for pollution control in the Great Bay drainage area. Soil surveys, technical standards, publications, pamphlets, videos, tapes, and speakers provided.

Nova Scotia

Atlantic Coastal Action Program (Environment Canada)

45 Alderney Drive
Dartmouth, NS B24 2N6
contact: Karen Swan, Project Officer
ph: 902-426-3766
fax: 902-426-4457
e-mail: swank@cpdar.dots.doe.ca
(see listing in New Brunswick portion of this section)

Community Contacts in Nova Scotia

Annapolis:
Stephen Hawboldt
Clean Annapolis River Project
(see listing in section on nonprofit organizations)

Pictou:
Bob Christie
Pictou Harbour Environmental Protection Project
PO Box 1570
Pictou, NS B0K 1H0
ph/fax: 902-485-1999
e-mail: phepp@fox.nstn.ca

Mahone Bay - Lunenberg:
Mike Parker
Bluenose Atlantic Coastal Action Program
PO Box 10
Mahone Bay, NS B0J 2E0
ph: 902-624-9888
fax: 902-624-9818
e-mail: nstn1033@fox.nstn.ns.ca

Sydney:
Judy White
ACAP Cape Breton, Inc.
Box 28, Station A
Sydney, NS B1P 6G9
ph/fax: 902-567-6282

Canadian Coast Guard

Aids & Waterways
PO Box 1000
Dartmouth, NS B2Y 3Z8
contact: John Major
ph: 902-426-3939

Contributes to a safe and effective marine transportation system through vessel traffic services and aids to navigation. Provides governmental publications, a list of lights and fog signals and marine aids directives.

Canadian Park Service

Historic Properties
Upper Water Street
Halifax, NS B3J 1S9
contact: Larry Brown
ph: 902-426-2063

Provides professional expertise in managing and protecting resources of cultural and natural heritage.

Canadian Wildlife/Marine Wildlife Conservation Division

Atlantic Region Office
Bedford Institute of Oceanography
PO Box 1006
Dartmouth, NS B2Y 4A2
contact: Eric Hiscock, Chief
ph: 902-426-6314

Conducts research on colonial and pelagic aspects of seabirds and develops management plans for certain marine species. Technical advice, speakers and publications available (such as the *Gazetteer of Marine Birds in Atlantic Canada: An Atlas of Sea Bird Vulnerability to Oil Pollution*).

144

Council of Maritime Premiers
Box 2044
Halifax, NS B3J 2Z1
contact: Kim Thomson,
Information Officer
ph: 902-424-7590
fax: 902-424-8976
e-mail: premiers@fox.nstn.ns.ca

Ensures coordination and promotes joint undertakings among the provinces of Prince Edward Island, New Brunswick and Nova Scotia, working through agencies, interprovincial committees and task forces.

Nova Scotia Department of Fisheries and Oceans
Scotia-Fundy Region
Headquarters
PO Box 550
Halifax, NS B3J 2S7
contact: Neil Bellafontaine
ph: 902-426-2581

Manages fisheries in the Bay of Fundy, Scotia Shelf and Georges Bank and watershed areas. Provides publications such as *Beside the Sea* (which examines coastal areas of the Gulf region), and the *Adopt-a-Stream Manual*.

Nova Scotia Department of Fisheries and Oceans
Bedford Institute of Oceanography
Marine Assessment Liason
Division
PO Box 1006
Dartmouth, NS B2Y 4A2
contact: Brian Nicholls
ph: 902-426-3246

Conducts research on management and development of ocean resources (*e.g.*, fish stock surveys, toxic chemical risk assessment, and pollution stress in salmon) and provides publications, posters, speakers, films and a computerized global bibliography on oil pollution and aquatic environments.

**Environment Canada —
Atlantic Region**
Queen Square, 45 Alderney Drive
Dartmouth, NS B2Y 2N6
contact: Edward Norrena
ph: 902-426-7155
fax:902-426-3574

Implements federal environmental policy and administers the Canadian Marine Environmental Quality Program, the Integrated Resource Management Program, and the Sustainable Development Program. Provides public and industry advisory documents, technical advice and project support through existing funding programs. Environmental Canada's Water Campaign Environmental Learning Program (ph: 819-953-9427) provides many free educational resources such as *From the Mountains to the Sea: A Journey in Environmental Citizenship* (for ages 3-8); *Use Water Wisely; Water Conservation: Every Drop Counts; Water-saving Devices;* and *Water — the Transporter*.

Nova Scotia Department of the Environment
PO Box 2107
Halifax, NS B3J 3B7
contact: Peter Underwood
ph: 902-424-5695
fax: 902-424-0503

Works to protect and enhance the province's natural environment through programs such as municipal sewage assistance, hazardous-waste management plans, legislation/regulations, environmental education materials, and reports (*e.g., Clean Water for Nova Scotia: New Directions for Water Resource Management*).

Nova Scotia Department of Fisheries
PO Box 2223
Halifax, NS B3J 3C4
contact: Art Longard
ph: 902-424-0347

Promotes industrial development, aquaculture, recreational fisheries, marketing, training and development of management plans. Offers a series of pamphlets on sensitive habitats.

Nova Scotia Land Use Policy Committee
PO Box 22540
Halifax, NS B3J 3C8
contact: C.D. Conrad
ph: 902-424-4963

Reviews matters related to land use (*e.g.*, beach land use, coastal zone mapping, comprehensive watershed management and municipal water supplies). Slide presentation on watershed protection and booklet entitled *Water, Water Everywhere: Protecting the Municipal Water Supply in Nova Scotia*.

Nova Scotia Department of Mines & Energy
PO Box 1087
Halifax, NS B3J 3C8
contact: Andrew G. Batcup
ph: 902-424-5933

Evaluates and regulates Nova Scotia's mineral resources, including joint management with the federal government of offshore petroleum resources.

MEDIA RESOURCES

Bullfrog Films
PO Box 149
Oley, PA 19547
ph: 1-800-543-FROG
fax: 610-370-1978
e-mail: bullfrog@igc.apc.org.

Film distributors with several dozen videos on ecological and marine topics that are available for rental or purchase. Sample titles include "Secrets of the Salt Marsh," "The Shoreline Doesn't Stop Here Anymore," "Troubled Waters," and "Pointless Pollution: America's Water Crisis." Free catalog.

Films for the Humanities & Sciences
PO Box 2053
Princeton, NJ 08543-2053
ph: 1-800-257-5126
fax: 609-275-3767

Distributes films on environmental science and policy issues, such as energy alternatives, global warming, oceanography, coastal erosion, waste disposal and an *Earthkeeping* series on environmental action. Free catalog.

Griesinger Films
7300 Old Mill Road
Gates Mills, OH 44040
ph: 216-423-1601
fax: 216-423-1601

Produces and distributes films on issues of sustainability. Titles include "Investing in Natural Capital" and "An Introduction to Ecological Economics."

Maine Department of Marine Resources
Fisherman's Library Video Collection
DMR Fisheries Laboratory
McKown Point
West Boothbay Harbor, ME 04575
ph: 207-633-9551
fax: 207-633-9641

Contains a library of 65 coastal and marine videos, on subjects such as fishing methods and gear; aquaculture; marine biology; and historical and sociological perspectives on fishing. Films may be borrowed for two weeks, free of charge.

Maine State Library
Educational Video Services
Station 64, LMA Building
Augusta, ME 04333-0064
ph: 207-287-5620
fax: 207-287-5624

Provides copies of video programs produced by the Maine Department of Inland Fisheries and Wildlife, available free to those who supply a blank videotape for each program.

National Film Board of Canada
PO Box 6100
Montreal, Quebec H3C 3H5
ph: 514-283-9000

Offers an extensive collection of films for rental or purchase. Ecology and conservation films include "Estuary," "Where the Bay Becomes the Sea" (about the Bay of Fundy) and "World in a Marsh." Catalog available for $9.

National Geographic Society
Educational Services
PO Box 98018
Washington, DC 20090-8018
ph: 1-800-368-2728
fax: 1-301-921-1575

Offers interactive videodiscs on ecological topics, including such titles as "Planetary Manager," "Habitats" and "Water." CD Rom reference resources include "Our Earth" and "Mammals." Videos and films (for grades K-adult) include "Riches from the Sea," "Pollution: World at Risk" and "Let's Explore a Seashore" (a 16-minute film about the Maine coast). Filmstrips, learning kits, books, atlases, maps, globes and games also available. Free catalog.

Northeast Historic Film
Bucksport, ME 04416-0900
ph: 207-469-0924 or 1-800-639-1636

Works to preserve and distribute moving images of northern New England, including historic films on traditional cultural activities such as logging, river-driving, ice-harvesting, schooner construction and maritime trades. Other titles include "Rachel Carson's Silent Spring" and "Marine Mammals of the Gulf of Maine." Free list of films.

Maine Coastal Program
State Planning Office
Station 38
Augusta, ME 04333-0038
ph: 207-287-3261
fax: 207-287-6489

Offers a free booklet, *Sightings*, which provides titles and descriptions for coastal/marine videos and slideshows available free or at low cost to schools and community groups throughout Maine. Includes resources available through the Maine Coastal Program, Maine State Library, Department of Marine Resources and University of Maine Sea Grant. The Coastal Program also has five traveling displays on coastal topics that may be borrowed by schools, libraries and community groups.

Turner Multimedia
105 Terry Drive, Suite 120
Newtown, PA 18940
ph: 1-800-344-6219
fax: 1-215-579-8589

Educational videos include titles such as "CNN Video Reports on the Wetlands," and "The Killing Tide" (about the life and death of America's waterways and wetlands). Live interactive "electronic field trips" offered on urban wetlands and biodiversity research through Turner Adventure Learning (which provides teachers with in-service training events and orientation programs).

MUSEUMS AND AQUARIUMS

Maine

Department of Marine Resources
McKown Point
West Boothbay Harbor, ME 04575
contact: Linda Mercer, Director
ph: 207-633-9500

Educates the public about the fish and fisheries of Maine through live displays, a touch tank and interpretive material. Open weekdays 8-5, weekends and holidays 9-5 from late May to mid-October.

Also located at 633-9500:
Library: Pamela-Shepard-Lupo
Public Aquarium: Jean Chenoweth

Gulf of Maine Aquarium
PO Box 7549
Portland, ME 04221
contact: Meg Handlin,
Administrative Manager
ph: 207-772-2321
fax: 207-772-6855
e-mail: lishness@saturn.caps.
maine.edu

Seeks to facilitate marine research and teach people about Maine's aquatic environments through construction of a waterfront aquarium. Current offerings include a poster ("Katahdin to the Sea"); on-line curriculum and teacher workshops and a "Learning from Satellites" teacher's guide; low-tide walks; a bimonthly member newsletter; and in-school programs on the Gulf of Maine, turtles and watersheds.

Maine Aquarium
Route One
PO Box 859
Saco, ME 04072
contact: Raymond Cronkite
ph: 207-284-4512

Provides exhibits and educational programs on local and exotic aquatic habitats and species, and offers year-round educational programs for schools and groups on topics such as lobstering, tide pools, fish, and penguins. Marine education workshops and curricula for teachers, and a hands-on computer exhibit with marine-related programs for all ages.

Maine Maritime Museum
243 Washington Street
Bath, ME 04530
contact: Public Relations & Marketing Manager.
ph: 207-443-1316
fax: 207-443-1665

Preserves and promotes Maine's maritime culture through exhibits, lectures, workshops and publications (on maritime history, sailing, lobstering, boat building and the Maine coast). Nineteenth-century shipyard with living history demonstrations and interpretive exhibits, library and historic vessels.

Maine State Museum
Cultural Building, Station 83
Augusta, ME 04333-0083
contact: Joseph R. Phillips,
Director
ph: 207-287-2301
fax: 207-287-6633

Works to preserve and present the heritage and history of Maine through gallery programs (*e.g.*, tidepool specimens, lobstering, sailmaking) and exhibits on natural history, shipbuilding, sailmaking and fishing. Open weekdays 9-5; Saturdays 10-4, and Sundays 1-4.

Mount Desert Oceanarium
Clark Point Road
PO Box 696
Southwest Harbor, ME 04609
contact: David and Audrey Mills
ph: 207-244-7330

Educates the public about marine life and commercial fishing through interpretive programs and exhibits. School group programs available at discount. Reservations needed for large groups. Open Monday through Saturday 9-5 from mid-May to mid-October.

Oceanarium: Bar Harbor
Route 3
Bar Harbor, ME 04609
contact: David & Audrey Mills
ph: 207-288-5005

Educational programs about lobsters, lobster fishing and harbor seals. Take a guided walk to a salt marsh.

Natural History Museum at COA
College of the Atlantic
Bar Harbor, ME 04609
contact: Dianne Clendaniel,
Director
phone: 207-288-5015
fax: 207-288-4126
e-mail: doc@ecology.coa.edu

Offers more than 50 exhibits depicting animals of the Gulf of Maine region and traveling natural history programs (Whales-on-wheels, Moveable Moose, Naugehyde Whale, Birds of New England) and traveling exhibits. On-site activities include museum tours and programs; a self-guided seaside nature trail; children's discovery corner; museum bookshop; summer field studies for grades K-12; courses and workshops on exhibit preparation; and a summer speakers' series.

Penobscot Marine Museum
PO Box 498
Searsport, ME 04974-0498
contact: Abigail Zelz, Education Coordinator
ph: 207-548-2529

Educates people about the maritime heritage of Maine, and particularly Searsport. Seven buildings contain exhibits on navigation, small craft, ship construction, marine art, and the Penobscot expedition. Activities include year-round educational programs (in schools and on-site); slide presentations; traveling programs; and a lecture and film series. Open May-October, seven days/week.

Seal Stranding Network

(An affiliate of the New England Aquarium)
University of New England
Department of Life Sciences
11 Hills Beach Road
Biddeford, ME 04005
contact: Eleanor Saboski
ph: 207-283-0171, ext. 2246
fax: 207-282-6379

Assists the New England Aquarium in rehabilitation of stranded seals and other marine mammals.

Massachusetts

Blue Hills Trailside Museum

Massachusetts Department of Education
1904 Canton Ave.
Milton, MA 02186
contact: Patty Steinman
ph: 617-333-0690

Offers hands-on natural history field trips for schools and groups (with overnight accommodations available at the Chickatawbutt Hill Education Center). Reservations required.

Cape Cod Museum of Natural History

PO Box 1710
Brewster, MA 02631
contact: Allan Morich, Director of Education
ph: 508-896-3867
fax: 508-896-8844

Works to increase knowledge of Cape Cod's human and natural history through educational programs (*e.g.*, oceanography cruises and estuary studies), field trips, exhibits, and a resource library.

Custom House Maritime Museum

25 Water Street
Newburyport, MA 01950
contact: Janet Howell, President
ph: 508-462-8681

Presents the maritime heritage of the Merrimack River Valley through exhibits on local ship-building, U.S. Coast Guard history, sea captains, local commerce, and trade and crafts. Publications, videos and a research library.

Essex Shipbuilding Museum

PO Box 277
Essex, MA 01929
ph: 508-768-7541

Maintains archives, exhibits, and educational programs concerning the history of shipbuilding in Essex. Offers a computerized list of vessels, research facilities, and a speaker's bureau.

Hull Lifesaving Museum

PO Box 221
Hull, MA 02045
contact: Judeth Van Hamm
ph: 617-925-2570

Provides school lectures, walking tours, a newsletter and library.

Museum of Science

Science Park
Boston, MA 02114-1099
contact: Courses and Travel Department
ph: 617-589-0340
fax: 617-589-0454

Fosters interest in science and technology through on-site programs and a "marine science field experience" for students age 13-15 at Suffolk University's Friedman Field Station in Edmunds, Maine (on Cobscook Bay).

National Marine Fisheries Service Aquarium

Water Street
Woods Hole, MA 02543
contact: Fred E. Nichy, Director
ph: 508-548-7684

Informs the public of marine concerns through educational tours, displays and a video entitled "Trashing the Oceans."

New Bedford Whaling Museum

18 Johnny Cake Hill
New Bedford, MA 02740
contact: Pat Howard, Secretary
ph: 508-997-0046

Preserves and exhibits artifacts relating to the cultural and economic history of whaling in the New Bedford area. Exhibits, year-round programs, a newsletter, and a research library with more that 1,100 logbooks of whaling voyages.

New England Aquarium

Central Wharf
Boston, MA 02110
contact: Rob Moir, Curator of Education
ph: 617-973-5200; 617-973-5232

Links research and education with advocacy on behalf of aquatic environments. Current projects include monitoring and research in Boston Harbor, a campaign to reduce marine debris and advocate for water quality regulations and toxics reduction. Resources include school curricula packages, reports, speakers, a volunteer program, programs for city youth, workshops, lectures, college courses and a Teachers' Resource Center.

Peabody Museum of Salem

East India Square
Salem, MA 01970
contact: Jane Winchell, Curator of Natural History
ph: 508-745-1876

Works to conserve and interpret the maritime history of New England and natural history of Essex County through exhibits, tours, lectures, library resources, workshops and a teacher-training institute.

148

New Brunswick

Huntsman Aquarium/Museum
Brandy Cove Road
St. Andrews, NB E0G 2X0
contact: James F. McElman, Manager
ph: 506-529-4285

Educates the general public and students in marine science through interpretive tours, day programs, beach walks, films, exhibits, a resident family of harbor seals, and a touch pool. Open 7 days/week, May-October.

New Brunswick Museum
277 Douglas Avenue
Saint John, NB E2K 1E5
contact: R.F. Miller, Head, Natural Sciences Division
ph: 506-643-2300

Collects, preserves and interprets the natural and human history of the Maritimes with exhibits; marine mammal research and publications; fossils; ship portraits; and study collection of natural science specimens and human artifacts.

New Hampshire

Strawberry Banke Museum
Portsmouth, NH 03801
contact: Pat Glidden
ph: 603-433-1100

Living history museum with 10-acre site containing historic homes, craft shops and boat-building facilities. Runs cruises aboard a traditional Piscataqua Gundalow; summer programs for children; and group tours for schools. Monthly calendar of events available.

Nova Scotia

Fisheries Museum of the Atlantic
Bluenose Drive
PO Box 1363
Lunenburg, NS B0J 2C0
contact: Jim Tupper, General Manager
ph: 902-634-4794

Displays exhibits on the fishing industry of the Atlantic Canadian coast, and maintains a reference library, photograph collection and register of shipping documents.

Nova Scotia Museum
1747 Summer Street
Halifax, NS B3H 3A6
ph: 902-429-4610

Offers publications such as *Springwatch* (an activity book for children).

NONPROFIT ORGANIZATIONS

Maine

Atlantic Salmon Federation
Fort Andross
14 Maine St.
Brunswick, ME 04011
contact: John Albright
ph: 207-725-2833

See New Brunswick entry for a description of activities.

Congress of Lake Associations
Box 391
Yarmouth, ME 04096
contact: Joan Irish
ph: 207-846-4271

A statewide network that works to protect and preserve Maine lakes by providing an informational clearinghouse, monitoring legislation, educating the public and supporting sound lake management.

Conservation Law Foundation, Inc.
119 Tillson Ave.
Rockland, ME 04841-3416
contact: Dan Sosland
ph: 207-594-8107
fax: 207-596-7706
e-mail: dsosland@clf.org

Promotes resource conservation through legal and economic advocacy on issues such as fisheries management, estuary protection and pollution control. Currently building a Gulf of Maine Ecosystem Advocacy Network.

Friends of Casco Bay
2 Fort Road
South Portland, ME 04106
contact: Joe Payne, Casco BayKeeper; Cheryl Seavey, Office Manager
ph: 207-799-8574
fax: 207-799-7224
e-mail: cascobay@keeper.org

Works to improve the environmental health of Casco Bay through stewardship, water-quality monitoring, oil-spill preparedness, clam-flat restoration and vessel pumpout alternatives. The BayKeeper [TM] works with citizens and businesses to cooperatively solve pollution problems and promote sound stewardship. The Portland Harbor Marine Debris Council, a project of FOCB, seeks to clean Portland Harbor through recycling efforts, waterfront cleanups, and a used oil collection center. FOCB offers a water-quality monitoring manual and a comprehensive volunteer database program.

The Green Institute
620 Back Road
North New Portland, ME 04961
contact: Jonathan Carter, Director
ph/fax: 207-628-5741

Sponsors educational programs (conferences, workshops and trips) that stress interrelationships among environmental, social and economic community-level concerns. Programs focus on topics such as "pollution in the Gulf of Maine bioregion" and forest management.

Island Institute
60 Ocean Street
Rockland, ME 04841
contact: Philip W. Conkling
ph: 207-594-9209
fax: 207-594-9314
e-mail: iinst@aol.com

Advocates balanced use of Maine islands and support for island communities through services such as natural resource consulting (*e.g.*, solid waste and water conservation studies, satellite imagery and remote sensing and forest management advice); community assistance *(e.g.*, affordable housing, island schools); periodicals (two bimonthly papers, *Inter-Island News* and *Working Waterfronts*, and an annual journal) and more than 500 technical papers.

Maine Aquaculture Innovation Center
141 N. Main Street, Suite 203
Brewer, ME 04412
contact: Mike Hastings
ph: 207-989-5310

Promotes aquaculture development through research and industry partnership. Publishes a quarterly newsletter, a research reports and an aquaculture publications list.

Maine Association of Conservation Commissions
PO Box 9005
Augusta, ME 04338
contact: Susan MacPherson, Executive Director
ph: 207-622-5330
fax: 207-622-6228

Provides educational and support services for member commissions and municipalities, including site visits, workshops, conferences, legislative monitoring and a quarterly newsletter. Publications include the *Maine Manual for Conservation Commissions* and *A Planning Tool for Maine Communities: Natural Resources Handbook*. Annual meeting/workshop each April.

Maine Audubon Society
Gilsland Farm
118 U.S. Route One
Falmouth, ME 04105
contact: Bill Hancock, educational programs
ph: 207-781-2330
fax: 207-781-6185

Promoting sound use of Maine's environment through education and advocacy. Numerous coastal sanctuaries; teacher's resource center for K-12 educators; field trips; nature day camp; school programs; and *Habitat*, a bimonthly journal.

Maine Coast Heritage Trust
167 Park Row
Brunswick, ME 04011

Second Office:
PO Box 426
Northeast Harbor, ME 04662
contact: James J. Espy, President
ph: 207-729-7366
fax: 207-729-6863

Protects shoreland areas of scenic, ecological, recreational and cultural significance by providing free conservation services to landowners, government agencies, local land trusts and communities. Publications include technical bulletins and *Conservation Options: A Guide for Maine Landowners*.

Maine Harbor Masters Association
Marine Trade Center
Portland Fish Pier, Suite 215A
Portland, ME 04101
contact: Al Trefry
ph/fax: 207-772-8121

Promotes training of harbor masters and effective harbor management through distribution of a management manual, training curriculum, and legal and educational guidance.

Maine Lobster Pound Association
HCR 77, Box 445
Hancock, ME 04640
contact: Herb Hodgkins, Executive Secretary
ph: 207-422-6238
fax: 207-422-9116

Works with other representative organizations to promote the lobster industry from the perspective of poundkeepers.

Maine Organic Farmers and Gardeners Association

PO Box 2176
Augusta, ME 04338
ph: 207-622-3118

Promotes organic and sustainable agriculture through education, legislation, and development of farmers' markets and community gardens. MOFGA sponsors summer garden tours and the annual Common Ground Country Fair (held each September).

Maine Science and Technology Foundation

87 Winthrop Street
Augusta, ME 04330
contact: Suzanne Watson
ph: 207-621-6350
fax: 207-621-6369
e-mail: watson@saturn.cape.maine.edu

Works to improve Maine industry's competitive performance through innovation and process development. Approximately one-quarter of the foundation's $1.5 million budget supports marine initiatives, such as the Maine Aquaculture Innovation Center and the Marine Research Board.

Maine Windjammer Association

PO Box 1144
Blue Hill, ME 04614
contact: Meg Maiden
ph: 207-374-2993
fax: 207-374-2952

Offers low-impact coastal cruises aboard traditional windjammers in Penobscot Bay. Brochures, videos and newsletter available.

Natural Resources Council of Maine (NRCM)

271 State Street
Augusta, ME 04330
contact: Judy Berk,
Communications Director
ph: 207-622-3101
fax: 207-622-4343

Protects Maine's environment through a program of advocacy, education and legal defense on issues such as coastal growth management, overboard discharge, and wetlands. Monthly newsletter, fact sheets and technical assistance available.

The Nature Conservancy — Maine Chapter

Fort Andross
14 Maine Street, Suite 401
Brunswick, ME 04011
contact: Bruce Kidman,
Communications Coordinator
ph: 207-729-5181

Works to identify and protect rare and endangered plant and animal species, habitats and natural communities. Maintains 55 island preserves (20 of which are open for careful day use) and a field trip program. Preserve brochures and guidebook available.

Penobscot River and Bay Institute

Box 214A
Brooksville, ME 04617
ph: 207-326-4822

Promotes the understanding and stewardship of the Penobscot River and Bay watershed and works to instill knowledge and skills leading to the conservation of the watershed's natural resources. Teacher guides and curriculum materials available.

RESTORE: The North Woods

7 North Chestnut St.
Augusta, ME 04330
contact: Jym St. Pierre
ph: 207-626-5635
fax: 207-622-9739

The purpose of this grassroots organization is to restore and preserve the natural integrity of the North Woods ecoregion of the United States and Canada through advocacy, public awareness and citizen action. Main Office in Massachusetts.

Sierra Club — Maine Chapter

192 State Street
Portland, ME 04101
contact: Joan Saxe (207-865-3648)
Ken Cline (207-288-3381)

Grassroots organizing to preserve the environment, promote awareness, and protect wildlife and wilderness. Conservation Committee works on local Maine issues.

Sustainable Maine

PO Box 676
Portland, ME 04104-0676
ph: 207-781-3947

Promotes strategies to support the ecological and economic health of Maine, and offers a primer on sustainability, other resource information and periodic conferences.

Massachusetts

American Fisheries Society

Southern New England Chapter
c/o National Marine Fisheries Service
Woods Hole, MA 02543
contact: Donald D. Flescher
ph: 508-548-5123
fax: 508-548-5124
e-mail: dflesch@whsun1.wh.whoi.edu

Evaluates educational, scientific and technological development in fisheries science and practice. Books and periodicals available.

Appalachian Mountain Club

5 Joy St.
Boston, MA 02108
ph: 617-523-0655
fax: 617-367-8878

Provides opportunities to hike, canoe and kayak, and to participate in maintaining AMC trails (primarily in the White Mountains of New Hampshire and adjacent Maine) and learn about the natural environment. A multi-faceted educational program is offered at the AMC's Pinkham Notch headquarters at the base of Mt. Washington.

151

American Littoral Society
New England Regional Office
PO Box 301
Woods Hole, MA 02543
contact: Don W. Bourne, Regional
Director
ph: 508-457-1499

Works to preserve and restore
coastal habitats and streams. Offers
educational programs, walks and
field trips, a magazine and two
newsletters, and scuba-dive trips.

**Atlantic Center for the
Environment/Quebec Labrador
Foundation**
39 South Main Street
Ipswich, MA 01938
contact: Kathleen Blanchard,
Executive Vice President
ph: 508-356-0038
fax: 508-356-7322
e-mail: atlantictr@igc.apc.org

Supports rural communities and
the environment of northern New
England and eastern Canada
through environmental education,
seabird research, publications,
community development assistance, international conservation
exchanges, conservation internships, land and river stewardship,
workshops and seminars.

The Coastal Society
PO Box 2081
Gloucester, MA 01930-2081
contact: Thomas E. Bigford
ph: 508-281-9209

Promotes better understanding and
sustainable use of the earth's coastal
resources by serving as a forum for
coastal resource professionals and
individuals. Holds biennial conferences and provides limited information on volunteer programs and
careers.

Cole Parkway Marina
100 Cole Parkway
Scituate, MA 02066
contact: Elmer Pooler,
Harbormaster
ph: 617-545-2130

Promotes effective coastal harbor
management by coordinating local
oil-spill cleanups and providing
coastal planning and permitting.

**Collaboration of Community
Foundations for the Gulf of
Maine**
One Boston Place, 24th Floor
Boston, MA 02108
contact: Lissa Widoff
ph: 617-723-7415
fax: 617-589-3616
e-mail: lwidoff@igc.apc.org

Supports community-based
approaches to regional issues in the
Gulf of Maine, such as the Gulf of
Maine Coastal Monitoring
Network and the Community
Fisheries Project.

**The Compact of Cape Cod
Conservation Trusts, Inc.**
PO Box 7
Barnstable, MA 02630
contact: Mark H. Robinson
ph: 508-362-9131
fax: 508-362-5335

Assists towns and private organizations to acquire and manage lands
for open space, and educates the
public about coastal planning, land
management and water quality
through workshops and advisory
services.

**Conservation Law Foundation,
Inc. (CLF)**
62 Summer Street
Boston, MA 02110-1008
contact: Peter Shelley
ph: 617-350-0990
fax: 617-350-4030
e-mail: pshelley@clf.org

Supports resource conservation
using legal and economic advocacy
on issues such as fisheries management, estuary protection, and pollution control in the Gulf of
Maine. Publications, fact sheets,
topical exhibits and a speakers'
bureau available.

**Environmental League of
Massachusetts**
3 Joy Street
Boston, MA 02108
contact: Paul Wingle, Vice
President, Legislative Affairs
ph: 617-742-2553
fax: 617-742-9654

Promotes environmental legislation such as a new open space bond
issue for Massachusetts. Legislative
information and a quarterly bulletin available.

**International Wildlife
Coalition/Whale Adoption
Project**
70 East Falmouth Highway
East Falmouth, MA 02536-5954
contact: Daniel J. Morast,
President
ph: 508-548-8328
fax: 508-548-8542

Works to protect endangered
wildlife worldwide and educate the
public through a "Whales of the
World" teacher's kit (for grades K-
5); newsletters and quarterly issues
updates; whale patrols; habitat use
surveys; and training of volunteers
(in the Cape Cod Stranding
Network).

**League of Women Voters of
Massachusetts**
133 Portland Street
Boston, MA 02114
contact: Myrna Hewitt, Chair of
Natural Resources
ph: 617-523-2999

Encourages citizen participation in
legislative action concerning land
use, toxins, water and solid waste.
Organizes the Coastweek celebra-
tion held each fall, and provides
legislative information and action,
lectures, tours, workshops, a speakers' bureau and newsletter.

**Massachusetts Aquaculture
Association**
PO Box 154
West Yarmouth, MA 02673
contact: Dick Nelson
ph: 508-362-2511

Offers educational, advisory and
referral services; lectures and
exhibits; and technical assistance
for growers.

Massachusetts Association of Conservation Commissions

10 Juniper Road
Belmont, MA 02178
contact: Tracy Lang
ph: 617-489-3930

Helps conservation commissions and interested citizens protect community natural resources by providing workshops, conferences, videos and slide shows, legal and technical assistance, a newsletter and speakers' bureau.

Massachusetts Audubon Society

South Great Road
Lincoln, MA 01773
contact: Holly Spousta
ph: 617-259-9500
fax: 617-259-8899

Promotes environmental education, advocacy, open-space preservation and biological conservation. Maintains 19 sanctuaries, and provides research reports, an environmental library and a catalog of publications.

Massachusetts Lobstermen's Association

PO Box 600
Scituate, MA 02066-0600
contact: William Adler, Executive Director
ph: 617-545-6984
fax: 617-545-7837

Fosters sensible harvesting and conservation methods; strengthens law enforcement; and promotes cooperation among lobstermen. Informational exchange, technical consulting, legal information and newsletter available.

Massachusetts Shellfish Officers Association (MSOA)

c/o Wellfleet Shellfish Department
300 Main Street
Wellfleet, MA 02667
contact: Paul Sommerville, President
ph: 508-349-0325
fax: 508-349-0305

Provides a forum for coastal municipalities' shellfish officers to exchange information about research, management, law enforcement and water quality. Public education and input to legislators offered concerning stormwater runoff; shellfish propagation, management and regulation; and aquaculture.

Massachusetts Water Watch Partnership and River Watch

Blaisdell House
Amherst, MA 01003
contact: Jerry Schoen
ph: 413-545-5532

Offers a training manual for river water-quality monitoring and consultation concerning river and lake water-quality monitoring.

Massachusetts Wildlife Federation, Inc.

PO Box 188
Concord, MA 01742
contact: Wayne Davis, President
ph: 508-759-7228

Promotes conservation education through a monthly newsletter and quarterly publication, National Wildlife Week, and legislative efforts.

Merrimack River Watershed Council, Inc.

694 Main Street
West Newbury, MA 01985
contact: Ralph Goodno
ph: 508-363-5777

Offers publications and a video on valley pollution issues; recreational maps; a quarterly newsletter; and recreational map and canoe guide.

Neponset River Watershed Association

2468 A Washington
Canton, MA 02021
contact: Ian Cooke
ph: 617-575-0354

A streams project curriculum and a interpretive watershed walk program are available.

New England Fisheries Development Association

451 D Street
Boston, MA 02210
contact: Ken Coons, Executive Director
ph: 617-443-9494
fax: 617-443-9499
e-mail: 77501,3402@compuserve.com

Works to improve handling of fish and shellfish to ensure product quality and safety. Conducts marine toxin research; provides consumers and industry with information on fish and shellfish, aquaculture, harvesting, processing and distribution, seafood contaminants and waste utilization. Electronic bulletin board, newsletter and educational programs available.

RESTORE: The North Woods

PO Box 440
Concord, MA 01742-0440
contact: David Carle
ph: 508-287-0320
fax: 508-287-5771

See listing under Maine Nonprofit Organizations for details.

Save the Harbor/Save the Bay

25 West Street
Boston, MA 02111
contact: Janey Keough
ph: 617-451-2860
fax: 617-451-0496

Works to protect and promote Boston Harbor and Massachusetts Bay through the BayWatch Project, Bays Advocacy Program and Harbor Crew Youth Program. Offers volunteer programs, internships, annual events (swim races, boat tours, meetings), and a video on Boston Harbor.

Stripers Unlimited, Inc.

PO Box 3045
South Attleboro, MA 02703
contact: Avis Boyd, Executive Secretary
ph: 508-761-7983
fax: 508-761-7973

Protects striped bass and its habitat through research and education about chemical pollution in the environment. Slide lectures and a newsletter available.

The Trust for Public Land (TPL)
New England Regional Office
33 Union Street
Boston, MA 02108
ph: 617-367-6200
fax: 617-367-1616

Facilitates protection of open space areas in urban and rural settings for public use (often acting as an interim buyer of threatened properties). Technical assistance and publications available.

The Trustees of Reservation
572 Essex Street
Beverly, MA 01915
ph: 508-921-1944

Preserves properties of exceptional scenic, historic and ecological value throughout Massachusetts. Manages numerous coastal reservations and refuges. Newsletter, calander of events, annual report, naturalist walks, workshops and conservation videos available.

New Brunswick

ACAP - Saint John
PO Box 6878, Station A
Saint John, NB E2L 4S3
contact: Allison Lowe, Director, Communications;
Patrick Desmond, Director, Technical Operations
ph: 506-652-2227
fax: 506-633-2184
e-mail: acapsj@mi.net

Working to develop a comprehensive management plan for the Saint John Harbor and its tributaries and involve stakeholders through environmental monitoring, pollution prevention, materials exchange and public education. Offers a resource center, videos, training sessions and a water-quality monitoring fair.

Atlantic Salmon Federation
PO Box 429
St. Andrews, NB E0G 2X0
ph: 506-529-4581
fax: 506-529-9189

Promotes education, research and international cooperation to support conservation and management of the Atlantic Salmon. Offers research papers, technical reports, audio-visual materials and *Fish Friends* (a curriculum supplement for grades 4-6).

Conservation Council of New Brunswick
180 St. John Street
Fredericton, NB E3B 4A9
contact: David Coon, Bay of Fundy Project Coordinator
ph: 506-458-8747
fax: 506-466-4033

Promotes education and advocacy that support the regions ecological integrity (currently assessing environmental impacts of saltwater aquaculture and developing an ecological fisheries program). Educational resources include a cassette tape ("Voices of the Bay: Changing Times along Fundy Shores"); *Turning the Tide — A Citizen's Guide to the Bay of Fundy*; slide shows and posters; school kits on marine debris; and a Bibliography of Scientific Research in the Bay of Fundy (five volumes).

The EarthWarden Program
327 Chartersville Road
Dieppe, NB E1A 1K5
contact: Shirley St. Pierre, Director
ph: 506-852-4483

Publishes the *EarthWarden Guide Book* ($10.00) and promotes environmental awareness and stewardship for school children.

Eastern Charlotte Waterways, Inc.
Main Street
St. George, NB E0G 2Y0
contact: Thomas E. Clark, Executive Director
ph: 506-755-6001
fax: 506-755-6187
e-mail: ecwinc@nbnet.nb.ca

Fosters community participation in joint environmental management of local watersheds through water-quality monitoring; economic valuation of intertidal zones; coastal resource mapping; remote video sensing; oil-spill contingency planning; and recreational fisheries management. Environmental resource center being developed with library of slides and aerial photography.

Fundy Guild Inc.
PO Box 150
Alma, NB E0A 1B0
ph: 506-887-2000

Promotes understanding and enjoyment of Fundy national park and the surrounding area; organizes two beach cleanups each year and distributes a beach guide, *We Live by the Sea* booklet, and posters.

The Kindness Club
65 Brunswick Street
Fredericton, NB E3B 1G5
contact: Jane Tarn
ph: 506-459-3379

Provides humane and environmental education for children, including classroom programs on marine debris, teachers' kits ($8, postpaid), information sheets, and a club structure that fosters local activities (*e.g.*, adopt-a-whale, trash cleanups, tree plantings). Quarterly newsletter ($3/yr. for children) and an annual essay contest.

Maritime Fisherman's Union
PO Box 1418
Shediac, NB E0A 3G0
contact: Michael Belliveau
ph: 506-532-2485

Promotes the interests of inshore fishermen.

The Nature Trust of New Brunswick, Inc.

PO Box 603, Station A
Fredericton, NB E3B 5A6
ph: 506-453-3488
fax: 506-457-7267
e-mail: hins@unb.ca

Acquires and protects the habitat of rare or endangered plants and animals and educates people about the importance of natural areas. Owns Mowat Island (in Deer Island Archipelago) and covenants on Barnes and Manowagonish islands in the Bay of Fundy. Brochures, newsletters and land consultations available.

New Brunswick Environmental Network

RR 4
Sussex, NB E0E 1P0
contact: Mary Ann Coleman
ph/fax: 506-433-6101
e-mail: nben@web.apc.org

Encourages cooperation and communication among citizen's environmental groups and between these groups and the government. Offers newsletter and database of 76 New Brunswick environmental groups.

New Brunswick Federation of Naturalists

RR 2
Albert, NB E0A 1A0
contact: Mary Majka

Facilitates communication among naturalists; promotes coastal cleanups; and offers interpretation and protection programs at shorebird nesting sites. Publishes *New Brunswick Naturalist* quarterly.

New Brunswick Wildlife Federation

PO Box 889
Moncton, NB E1C 8N8
contact: Richard DeBow
ph: 506-857-2110

Protects the wildlife and natural resources of New Brunswick.

Shore Watch

Cranberry Head Road, Box 628
Chance RR 2
Lepreau, NB E0G 2H0
contact: Mike Bursey
ph: 506-659-3414

Offers practical coastal educational programs and projects such as shore cleanups, salt marsh construction and protection, and a sustainable development initiative.

St. Croix Estuary Project

237 Water Street
St. Andrews, NB E0G 2X0
contact: Rob Ranier
ph: 506-529-4868
fax: 506-529-4878
e-mail: scepnet2nbnet.nb.ca

Seeks to develop a comprehensive environmental management plan for the St. Croix estuary. Current programs include environmental planning and monitoring, geographic mapping, and public education. Provides local expertise, maps, a slide collection and resource library.

St. John Port Corporation

PO Box 6429, Station A
Saint John, NB E2L 4RB
contact: Peter Clark, Director of Marketing
ph: 506-636-4869

Works to enhance international trade via the Port of Saint John, creating economic benefits for the community. Video, fact sheets and newsletter available.

New Hamphire

Audubon Society of New Hampshire

3 Silk Farm Road
Concord, NH 03301-8200
contact: Scott Fitzpatrick,
Education Director
ph: 603-224-9909
e-mail: nhaudubon@igc.org

Protects and conserves wildlife and their habitat in New Hampshire through events, publications,

exhibits, and educational programs at the Seacoast Science Center/Odiorne State Park in Rye. Publications include *Method for the Inventory and Evaluation of Vegetated Tidal Marshes in New Hampshire.*

Great Bay Estuarine System Conservation Trust

PO Box 34
Durham, NH 03824
contact: William D. Penhale, Newsletter Editor
ph: 603-868-2952

Preserves the natural resources of the Great Bay Estuary through review and action on current and prospective activities related to the bay. Speakers, educational activities and a quarterly newsletter available.

Interstate Passenger Boat Association

PO Box 250
East Kingston, NH 02837
contact: Brad Cook, President
ph: 603-394-7008

Responds to administrative and legislative activity affecting the passenger vessel industry; conducts ongoing whale research.

The Nature Conservancy: New Hampshire Chapter

2 1/2 Beacon Street, Suite 6
Concord, NH 03301
contact: Henry Tepper, State Director
ph: 603-224-5853
fax: 603-228-2459

Preserves the habitats of diverse plants, animals and natural communities through land protection and biodiversity surveys. Publications and field trips offered.

New Hampshire Association of Conservation Commissions

54 Portsmouth Street
Concord, NH 03301
contact: Marjory M. Swope, Executive Director
ph: 603-224-7867

Fosters conservation and sound use of New Hampshire's natural resources through the formation and support of conservation

commissions. Facilitates communication among conservation commissions and between commissions and governmental agencies. Offers a *Handbook for Municipal Conservation Commissions in NH*, a quarterly newsletter and periodic conservation news bulletins.

New Hampshire Commercial Fishermen's Association

PO Box 601
Rye, NH 03870
contact: Eric Anderson, President
ph: 603-431-1779

New Hampshire Wildlife Federation

PO Box 239
Concord, NH 03301
contact: Mary Shriver
ph: 603-224-5953

Protects natural resources through conservation, education and legislation. Bimonthly newspaper for members.

The Northern Forest Forum

PO Box 6
Lancaster, NH 03584
contact: Jamie Sayen, Editor
ph: 603-636-2952

Published six times a year ($15. subscription fee) the *Forum*'s mission is to promote sustainable natural and human communities for the northern forest region. Focuses on wilderness issues, establishment of large eco-reserves, reforming unsustainable forest practices, economic issues, establishing communications with timber industries and promoting "cultural restoration" of the forest region.

Propeller Club of the U.S.

Port of Portsmouth, NH
PO Box 1436
Portsmouth, NH 03802-1436
contact: Whitcomb Wells
ph: 603-772-2245

Promotes the merchant marine, shipyards and allied industries, and supports the UNH Sea Grant Program.

Society for the Protection of New Hampshire Forests

54 Portsmouth Street
Concord, NH 03301
contact: Sylvia Bates, Director of Land Protection
ph: 603-224-9945
fax: 603-228-0423

Promotes conservation and appropriate use of New Hampshire's natural resources through education, advocacy, land protection and forest management. Information and workshops available on land protection and forest management issues, as well as two videos ("Land in Trust" and "Logging Aesthetics") and a quarterly magazine, *Forest Notes*.

The Strafford Rivers Conservancy

PO Box 623
Dover, NH 03820
contact: Peggy McLaughlin
ph: 603-742-9434

Preserves the Strafford region's natural resources through fee simple acquisition, conservation easements, and identification of priority conservation areas along local rivers.

Nova Scotia

Annapolis Field Naturalists

PO Box 576
Annapolis Royal, NS B0S 1AO
contact: Gini Proulx
ph: 902-467-3235

Promotes greater understanding of Nova Scotia's natural history and supports environmental protection. Conducts periodic beach sweeps and field trips, and offers monthly public programs.

Annapolis Fly Fishing Association

PO Box 1594
Middleton, NS B0S 1P0
contact: Brian Feener
ph: 902-825-4424

Works to improve fishing in the Annapolis Valley region through education on conservative fishing methods.

Clean Annapolis River Project

PO Box 395
Annapolis Royal, NS B0S 1A0
contact: Stephen Hawboldt, Program Director
ph: 902-532-7533
fax: 902-678-1253
e-mail: shawbold@fox.nstn.ca

Works to develop and implement an integrated resource management strategy for the Annapolis watershed and estuary. Programs include development of coastal zone management software; constructed wetlands; volunteer environmental monitoring; fish habitat restoration; environmental quality assessment; and private stewardship. Public education materials, maps, visual aids and developmental software available.

The Clean Nova Scotia Foundation

POB 2528
Central Halifax, NS B3J 3N5
contact: Martin Janowitz, Executive Director
ph: 902-420-3474
fax: 902-424-5334
e-mail: cnsf@fox.nstn.ca

Works to cooperatively develop a sustainable and healthy society in Nova Scotia through such efforts as Envirotown (a community sustainability project); the Moosehead Maritimes Beach Sweep (involving 15,000 volunteers); a coastal ecosystem education kit; EcoIsland (an interactive elementary education computer game) and a wetlands simulation game (for junior/senior high level); school workshops; community environmental action guides; waste reduction guides; environmental games, posters, a news magazine and a resource library. Publications include the *Adopt-a Beach* booklet, *Beach Sweep and Litter Survey* (an activity guide for junior high students), and *Frogwatch* (on frog habitats).

Ducks Unlimited Canada

PO Box 430, 9 Havelock Street
Amherst, NS B4H 3Z5
contact: Al Glover, Maritime
Provincial Manager
ph: 902-667-8726

Increase waterfowl resources
through preservation and restoration of prime habitat. Film available on estuaries and coastal
wetlands.

Ecology Action Centre

1553 Granville Street
Halifax, NS B3J 1W7
contact: Fred Gale, Chair
ph: 902-429-2202

Works to protect and enhance
Nova Scotia's natural environment
by organizing the Halifax Harbour
Clean-up and providing books
reports, pamphlets, videos and a
newsletter.

Friends of Nature Conservation Society

PO Box 281
Chester, NS B0J 1J0
contact: Martin R. Haase,
Executive Secretary
ph: 902-275-3361

Preserves natural areas through
ownership of wilderness sanctuaries (on the Maine and Nova Scotia
coasts).

Independent Seafood Processors Association of Nova Scotia

PO Box 40
Yarmouth, NS B5A 4B1
contact: Garth L. Dalton,
Secretary/Manager
ph: 902-742-1960
fax: 902-742-1961

Represents the interests of small
fish-processing plants in Nova
Scotia.

Maritime Fishermen's Union Clean Ocean Campaign

RR5
New Glasgow, NS B2H 5C8
ph: 902-922-3314
fax: 902-922-2283

contact: Ishbel Munro
e-mail: nsen@web.apc.org

Works to reduce the amount of
plastic debris in the ocean through
a Ship-to-Shore Trash Campaign,
permanent wharf signage and
posters.

Nova Scotia Environmental Network

PO Box 223
Pictou, NS B2A 3L8
ph: 902-794-9849

Encourages cooperation and communication among citizen's environmental groups and between
these groups and the government.

Nova Scotia Wildlife Federation

PO Box 654
Halifax, NS B3J 2T3
contact: Tony Rodgers
ph: 902-423-6793

Fosters sound management of
Nova Scotia's renewable resources
through projects done by 33 member clubs.

Sackville Rivers Association

PO Box 45071
Lower Sackville, NS B4E 2Z6
contact: Beth Lenentine
ph: 902-865-9238
fax: 902-864-3564

Offers an inventory of aquatic education resources in Nova Scotia (on
disk), with listings for books, manuals, handbooks, fact sheets,
brochures, magazines, reports,
newsletters, programs, videos and
internet references.

Seafood Producers Association of Nova Scotia

PO Box 991
Dartmouth, NS B2Y 3Z6
contact: Roger Stirling, President
ph: 902-463-7790
fax: 902-469-8294

Represents the interests of seafood
producers and fishing vessel operators in Nova Scotia.

PARKS AND SANCTUARIES

Maine

Acadia National Park

PO Box 177
Bar Harbor, ME 04609
contact: Laurie Olson,
Environmental Education
Coordinator
ph: 207-288-3893 or 5459
fax: 207-288-5507

Available as an outdoor classroom
for all educators. Offers up to 120
interpretive programs each week
on Acadia's natural and cultural
history, and monitors and protects
park resources through a resource
management and science program.
Environmental education programs
for grades 3-6. Presents "Resource
Acadia," 2-day seminars exploring
resource management issues.
Offers an "activity Guide" to
teachers and youth leaders bringing groups to the Park.
Internships/volunteer work available. Publications list provided on
request.

Gray Game Farm and Visitor's Center

Maine Department of Inland
Fisheries & Wildlife
Route 26
Gray, ME 04104-3553
contact: Lisa J. Kane, Nature
Educator
ph: 207-287-3303

This wildlife and conservation education facility offers a demonstration wetland, wildlife gardens, picnicking facilities, and an interpretive building with interactive
exhibits and displays.

Maine Audubon Society Sanctuaries

(see listing in nonprofit organizations section)

Maine State Parks

(see listing for Maine Department of
Conservation/Bureau of Parks and
Recreation in governmental agencies
section and chart on opposite page)

Maine Bureau of Parks and Recreation
State House Station #22
Augusta, Maine 04333-0022
Telephone: 207-287-3821
TDD: 207-287-2213

STATE PARK	LOCATION	TELEPHONE	Camping	Cross-Country Skiing	Scenic Road	Picknicking	Swimming	Boat Launcing	FIshing	Snowmobiling	Fee Charged	Hiking	Guided Programs	Self-guiding Programs	Interpretive Signs/Trails	Mountain	Forest	Field	Marsh/Bog/Swamp	Pond/Lake	Stream/River	Bay/Ocean Beach	Rocky Shore	Salt Marsh/Mud Flat
Aroostook	Presque Isle	207-768-8341	•	•		•	•	•	•	•	•	•				•	•	•		•				
Bradbury Mountain	Pownal	207-688-4712	•	•		•					•	•	•			•	•	•						
Camden Hills	Camden/Lincolnville	207-236-3109	★	•	•	•					•	•	•		•	•	•	•				•	•	
Cobscook Bay	Edmunds Twp.	207-726-4412	•	•	•	•		•	•		•	•		•			•	•					•	•
Cresent Beach	Cape Elizabeth	207-767-3625				•	•		•		•						•	•				•	•	•
Damariscotta Beach	Jefferson	207-549-7600		•		★	•		•		•						•	•		•				
Ferry Beach	Saco	207-283-0067				★	•				•	•	•	•	•		•		•	•	•			
Grafton Notch	Grafton Twp.	207-824-2912			•	•			•		•	•			•	•	•	•			•			
Holbrook Is. Sanctuary	Brooksville	207-326-4012		•		•					•	•	•		•	•	•	•	•	•	•	•	•	•
Lake St. George	Liberty	207-589-4255	•	•		•	•	•	•	•	•	•				•	•	•		•				
Lamoine	Lamoine	207-667-4778	•			•		•	•		•			•			•					•	•	
Lily Bay	Beaver Cove Twp.	207-695-2700	•			•	•	•	•	•	•	•		•			•	•	•					
Moose Point	Searsport	207-548-2882		•		•					•			•			•	•				•	•	
Mt. Blue	Weld/Avon	207-585-2347	•	•		•	•	•	•	•	•	•	•		•	•	•	•		•				
Peacock Beach	Richmond	207-582-2813				•	•				•						•			•				
Peaks-Kenny	Dover-Fxcrft/Bowrbank	207-564-2003	★			★	•		•		•	•				•	•			•				
Popham Beach	Phippsburg	207-389-1335				★	•				•			•	•		•					•	•	
Quoddy Head	Lubec	207-773-0911				•					•	•		•	•	•		•					•	•
Range Ponds	Poland	207-998-4104		•		★	•	•	•		•				•	•	•	•	•	•				
Rangeley Lake	Rangeley/Rangeley Plt.	207-864-3858	★			•	•	•	•	•	•					•	•	•		•				
Reid	Georgetown	207-371-2303		•		★	•		•		•			•	•		•		•		•	•	•	•
Roque Bluffs	Roque Bluffs	207-255-3475				•	•		•		•			•			•	•	•		•	•		
Sebago Lake	Naples/Casco	207-693-6615	•	•		•	•	•	•		•		•		•		•	•		•				
Shackford Head	Eastport	207-726-4412				•					•											•	•	
Swan Lake	Swanville	207-525-4404				★	•		•		•						•	•		•				
Two Lights	Cape Elizabeth	207-799-5871				•					•			•			•	•				•		
Warren Island	Isleboro	207-596-2253	•			•			•		•	•		•			•	•					•	
Wolfe's Neck Woods	Freeport	207-865-4465				★					•	★	★	•	★		•	•				•	•	•

For information on the Allagash Waterway and the Penobscot River Corridor, call 207-287-3821

HISTORIC SITES	whose mission is primarily historical, also have natural environments																							
Colonial Pemaquid (Fort William Henry)	Bristol	207-677-2423				•		•	•		•		•	•	•		•					•	•	
Eagle Island	Harpswell	207-693-6231				•					•		•	•		•						•	•	
Fort Edgecomb	Edgecomb	207-882-7777				•			•		•		•	•			•						•	
Fort Halifax	Winslow	207-645-4217				•								•			•				•			
Fort Kent	Fort Kent	207-764-2041				•							•	•			•				•			
Fort Knox	Prospect	207-469-7719				•					•		•	•	•		•				•			
Fort McClary	Kittery	207-439-2845				•					•	•	•	•			•		•				•	
Fort O'Brien/ Fort Machias	Machias	207-764-2041				•								•			•				•			
Fort Point/Fort Pownall	Stockton Springs	207-596-2253							•				•	•			•					•	•	
Fort Popham	Phippsburg	207-389-1335				•			•					•			•						•	
Katahdin Iron Works	T6 R9 NWP	207-564-2003				•								•			•			•				
Vaughan Woods	South Berwick	207-384-5160				•			•	•				•		•	•				•			

•• Please contact the Park before any group visit   ★ indicates barrier-free facility   12/94

From the Maine Environmental Education Matrix, 1995. *Compiled by Earthminders, Partners in Environmental Education and the Maine Environmental Education Association*

Moosehorn National Wildlife Refuge

U.S. Fish and Wildlife Service PO Box 1077
Charlotte Road
Calais, Maine 04619
contact: refuge manager
ph: 207-454-3521
fax: 207-454-2550

The Refuge includes the 16,080 acre Baring Unit and the 6,665 acre Edmunds Unit. It is the northernmost in the USFWS chain of migratory bird refuges that extends from Maine to Florida. At Moosehorn the American woodcock is intensively studied and managed. Bald eagles, black bear, migratory and breeding water fowl and migratory shorebirds are also protected here. Bird lists, trail guides and special programs are available on request.

The Nature Conservancy Preserves

(see listing in nonprofit organizations section)

Petit Manan National Wildlife Refuge

PO Box 279
Milbridge, ME 04658
contact: Stan Skutek, Refuge Manager
ph: 207-546-2124

Preserves and manages habitat for migratory birds and endangered species, and promotes environmental education. Colonial seabird management programs on Petit Manan and Seal islands and interpretive displays and hiking trails on Petit Manan Point, Steuben.

Rachel Carson National Wildlife Refuge

RR 2, Box 751
Wells, ME 04090
(location: along Route 9 East)
contact: Ward Feurt
ph: 207-646-9226

The refuge includes ten separate divisions located along the coast between Kittery and Cape Elizabeth. Approximately 4,600

acres have been acquired since it was established in 1966. The only developed public-use facilities are at Refuge headquarters in Wells, where there is a mile-long wheelchair-accessible estuarine trail. Bird lists, trail guide and other publications available. Refuge trail is open from sunrise to sunset, year-round.

Sunkhaze Meadows National Wildlife Refuge

U.S. Fish & Wildlife Service
1033 South Main Street
Old Town, ME 04468
contact: Mark Sweeny
ph: 207-827-6138
fax: 207-827-6099
e-mail: r5rw_shmnwr@mail.fws.gov

Manages refuge and unique peat-dominated wetland complex contained within its boundaries. Works to provide and enhance habitats for waterfowl, raptors, neotropical migratory birds, and resident wildlife species.

Roosevelt-Campobello International Park

PO Box 97
Lubec, ME 04652
ph: 506-752-2922

Site of Franklin Delano Roosevelt's 34-room summer "cottage." Park also includes picturesque ponds, bogs, beaches, rocky shore and trails.

Wells National Estuarine Research Reserve

(see listing in research programs and organizations section)

Massachusetts

Boston Parks and Recreation

1010 Massachusetts Avenue
Boston, MA 02118
ph: 617-635-4505

Manages a string of nine continuous parks in urban Boston, including Boston Common and the Public Garden. Programs available at the Arnold Arboretum, Franklin Park Zoo and other sites. Guidebook with map available.

Cape Cod National Seashore

South Wellfleet, MA 02663
contact: Maria Burks, Superintendent
ph: 508-349-3785

Offers ongoing ranger-guided walks and talks on the natural, historic and scientific features of Cape Cod; provides educational opportunities for school groups; conducts a marine debris survey; and offers an environmental education guide, bookstore and library (for use by appointment).

Division of Forests and Parks

Massachusetts Department of Environmental Management
100 Cambridge Street, 19th Floor
Boston, MA 02202
ph: 617-727-3180 or 1-800-831-0569 (in Mass.)

Manages 270,000 acres of public land in state parks and forests. Informational brochures available.

Great Meadows National Wildlife Refuge

U.S. Fish & Wildlife Service
Weir Hill Road
Sudbury, MA 01776
contact: refuge manager
ph: 617-443-4661
fax: 508-443-2898

The Refuge includes valuable freshwater wetlands flanking 12 miles of the Concord and Sudbury Rivers. The Refuge protects and manages habitat for wildlife, with special emphasis on migratory birds. Hiking trails and canoeing offer excellent wildlife viewing opportunities. Educational program available in spring and fall.

Massachusetts Audubon Society Sanctuaries

(see listing in nonprofit organizations section)

Monomoy National Wildlife Refuge

Wikis Way
Morris Island
Chatham, MA 02633
contact: Sharon Ware
ph: 508-945-0594 or 508-443-4661
fax: 508-945-9559

The 2,750 acres of barrier beach island Refuge is located on the "elbow" of Cape Cod. It includes sand dunes, freshwater ponds and salt and freshwater marshes. Habitat is managed for wildlife with a special emphasis on migratory birds.

North Atlantic Region
National Park Service
15 State Street
Boston, MA 02115
contact: Education Specialist
ph: 617-223-5062

Provides information on National Parks and Historic Sites in the Northeast.

Parker River National Wildlife Refuge
U.S. Fish and Wildlife Service
Plum Island
Northern Boulevard
Newburyport, MA 01950
contact: Kim Johnson, Outdoor Recreation Planner
ph: 508-465-5753

Preserves the natural diversity of mammals and birds on refuge land through beach management programs and educational outreach (*e.g.*, annual teacher workshops.)

Stellwagen Bank National Marine Sanctuary
(see listing in governmental agencies section)

Trustees of Reservations Reserves
(see listing in nonprofit organizations section)

New Brunswick

Fundy National Park
PO Box 40
Alma, NB E0A 1B0
contact: A. Bardou, Chief Interpreter
ph: 506-887-6000
fax: 506-887-6011

Offers programs on the shore, tides and land/sea interface. Open year-round.

New Brunswick Parks and Sites
Canadian Heritage, Atlantic Region
Historic Properties, Upper Water Street
Halifax, NS B3J 1S9

Provides information on national parks and historic sites in the Atlantic provinces.

Roosevelt Campobello International Park
(see listing under Maine in this section)

New Hampshire

Division of Parks and Recreation
New Hampshire Department of Resources and Economic Development
PO Box 1856
Concord, NH 03302-1856
ph: 603-271-3556
fax: 603-271-2629

Manages New Hampshire's 42 state parks and 12 historic sites. Informational brochure available.

Great Bay National Wildlife Refuge
U.S. Fish & Wildlife Service
601 Spaulding Turnpike, Suite 17
Portsmouth, NH 03801
contact: Sharon Vaughn
ph: 603-431-7511

The Refuge includes 6 miles of undeveloped Great Bay shoreline, the largest undisturbed expanse in the Great Bay estuarine system. The Refuge protects one of New Hampshire's finest areas of wildlife habitat.

Lake Umbagog National Wildlife Refuge
U.S. Fish & Wildlife Service
P.O. Box 280
Errol, NH 03579
contact: Steve Breeser, Refuge Manager
ph: 603-482-3415
fax: 603-482-3308

The Refuge preserves and manages the largest freshwater marsh complex remaining in New Hampshire. The ten-mile long lake runs along the Maine/New Hampshire border, with an average depth of only 15 feet. The lake, islands, wetlands and marshes along rivers, forested swamplands and uplands provide excellent habitat for migratory birds, endangered and threatened species, resident wildlife and rare plants. Environmental education, hiking, wildlife observation, hunting, fishing, canoeing and pleasure boating are all encouraged on the Refuge.

Odiorne State Park (and Fort Dearborn)
Route 1A
Rye, NH 03870
ph: 603-436-6607

Interpretive center with brochures, exhibits and library with marine/coastal programs run by Audubon Society of New Hampshire and University of New Hampshire Sea Grant.

Society for Protection of New Hampshire Forests Preserves
(see listing in nonprofit organizations section)

Nova Scotia

Kejemakujik National Park
PO Box 36
Maitland Bridge, NS
ph: 902-682-2770

Nova Scotia Department of Natural Resources
RR1
Belmont, NS B0M 1C0.

Provides information on Nova Scotia's 123 Provincial Parks.

Nova Scotia Parks and Sites
Canadian Heritage, Atlantic Region
Historic Properties, Upper Water Street
Halifax, NS B3J 1S9

Provides information on national parks and historic sites in the Atlantic provinces.

RESEARCH PROGRAMS AND ORGANIZATIONS

Maine

AlgaeTech
RR1, Box 60
Topsham, ME 04086
contact: Andrew Bertocci, President
ph: 207-729-6812
fax: 207-798-5060
e-mail: algaetech@maine.com

Works to further the understanding of and appreciation for the seaweed resource, and promotes its responsible use.

Allied Whale
College of the Atlantic
105 Eden Street
Bar Harbor, ME 04609
contact: Peter Stevick, Moira Brown
ph: 207-288-5644
fax: 207-288-4126

Conducts research on population dynamics, migrations and life histories of whales, porpoises and seals. Provide speakers by arrangement; a video "Marine Mammals on the Gulf of Maine" ($29.95); and an adopt-a-whale program ($30).

Beals Island Regional Shellfish Hatchery
PO Box 83
Beals, ME 04611
contact: Brian Beal
phone: 207-255-3313 or 207-497-5769
fax: 207-255-4864
e-mail: bbeal@maine.maine.edu

Works to enhance unproductive intertidal areas with soft-shell clams reared in a hatchery setting. Supports stock enhancement efforts in coastal towns throughout Maine. Resources include curricula, videos, posters, fact sheets, workshops, tours and exhibits.

Bigelow Laboratory for Ocean Sciences
McKown Point
West Boothbay Harbor, ME 04575
contact: Fran Scannell
ph: 207-633-9600
fax: 207-633-9641

Pursues research on a broad spectrum of topics, including coastal pollution, sea-level rise, ultra-violet radiation and the ozone layer, and factors affecting productivity in the Gulf of Maine. Resources include a marine research library, workshops, a biannual newsletter, a year-round lecture series, and the Gaia Crossroads Project (a pilot educational program that explores uses of satellite imagery for learning in grades K-12).

Darling Marine Center (University of Maine)
25 Clark's Cove Road
Walpole, ME 04573
contact: Timothy Miller, Program Coordinator
phone: 207-563-3146, ext. 218
fax: 207-563-3119
e-mail: temiller@mail.caps.maine.edu

Serving as the University of Maine's marine laboratory, the Center does research on aquaculture hatchery techniques, ecology of marine plankton and benthos; coastal geomorphology; shellfish genetics; salt marshes; lobster behavior; and toxics. Resources include a marine library; summer tours; summer courses; marine science recertification workshops for teachers; a "semester by the sea" for undergraduates; laboratories, classrooms, and limited dorm facilities; a flowing seawater building; and a fleet of small boats.

Maine Cooperative Fish and Wildlife Research Unit
University of Maine
5755 Nutting Hall, Room 240
Orono, ME 04469-5755
contact: Bill Krohn (wildlife), John Moring (fish)
phone: 207-581-2870 (wildlife)
207-581-2582 (fish)

Conducts research projects (*e.g.*, on marine seabirds or tidepool fishes) for cooperators, mainly federal and state fish and wildlife agencies. Annual report and scientific publications available.

Marine Environmental Research Institute
Resource Center
PO Box 300
Brooklin, ME 04616
contact: Reg Hoyt, Program Director
ph: 207-359-8078
fax: 207-359-8079

Conducts multidisciplinary research on the relationship between environmental pollution and health effects in marine mammals. The Brooklin Resource Center offers a marine library and reading room for public use, and is compiling a database of information and resources on marine wildlife and marine pollution. MERI also offers traveling exhibits, field trips for children, eco-cruises for adults/families, and a summer lecture series.

Marine Law Institute
University of Maine School of Law
246 Deering Ave.
Portland, ME 04102
contact: Alison Rieser, Director
phone: 207-780-4474
fax: 207-780-4913
e-mail: bbsmith@payson.usmacs.
maine.edu

Conducts legal and policy research in the field of marine and coastal law, particularly public access and coastal right-of-way issues; aquaculture regulation; growth management; protection of water-dependent uses; and fisheries management. Numerous publications available, including *Territorial Sea Journal*, *North Atlantic Water Dependent Use Study* and *East Coast Fisheries Law and Policy*.

Wells National Estuarine Research Reserve
RR2, Box 806
Wells, ME 04090
contact: James T. List
ph: 207-646-1555
fax: 207-646-2930

Conducts research in nearshore areas and conveys findings to coastal decision-makers. Visitor's center includes interpretive exhibits, 7 miles of trails, and classroom and research space.

Massachusetts

Atlantic Cetacean Research Center
PO Box 1413
Gloucester, MA 01930
contact: Steve Frohock
ph: 508-283-2708

Conducts research on whales of Massachusetts Bay and provides public education through commercial whale watches, speakers and internships.

Batelle Lab
397 Washington St.
Duxbury, MA 02332
contact: Joan Sundstrom
ph: 617-934-0571

Provides reference library on marine and coastal pollution for scientists.

Center for Coastal Studies
PO Box 1036
Provincetown, MA 02657
contact: David DeKing, Executive Director
ph: 508-487-3622

Pursues cetacean research and provides research reports, a curriculum guide, a field guide to humpback whales, speakers, slide shows, guided field walks and a newsletter.

Cooperative Fish & Wildlife Research Unit
University of Massachusetts
Holdsworth Natural Resource Center
Amherst, MA 01003
contact: Rebecca Field, Unit Leader
ph: 413-545-0398

Conducts research projects for state and federal fishery and wildlife agencies and private groups using university graduate students. Provides technical information and a newsletter.

Earthwatch
PO Box 403
Watertown, MA 02272
contact: Blue Magruder, Director of Public Affairs
ph: 617-926-8200 or 1-800-776-0188
fax: 617-926-8532
e-mail: info@earthwatch.org
http://www.earthwatch.org

Recruits citizen volunteers and university students to help with environmental research and field work worldwide. Publishes *Earthwatch* magazine bimonthly.

Manomet Observatory, Inc.
PO Box 1770
Manomet, MA 02345
contact: Karen Grey, Chief Administrative Officer
ph: 508-224-6521
fax: 508-224-9220

Conducts scientific research to facilitate environmental decision-making and works collaboratively to improve conservation of natural resources. Educational programs include "Taking Stock of Our Fisheries," "Save Our Migratory Birds," and "Shorebird Migration Game."

Marine Biological Laboratory
Water Street
Woods Hole, MA 02543
contact: Pamela Clapp, Director of Communications
ph: 508-289-7423
fax: 508-457-1924
e-mail: lmoorhou@mbl.edu

Conducts research in coastal ecosystems (*e.g.*, eutrophication effects, nutrient cycling; benthic ecology; and biogeochemistry in sediments and the water column). Library with 200,000 volumes; laboratories; marine specimens; graduate and post-graduate courses; conferences; newsletter; and a summer tour program.

Massachusetts Institute of Technology

Sea Grant College Program
292 Main Street, Building E38-300
Cambridge, MA 02139
contact: Karen Hartley, Public
Information Director
ph: 617-293-3461

Pursues research in automation
and manufacture of marine systems, marine biotechnology, ocean
and coastal processes and ocean
engineering. Publications include
biannual research reports, quarterly newsletters, a biannual magazine, and a *Citizen's Guide to Sources
of Marine and Coastal Information in
Massachusetts.*

Northeastern Regional Aquaculture Center

University of Massachusetts —
Dartmouth
285 Old Westport Road
North Dartmouth, MA 02747-
2300
contact: Victor J. Mancebo,
Executive Director
ph: 508-999-8157
fax: 508-999-8590
e-mail: vmancebo@umassd.edu

Supports aquaculture research,
development, demonstration and
extension education and networking. Fact sheets, videos, and a
report on the northeastern situation/outlook are available.

Plymouth Marine Mammal Research Center

PO Box 1328
Plymouth, MA 02362
contact: David Wiley
ph: 508-224-8477

Conducts research on marine
mammals, especially the feeding
and foraging strategies, song patterns and distribution of baleen
whales.

Urban Harbors Institute

University of Massachusetts -
Boston
Boston Harbor Campus
Boston, MA 02125-3393
contact: Richard Delaney, Director
ph: 617-287-5570

Conducts multidisciplinary
research on urban harbor issues
(*e.g.*, transportation, port environmental and safety issues, and water
quality) and develops marine science curricula for secondary
schools. Resources include a
research and slide library, technical
assistance, speakers, lectures and a
research vessel.

Whale Conservation Institute

191 Weston Road
Lincoln, MA 01773
ph: 617-259-0423
fax: 617-259-0288
e-mail: wci@vmsvax.simmons.edu

Conducts research on whales in the
Gulf of Maine and offers volunteer
internships and a newsletter.

Woods Hole Oceanographic Institute

Water Street
Woods Hole, MA 02543
contact: Lee Campbell,
ph: 508-548-2000, ext. 2270
Pursues research in marine science,
marine policy, and marine exploration. Offers a library, conference
facilities and publications (technical
reports, a newsletter and *Oceanus*
magazine).

Environmental Sciences Research Centre

Department of Biology
Universite de Moncton
Pavillon Remi-Rossignol
Moncton, NB E1A 3E9
contact: Andrew Boghen
ph: 506-858-4321
fax: 506-855-0177
e-mail: boghena@umoncton.ca

Conducts research in coastal
ecology, including effects of habitat
damage on aquatic ecosystems.
Conferences, seminars, books,
reports and posters relating to
research are available.

Huntsman Marine Science Centre

Brandy Cove Road
St. Andrews, NB E0G 2X0
contact: John H. Allen
ph: 506-529-1200
fax: 506-529-1212
e-mail: huntsman@nbnet.nb.ca

Provides public education to
engage community participation in
coastal zone management and conducts marine research (*e.g.*, on ecological effects of salmon cage farming on benthic communities).
Facilities include wet labs, dive
center, hatchery, cage site, research
vessels and workshop settings.
Summer field courses offered.

St. Andrews Biological Station (Department of Fisheries and Oceans)

St. Andrews, NB E0G 2X0
contact: Dr. Wendy Watson-
Wright, Director
ph: 506-529-8854
fax: 506-529-5862
e-mail: michele@sta.dfo.ca

Conducts scientific research in
support of capture fisheries and
aquaculture (*e.g.*, stock assessments;
culture of salmonids, marine finfish
and invertebrates; monitoring of
phytoplankton, organic chemicals
and marine toxins). Resources
include research reports, library
and computer databases.

University of New Brunswick
Environment and Sustainable
Development Research Centre
PO Box 4400
Fredericton, NB E3B 5A3
contact: Jessie Davies, Director
ph: 506-453-4886
fax: 506-453-4883
e-mail: enviro@unb.ca

Works in partnership with industry, nongovernment organizations, and government to facilitate research and development on environment and sustainable development issues. Coordinates environmental and sustainable development education. Conducts research directed at issues in the Gulf region (*e.g.*, the brood ecology of breeding eiders, seabird-plankton interactions, and loon-mercury interactions through the Atlantic Cooperative Wildlife Ecology Research Network. Undergraduate and graduate courses available, with masters programs in Environmental Studies and Environmental Management offered.

University of New Brunswick
Marine Research Group - Biology
Department
PO Box 5050
St. John, NB E2L 4L5
contact: Jack Terhune, Chair
ph: 506-648-5565

Conducts marine and coastal research and offers a B.S. degree with specialization in marine biology. Research vessel, library resources and extensive underwater video material (8 mm.) of the Quoddy region available.

New Hampshire

Great Bay National Estuarine Research Reserve
89 Depot Road
Stratham, NH 03885
contact: Peter Wellenberger
(research; Betsy Franz (education)
ph: 603-778-0015 for education
603-868-1095 for research
fax: 603-778-0031

The Reserve conducts research activities in Great Bay and provides information on its activities. The Sandy Point Discovery Center offers educational programs to school groups. Trails include a handicapped accessible boardwalk trail through a salt marsh. Indoor and outdoor exhibits. Grounds open sunrise to sunset. Call for building hours.

Jackson Estuarine Lab
Adams Point Road
Durham, NH 03824
contact: Stephen Jones, Larry Ward
ph: 603-862-2175

Conducts water-quality monitoring in Great Bay and Wells estuaries and bathymetric and marsh mapping in Great Bay. Digitized maps of upper Great Bay estuary; computerized data; research bibliography and various publications available.

Office of Fishery Assistance at Laconia
U.S. Fish & Wildlife Service
Federal Building, Room 124
Laconia, NH 032246
contact: Joe McKeon
ph: 603-528-8750
fax: 603-528-8729

Conducts research and provides management support on fish populations.

Regional Association for Research on the Gulf of Maine (RARGOM)
Dartmouth College
Thayer School of Engineering
Hanover, NH 03755
contact: Genie Braasch, Associate Director
ph: 603-646-3480
fax: 603-646-3856
e-mail: braasch@dartmouth.edu

Facilitates a coherent program of regional research around the Gulf of Maine and communicates scientific findings to the public. Works to encourage development of community-owned modeling systems and a regional information system to serve scientists and resource managers. Members include universities, research laboratories, and governmental agencies.

Seacoast Science Center, Odiorne Point State Park
570 Ocean Boulevard
Rye, NH 03870
contact: Steve Miller, Director of Programs
ph: 603-436-8043
fax: 603-433-2235

Provides programs and exhibits to spark understanding of the cultural and natural history of Odiorne Point State Park. The Center is active in several coastal and Gulf of Maine programs with a focus on education. Teacher guides and outreach programs are available for schools, scout, and youth groups. Programs offered on coastal resources, salt marsh ecology, wildflowers, pond life, and history and walks are held on weekends and in summer. Children's camps scheduled throughout the summer and during school vacations. The Center's bimonthly newsletter, The Seacoast Sun, is distributed to Center members.

164

Sea Grant College Program
Kingman Farm - University of
New Hampshire
Durham, NH 03824
contact: Brian E. Doyle, Sharon
Meeker
ph: 603-749-1565
fax: 603-743-3997
e-mail: brian.doyle@unh.edu.

Supports Great Bay Citizen's
Water Quality Monitoring Project,
a docent outreach program, and
research/education on aquaculture,
commercial fishing, marine pollution and coastal issues. Technical
reports, videotapes, and other
library resources available.

Shoals Marine Laboratory
G-14-E Stimson Hall
Cornell University
Ithica, NY 14853-7107
ph: 607-255-3717
(Laboratory location: Appledore
Island, Isles of Shoals)

Offers field-oriented credit and
noncredit courses in the marine
sciences each summer through
Cornell University and the
University of New Hampshire.
Course catalog available.

Nova Scotia

Acadia Centre for Estuarine Research
Acadia University
Wolfville, NS B0P 1X0
contact: Graham R. Daborn
ph: 902-542-2201

Fosters estuarine research, especially in the Bay of Fundy/Gulf of
Maine system on topics such as
sediment dynamics, community
structure, fish and shellfish ecology, human impacts, and aquaculture. Publications available on
effects of human impacts, tidal
power, and sea-level rise.

Acadia University
Wolfville, NS B0P 1XO
contact: M.J. Dadswell
ph: 902-542-2201

Provides marine education and
conducts research on estuaries and
inshore fisheries and aquaculure.
Publications and audio-visual
materials available.

Brier Island Ocean Study (BIOS)
Westport, NS B0V 1H0
contact: Carl Haycock
ph: 902-839-2960

Conducts cetacean research and
education in the lower Bay of
Fundy, including photo identification of humpback whales, data-
sharing, public and school education programs, and an "Adopt-a-
Fundy Whale Program."

Canadian Institute of Fisheries Technology
Technical University of Nova
Scotia
Box 1000
Halifax, NS B3J 2X4
contact: Marvin A. Tung, Director
ph: 902-420-7758

Provides for graduate education,
research and development in food
and seafood science and fisheries
engineering. Analytical laboratory,
process engineering pilot plant,
and food rheology and texture laboratory available.

Centre for Marine Geology
Dalhousie University
Halifax, NS B3H 3J5
contact: Paul T. Robinson
ph: 902-494-2361

Fosters research in all aspects of
marine geology (including sea levels, ocean drilling, coastal and shelf
sedimentation, and coastal and
estuarine environmental change).

Halifax Fisheries Research Lab
PO Box 550
Halifax, NS B3J 2S7
contact: J. D. Pringle, Director
ph: 902-426-6138
fax: 902-426-1862
e-mail: j_pringle@bionet.bio.dfo.ca

Provides biological advice to
resource managers, industry and
the public on invertebrates and
marine plant species. Conducts
stock assessments, aquaculture
research and disease diagnostics.
Scientific research and topical
slides and videos available.

Institute for Marine Biosciences
National Research Council
1411 Oxford Street
Halifax, NS B3H 3Z1
contact: D. Viger, Program
Services Office Manager
ph: 902-426-6829
fax: 902-426-9413
e-mail: vigerdj@imb.lan.nrc.ca

Promotes research and development in marine biotechnology for
economic benefits. Marine biology
section works on aquaculture,
DNA sequencing, and microbiolo-
gy while marine chemistry section
focuses on organic, analytical and
natural products. Fact sheets,
research publications and technical
reports produced.

School for Resources and Environmental Studies
Dalhousie University
Halifax, NS B3H 3E2
Contact: Roy Cole
ph: 902-494-3632
fax: 902-494-3728

ANNUAL EVENTS

Maine

March

Water-quality Monitoring Fair. Contact Kathleen Leyden, Shore Stewards Partnership, Maine Coastal Program, 207-287-3261.

April

Maine Association of Conservation Commissions annual meeting/workshop. Contact MACC, 207-622-5330.

Maine Environmental Education Association's annual conference. Contact Don Hudson/Dot Lamson, 207-882-7323.

July

Lakeweek (a week of educational events celebrating Maine's lake resources). Contact Barbara Welch, MDEP, 207-287-7688.

September

Coastweek (a nationwide week of educational events celebrating the coast, with dozens of activities in Maine). Contact Coastweek Coordinator, Maine Coastal Program, 207-287-3261.

Coastal Cleanup (a statewide volunteer cleanup of beaches and shores).Contact Coastal Cleanup Coordinator, Maine Coastal Program, 207-287-3261.

Common Ground Country Fair (focused on sustainable and organic agriculture). Contact Maine Organic Farmers and Gardeners Association, 207-622-3118.

October

Gulf of Maine Marine Educator's Annual Conference. Contact Mary Cerullo, 207-799-6406.

Island Institute Conference contact: Philip Conkling, 207-594-9209

November

Land Conservation Conference contact: Rupert Neily, 207-729-7366

Massachusetts

March

New England Environmental Conference. Contact Nancy Anderson, New England Environmental Network, 617-381-3451.

April

Massachusetts Marine Environment Symposium. Contact Roger Stern, Massachusetts Bay Marine Studies Consortium, 617-287-6540.

September/October

Coastsweep Statewide Beach Cleanup. Contact Anne Donovan, Massachusetts CZM Office, 617-727-9530, ext. 420.

New England Environmental Education Alliance conference. Contact Jeff Schwartz, NEEEA, 207-865-3066.

December

Massachusetts Bays Educators Conference. Contact Faith Burbank, Mass Bays Education Alliance, 617-740-4913

Other Annual Events

Envirothon. Contact MA Division of Conservation Services.

Massachusetts Marine Educators Annual Meeting. Contact MME.

Mass Bays Symposium and WET workshops. Contact Mass Bays.

NOTES

NOTES